DE PROPRIETATIBUS LITTERARUM

edenda curat

C. H. VAN SCHOONEVELD

Indiana University

Series Maior, 12

STRUCTURE
IN
MEDIEVAL NARRATIVE

by

WILLIAM W. RYDING

1971

MOUTON

THE HAGUE · PARIS

LIBRARY OF CONGRESS CATALOG CARD NUMBER: 72-154531

Printed in The Netherlands by Mouton & Co., Printers, The Hague.

PREFACE

This essay is, I believe, the first attempt to study the structure of medieval narrative in a general way. Specialized treatments of this subject have, of course, appeared in scholarly journals and books, but specialists are still in considerable disagreement about fundamental issues, and nobody has so far undertaken to synthesize and extend our present knowledge of the subject as a whole. The nonspecialist, familiar in most cases with only a few examples of medieval story, and these known often only in abridged or abbreviated translations, is likely to feel that what most characterizes medieval narrative is precisely its lack of structure. This is not surprising since, in general, our ideas about narrative structure derive directly from neoclassical notions that were originally used by the literary theoreticians of the Renaissance in order to point up the failings of the narrative works of the Middle Ages.

What this study purports to show is that there is a more or less consistent development of narrative forms, quite independent of and unrelated to Aristotelian notions, which extends from the beginnings of the vernacular tradition – as early, it would appear, as *Beowulf* – to well into the sixteenth century when, in Italy, it becomes the object of critical attacks from the Aristotelian quarter and culminates in Tasso's *Discorsi del poema eroico*. In various ways, however, the problems posed by the increasing complexity of narrative structure had already been resolved by Boccaccio in the fourteenth century, and, independently and differently in England a century later, as we may infer from Malory's handling of his French sources. *Beowulf*, Boccaccio, and Malory have thus been drawn into this study because they provide the framework for the development I have chosen to discuss. Yet the special focus of this study is on the narrative practices prevailing in Old French literature during the twelfth and thirteenth centuries. It is this period that I believe to be critical for the history of the subject.

Even here, however, because of the extensiveness of the period and the unusual length and complexity of its narrative productions, I have declined to attempt anything like an exhaustive treatment of the material. Even to have tried to do so would, I believe, have unnecessarily complicated and obscured a tradition that emerges with some clarity when we stand back and view in a simple and unprejudiced way the central narrative tradition extending from the *Vie de Saint Alexis* through the early *chansons de geste* and the courtly romances of Chrétien de Troyes to the complex and voluminous Arthurian Vulgate.

I should like to add that much of what I say here has been expressed or implied in the studies of those who have worked before me in this field. I think particularly of Professors Jean Frappier and Eugene Vinaver, whose work lightened my burden considerably. Professor W. T. H. Jackson provided many valuable suggestions. My teacher, Professor Maurice Valency, who first set me to thinking about these matters, provided advice and encouragement that were particularly precious.

CONTENTS

CONTENTS

INTRODUCTION

In the latter half of the sixteenth century there occurred in Italy what might be described as a crisis in the concept of narrative structure. The controversy raged in literary circles from 1548 until the end of the century. When it was over a revolution of sorts had been accomplished. The authority of Aristotle in matters of narrative form was firmly established as it was to remain down to our own times. Matters we now take for granted – the idea, for example, that properly constructed narrative has a beginning, middle, and end within which events succeed one another logically – were for the first time formulated for application to the western vernacular literary tradition. With few exceptions, all narratives written before the Italian controversies of the sixteenth century might fairly be described as belonging to a tradition that for the purposes of this paper will be called medieval, although in some ways non-Aristotelian would be a better term. The narratives of the period following might then simply be called modern.

This period is of such importance, not only for the understanding of subsequent literary developments, but also of the anterior literary traditions of narrative form, that it deserves close preliminary consideration.

When Aristotle set himself the task of describing the structure of well-made narrative, his task was relatively simple: he formulated the practice of the writers he knew and liked, Homer and the Greek dramatists; that is, the philosopher simply codified what had come to be standard practice. The idea of well-made narrative during the late Renaissance had no such organic growth. Aristotle's ideas entered the cultural stream of the sixteenth century in direct opposition to the prevailing notions of narrative structure. The most widely admired narrative of the period, Ariosto's *Orlando furioso*, represents the culmination of a long narrative tradition beginning in twelfth-century France. It combines the two major genres of the Middle Ages, epic and romance, in a long and complex form characterized by multiplicity and surprise rather than by the classical virtues of economy, unity, and inevitability.

This tradition had developed over a period of nearly four hundred years, a period as long as that which separates us from Tasso, Aristotle's greatest Renaissance commentator. It is perhaps a mistake to assume that the freedom of this development from classical interference was entirely due to widespread ignorance of Aristotle's *Poetics* or to the general unavailability of the text. The Moslem philosopher Averroës had done an abridged version of the *Poetics* in Arabic in the twelfth century; his version had in turn been translated into Latin by a German named Hermann in 1256. In that form it appears to have circulated considerably during the Middle Ages without having the slightest effect on narrative theory or practice. In fact, even when Giorgio Valla published a translation of the *Poetics* in Latin in 1498, there was not much in the way of a general movement to adapt Aristotle's principles to the writing of contemporary narrative. It was only with the appearance of Robortelli's edition and commentary in 1548 that the question became a burning issue. It is, indeed, difficult to understand why, although the authoritarian influence of the Council of Trent has sometimes been alleged as a contributing factor.[1]

Robortelli, at any rate, was able to speak of the *Poetics* as a book generally neglected up to his time: "Jacuit liber hic neglectus, ad nostra fere haec usque tempora", a sentiment echoed a year later by Bernardo Segni in his Italian translation.[2]

It was an important historical juncture, a meeting of the old and the new, the watershed between medieval and modern narrative. It was here that the form of narrative first came up for serious theoretical consideration. And it is important to recognize that Aristotle's ideas took on a more systematic and absolute form at this time because they were hardened in the fires of controversy and used to attack the system of medieval narrative as it appeared in Ariosto's *Orlando furioso*.

Tasso's discussion of narrative form is by far the most lucid and thoughtful of those written during this period. He sketched out the main lines of his theory in 1564 in the *Discorsi dell' arte poetica*, when he was only twenty, but his work in literary theory is best known to

---

[1]   J. Cottaz, *Le Tasse et la conception épique* (Paris, 1942), p. 328.
[2]   J. Spingarn, *History of Literary Criticism in the Renaissance* (2nd ed.; New York, 1908), pp. 16-17. Spingarn presents an excellent discussion of the controversy about narrative structure on pp. 107-124.

posterity in a later recension, the *Discorsi del poema eroico* (1594), which was written when he was quite mad.[3] His remarks on narrative structure appear in the third book of the *Discorsi del poema eroico* and fall into three general categories: the question of beginning, middle, and end; the question of length; and the question of unity, a division I find so useful that I have adopted it as the general basis of this inquiry.

Tasso begins his discussion, appropriately enough, with the question of beginning, middle, and end. At first, he defines these terms in the same rather irritatingly tautological way as Aristotle: the beginning necessarily leads to something else, but is not necessarily preceded by anything else; the end necessarily follows other things, but does not necessarily have anything after it; the middle, naturally, stands between these two, necessarily preceded and followed by other things.[4]

But Tasso is not entirely satisfied with this rather flat restatement of Aristotle; he amplifies his definition to make its meaning quite clear. A complete story, he says, must contain everything necessary to its being understood: the causes and the origins of the matter being treated, and the stages through which the action necessarily passes before arriving at the end, which, in turn, must leave nothing unresolved.[5]

Tasso now directs his first criticism at the *Orlando furioso*: it has no beginning; Boiardo's *Orlando innamorato*, on the other hand, has no end. This is true as far as it goes. Boiardo had died (1494) before carrying the *Innamorato* to its conclusion. Ariosto had picked up the narrative in 1506 where his predecessor had left it, calling his continuation the *Orlando furioso*. Tasso's objection, as he knew perfectly well, was somewhat specious. The two works were meant to be considered as one poem, of which the *Innamorato* supplies the beginning, the *Furioso* the end: the one was a sequel to the other. But there is an important point to be made here with respect to the composition of medieval narrative, namely that the practice of writing narrative sequels and preludes had an annoying way of blurring the concept of beginning, middle, and end.

[3] Both essays appear in *Torquato Tasso: Prose*, ed. Ettore Mazzali (Milan, 1959). Subsequent page references will be to this edition.
[4] "Principio è quello che necessariamente non è dopo altra cosa, e altre cose sono dopo lui. Il fine è quello che è dopo altre cose, nè altra cosa ha dopo sè. Il mezzo è posto fra l'uno e l'altro, ed egli è dopo alcune cose, ed alcune cose n'ha dopo se." Tasso, pp. 568-569. *Cf.* Aristotle, *Poetics* 7. 1450b.
[5] "Intiera è quella favola che in sè stessa ogni cosa contiene ch'a la sua intelligenza sia necessaria: e le cagioni e l'origine di quella impresa che si prende a trattare, vi sono espresse, e per li debiti mezzi si conduce ad un fine, il quale niuna cosa lassi o non ben conclusa, o non ben risoluta." Tasso, p. 569.

While many writers of the Middle Ages wrote their stories as separate, self-contained units, there were many others who spent their creative energies writing nothing but preludes and sequels, never thinking of writing a story they might care to call their own. This leads to obvious problems, for the very concept of beginning, middle, and end presupposes that the writer has it in mind to compose a complete, self-subsistent work, not merely an addition to an already existing narrative corpus. I am thinking, of course, of that vast body of medieval literature that is classed as 'cyclic', the epic cycles, the *Roman de Renart*, and the Arthurian cycle, which together make up a heavy percentage of medieval narrative. What Tasso was criticizing, therefore, was the practice of formulating works as prologues, continuations, and sequels, a practice which necessarily negated the concept of the poetic unity of a work of art.[6]

On the question of length, Tasso follows Aristotle quite closely. Both agree that length is a virtue: "The longer a story is", wrote Aristotle, "consistently with its being comprehensible as a whole, the finer it is by reason of its magnitude" (*Poetics* 7. 1451a). For Tasso, a short poem may be praised for its grace or its point, but not for its perfection or beauty. For that, magnitude is necessary.[7]

Since, within Aristotle's view, the limiting factor on length is total comprehensibility, the reader's memory becomes a major determinant. The story should be of a length such that it may be taken in by the memory. Aristotle further specifies that it should be long enough "to allow of the hero's passing by a series of probable or necessary stages from misfortune to happiness, or from happiness to misfortune" (*Poetics* 7. 1451a). Three separate things are thus included in the formulation: the reader's memory, logical sequence, and a reversal of fortune. Only the first two appear in Tasso's discussion, and there is a slightly altered emphasis, for while in Aristotle the matter of logical sequence comes up rather extraneously, Tasso makes it clear that it is logical progression that makes it possible for the reader to remember how everything fits together in the story. Without the mnemonic aid of logical sequence, the reader could not reason his way back to the beginning, and therefore he could never get a fully unified impression of the action.

Tasso therefore defines proper length as one that does not unduly

---

[6] *Cf.* Chapter I, *infra*, pp. 38-61.

[7] "Ne le picciole poesie si loda più tosto la grazia e l'acume che la bellezza o la perfezione. E necessaria dunque la grandezza." Tasso, p. 572.

tax the reader's capacity to remember. The writer has wasted his time if the reader, once arrived at the middle of the story, has already forgotten the beginning. Thus it is at this point, in connection with the problem of length, that Tasso asserts that the principal perfection of the poet is nothing less than his ability to make one event follow another according either to probability or to necessity.[8]

Tasso now delivers his second major objection to the *Innamorato-Furioso*: even if it is considered as a single work, the ensemble will not qualify as an artistic success, since a person of average memory could hardly be expected to keep the whole thing, about 80,000 verses, in his head.[9]

Tasso does not press the issue of logical sequence here, although he might very well have done so. For him, the sheer physical length of the compound romance constituted sufficient proof of its inacceptability.[10]

The matter of length is crucial to the understanding of the development of medieval story. I suspect that if it had not been for the medieval writers' conviction that length was a necessary condition of excellence, medieval narrative would not have taken on some of the forms it did.[11]

The third and last of Tasso's structural concerns was the matter of unity, a subject that was just as slippery then as it is now. It is in this area that Tasso's powers of synthesis are shown most clearly.

Trissino had begun the controversy about unity by writing an imitation classical epic, *Italia liberata dai Goti* (1548), accompanied by a dedicatory epistle to Charles V in which he condemned all heroic narratives that did not conform to the classical ideal of a single action. He specifically criticized the *Orlando furioso*, which interweaves three major epic actions involving three central heroes into a complex narrative tapestry, a form of story-telling very much in vogue in the mid-

---

[8] "Grande dunque sarà convenevolmente quella poesia in cui la memoria non si perda nè si smarrisca, ma tutta unitamente comprendendola, possa considerare come l'una cosa con l'altra sia congiunta, e da l'altra dependente. Viziosi senza dubbio sono quei poemi ... ne' quali di poco ha il lettore passato il mezzo che del principio si è dimenticato; però che vi si perde quel diletto che dal poeta, come principale perfezione dee ... esser ricercato. Questo è come l'uno avvenimento dopo l'altro necessariamente o verisimilmente succeda." *Ibid.*

[9] "E peraventura che l'*Innamorato* e'l *Furioso* come un solo poema considerasse, gli potria parer la sua lunghezza soverchia anzi che no, e non atta ad esser contenuta da una mediocre memoria." *Ibid.*

[10] Ariosto seems not to have been at all disturbed by the extensive complexities of his story. He revels in them, pretending on occasion to have lost track of his story himself (*Orlando furioso*, xxxii, 1-3).

[11] *Cf.* Chapter II, *infra.*

sixteenth century. Trissino's attack seemed ridiculous to Giraldi, who wrote a sensible rebuttal, the *Discorsi intorno al comporre dei romanzi* (1549), in which he distinguished three types of heroic poetry, the first having to do with one action of one man, the second with many actions of one man, and the third with many actions of many men. The first defines classical epic, the second biographical romance, and the third the romantic epic in the manner of Ariosto. All three, Giraldi held, were separate and equally legitimate genres.[12]

Tasso's approach to the matter was cautious. He had taken Aristotle's side in the controversy, but he knew that Trissino's poem was a poor job, the work of a pedant rather than of a narrative artist. He also knew that his countrymen had little taste for the great classical writers of epic. The classical writers were able to succeed in writing epics of one action, because audiences in those days had a more robust taste. That of Tasso's time was refined and decadent:

Non era peraventura così necessaria questa varietà a' tempi di Virgilio e d'Omero, essendo gli uomini di quel secolo di gusto non così isvogliato; però non tanto v'attesero: maggiore nondimeno in Virgilio che in Omero si ritrova. Gratissima era a' nostri tempi; e perciò devevano i nostri poeti co' sapori di questa varietà condiri i loro poemi, volendo che da questi gusti sì delicati non fossero schivati.[13]

(It seems that variety was not so necessary in the times of Virgil and Homer, for the taste of the men of those times was not so satiated as to require it. These poets, therefore, did not achieve variety, although there is more in Virgil than in Homer. In our own time, variety has afforded the greatest pleasure, and because of this, our poets have been obliged to season their poems with the spice of variety, not wishing to fail those of the most refined tastes.)

Tasso's problem, clearly, was that of reconciling unity of action with variety of incident. He solved the problem by postulating an analogy between the epic poem and the universe itself, which, for all its variety, remains one in form and essence:

Con tutto ciò uno è il mondo che tante e sì diverse cose nel suo grembo rinchiude, una la forma e l'essenza sua, uno il nodo dal quale sono le sue parte con discorde concordia insieme congiunte e collegate.[14]

(Although the world contain so many and such various things in its bosom, its form and essence are one, and there is one knot that gathers together and binds its parts, from discord into harmony.)

[12] G. B. Giraldi Cintio, *Scritti Estetici: De' romanzi, delle comedie e delle tragedie*, ed. G. Antimaco (Milan, 1864), I, 24-52.
[13] Tasso, p. 588.
[14] *Ibid.*, pp. 588-589.

The artist, like the Supreme Artificer, must so construct his little world that it will have a unity analogous to that of the cosmos:

Giudico che da eccelente poeta . . . un poema formar si possa, nel quale, quasi in un picciolo mondo, qui si leggano, ordinanzi di eserciti, qui battaglie terrestri e navali, qui espugnazioni di città, scaramucce e duelli, qui giostre, qui descrizione di fame e di sete, qui tempeste, qui incendi, qui prodigi; là si veggiano sedizioni, là discordie, là errori, là venturi, là incanti; là opere di crudeltà, di audacia, di cortesia, di generosità, là avvenimenti d'amore, or felici, or infelici; or lieti, or compassionevoli: ma che nondimeno uno sia il poema che tanta varietà di materie contegna, una la forma e l'anima sua; e che tutte queste cose sieno di maniera composte, che l'una l'altra riguardi, l'una a l'altra corrisponda, l'una da l'altra o necessariamente o verisimilmente dependa, sì che una sola parte o tolta via o mutato di sito, il tutto si distrugga. E si ciò fosse vero, l'arte del comporre il poema sarebbe simile a la ragion dell'universo, la qual è composta de' contrari, come la ragion musica: perchè s'ella non fosse moltiplice, non sarebbe tutta, nè sarebbe ragione, come dice Plotino.[15]

(I judge that by an excellent poet . . . a poem can be formed in which, as in a microcosm, there would be read here arrays of armies, here battles on land and sea, here stormings of cities, skirmishes and joustings, here descriptions of hunger and of thirst, here storms, conflagrations, prodigies; there would be found seditions, discords, errors, adventures, magic spells; there deeds of cruelty, of audacity, of courtesy, of generosity; there experiences of love, sometimes happy, sometimes unhappy, sometimes joyous, sometimes pathetic; but may the poem that contains so great a variety of matter be one in form and soul, and may all its elements be put together in such a way that if one part is taken away, or its position changed, all is destroyed. And if this is true, the art of composing a poem is like the principle of the universe, which goes by contraries, like the principle of music, for if there were no multiplicity, there would be no whole and no law, as Plotinus says.)

Tasso's universe, necessarily reflecting the perfect logical order of the divine mind, is like a complex piece of machinery in which every gear and lever performs a necessary function with respect to the whole. Take out a part or change its position, and the machine is destroyed. Similarly, the ideal epic reflects the logical order of the artist's mind; logic, in the form of probability or necessity, holds everything together. Remove a single motivating factor and the entire work falls to pieces.

To write a work that would satisfy so elevated an ideal of narrative coherence would require an unusually gifted artist, one who, in his willingness to assume the responsibility of constructing a totally coherent universe, aspires to achievement beyond the capacities of mortal men. And indeed, Tasso's final criticism of Ariosto's narrative tech-

---

[15] *Ibid.*, p. 589.

nique is that Ariosto took the easy way out, settling for variety without troubling himself about coherence:

E certo assai agevol cosa e di niuna industria il far che 'n molte e separate azioni nasce gran varietà di accidenti; ma che la istessa varietà in una sola azione si trova, *hoc opus, hic labor est.*[16]

(It is indeed a very easy thing, requiring no effort, to achieve a great variety of incident from many separate actions, but to achieve the same variety in a poem of one action, *hoc opus, hic labor est.*

The technique that Tasso criticizes here, that of interlaced narrative, is in fact rather difficult to handle. Ariosto's story, we remember, consists of three relatively independent major actions, all of which are carefully adumbrated in the opening stanzas of his poem. First, there is the epic action, the war of Agramante of Africa on the Emperor Charlemagne; second, a sentimental action, Orlando's love for the pagan princess Angelica and the madness to which it drives him; and third, an action of dynastic significance, the love of the pagan prince Ruggiero and Rinaldo's sister Bradamante, from whose union the great house of Este is to derive. These major actions are considerably complicated by minor ones, Mandricardo's invasion of France in quest of Orlando's sword Durindana, and the invasion by Gradasso of Sericania in search of Rinaldo's charger, Baiardo. Ariosto tells all these stories at once, moving from one action to another, interrupting an episode from one sequence to launch into the matter of another, from which he then breaks off to return to the suspended narrative line. The various story threads tangle and untangle, cross and recross, in accordance with a carefully prearranged plan of narrative coincidences and interdependencies. This is not, obviously, a convergent pattern in which the various threads of the story move insistently toward a major knot, as in wellmade narrative; the threads diverge to form a broad and spacious tapestry; and yet Ariosto has so arranged his story that the various parts are in fact structurally dependent on one another. To take but a single instance: Orlando's love for Angelica is strongly related to the epic action; this keeps him from participating in the epic struggle, and is thus structurally analogous to Achilles' delayed entry into the Trojan War as a result of his quarrel with Agamemnon.

Ariosto did not invent narrative interlacing; he took it over from Boiardo, who in turn may have got it from the best example of its use in Old French literature, the prose romances of the Arthurian Vulgate

---

[16]   *Ibid.*, pp. 589-590.

cycle. The story of its origin and development is an important chapter in the history of medieval narrative form. It is, as one critic has said, "one of the fundamental esthetic issues of thirteenth-century literature".[17]

Tasso's ideas, although specifically directed at Ariosto, had their inevitable effect on almost all future critical reactions to medieval narrative literature. Tasso's ideal narrative poem, constructed as carefully as a watch, every part a necessary piece of a functioning whole, made most medieval narratives look structurally analogous to a sack of potatoes, episodic hodge-podges, thrown loosely into containers of no fixed shape.

Before Tasso, in France, critics can scarcely be said to have been particularly disturbed by the form of medieval narrative. Rabelais, for all his disdain of Gothic barbarousness, was still writing in accordance with late medieval forms. In composing the *Pantagruel* as a sequel to another man's book, the *Grandes et inestimables chronicques de l'énorme géant Gargantua*, he was following a standard medieval practice, beginning a narrative cycle.[18] The *Gargantua* and the *Pantagruel* are loosely constructed biographical romances, while the matter of Rabelais' later books, built around the quest for the *Dive Bouteille*, may be taken as a more or less conscious travesty of the quest for the Holy Grail.

In 1549, Joachim du Bellay, in no less a document than the *Deffence et Illustration de la langue françoise*, heralding the advent of a new, classically oriented French literature, was still able to speak with pride of "ces beaux vieulx romans françois, comme un *Lancelot*, un *Tristan*, ou autres".[19]

Even such a classicist as Jacques Peletier du Mans could, as late as 1555, praise narrative interlacing, the basic structural pattern of Ariosto's narrative and of the Old French prose *Lancelot*:

Il fait bon voir, comment le Poète, après avoir quelquefois fait mention d'une chose mémorable ... la laisse là pour un temps, tenant le lecteur en suspens, désireux d'en aller voir l'évènement. En quoi je trouve nos Romans bien inventés. Et je dirai bien ici en passant, qu'en quelques-uns de ceux-ci bien choisis, le Poète Héroïque pourra trouver à faire son profit: comme sont les aventures des chevaliers, les amours, les enchantements, les combats,

---

[17] E. Vinaver, "The Prose Tristan", in *Arthurian Literature in the Middle Ages*, general ed. R. S. Loomis (Oxford, 1959), p. 345. *Cf.* also *infra*, chap. III, pp. 142 ff.
[18] See Rabelais' prologue to the *Pantagruel*.
[19] *Deffence et Illustration*, II, v.

et semblabes choses, desquelles l'Arioste a fait emprunt de nous, pour trans-
porter en son livre.[20]

By 1580, however, things had changed considerably. Montaigne, no
doubt fully abreast of the Italian controversy, was one of the first to
deride medieval narrative forms. As a well-grounded classicist, he
boasts of never having read the old romances of chivalry:

> Car des *Lancelots du Lac*, des *Amadis*, des *Huons de Bordeaux*, et tel fatras
> de livres à quoy l'enfance s'amuse, je n'en connoissois pas seulement le nom,
> ni ne fais encore le corps, tant exacte estoit ma discipline.[21]

Montaigne's contribution to the Italian controversy is the following
unfavorable comparison of Ariosto's technique of interlaced narrative
to Virgil's determined concentration on one man and one action:

> Celuy-là [Virgil], on le voit aller à tire d'aisle, d'un vol haut et ferme, suyvant
> toujours sa pointe; cettuy-ci [Ariosto] voleter et sauteler de conte en conte,
> comme de branche en branche, ne se fiant à ses aisles que pour une bien
> courte traverse, et prendre pied à chaque bout de champ, de peur que
> l'haleine et la force luy faille.[22]

At the beginning of the seventeenth century, Cervantes put into the
mouth of his Canon of Toledo a severe judgment of the medieval
romances, one that has been frequently quoted since, and that seems to
have served as something of a model for such criticism during the
seventeenth and eighteenth centuries:

> No he visto ningún libro de caballerías que haga un cuerpo de fábula entero
> con todos sus miembros, de manera que el medio corresponda al principio
> y al fin; sino que los componen con tantos miembros, que más parece que
> llevan intención a formar una quimera o un monstruo que a hacer una
> figura proporcionada.[23]

Boileau, in 1673, referred with unmistakable scorn to the "art confus
de nos vieux romanciers",[24] while Huet, the learned Bishop of
Avranches, described medieval romance as "un amas de fictions gros-
sièrement entassées les unes sur les autres".[25]

---

[20] J. Peletier du Mans, *L'Art Poétique*, ed. A. Boulanger ("Publications de la
Faculté des Lettres de l'Université de Strasbourg", LIII, 1930), p. 201. I have
modernized Peletier's highly peculiar orthography.
[21] *Montaigne: Essais*, ed. M. Rat (Paris, 1948), I, xxvi, 190.
[22] *Ibid.*, II, x, 89.
[23] *Don Quixote*, I, xlvii.
[24] *Art Poétique*, I, v, 118.
[25] Letter to Segrais (1673), cited in A. Pauphilet, *Le Legs du moyen âge* (Melun,
1950), p. 29.

After the time of Tasso, critical reactions to the structure of medieval narrative may be said to divide into three major phases. The first extends through the seventeenth and most of the eighteenth century, and is a decidedly negative phase during which the narrative works of the Middle Ages are judged generally on the assumption of their having been produced by definite authors, however inept. The second phase, which covers all of the nineteenth and part of the twentieth centuries, up to the period 1908-1913, may be called the romantic phase. Over this period, the narrative productions of the Middle Ages were considered to be the result of centuries of accumulation and accretion. In place of the one author there now appeared an anonymous group slowly elaborating the elements with no consistent plan in mind, gradually molding quantities of short lyric narratives into extended productions that came to be written down from the late eleventh century onward. The third critical phase is that inaugurated by Joseph Bédier in the four volumes of his book *Les Légendes épiques*, published from 1908-1913, in which he systematically attacked the basis of the romantic theories, resurrected the medieval poet, and made it necessary once again to evaluate medieval literature as the product of the conscious will of literary artists.

The fact that Tasso's standards of unity and coherence were set so high in the first place, and refined and dogmatized even further during the seventeenth century by Tasso's French successors in literary theory, made it curiously possible for the men of the eighteenth century to look back on the Homeric epics with a certain feeling of superiority. Homer's works began to look like rather patchy productions composed of oddly discordant elements not properly integrated into a whole. Classical scholars therefore began to theorize about the origins of epic literature, particularly the primitive or primary epic, as distinguished from the learned or secondary epic tradition represented in such poems as the *Aeneid*, the *Franciade*, and *Paradise Lost*. Such speculations ultimately came to have a profound effect on ideas about medieval narrative structure.

As early as 1713, Richard Bentley had attempted to explain the discrepancies and lacunae in the Homeric epics by proposing that they were not originally composed as whole poems, but that they represented a late accumulation of originally independent short songs:

Homer wrote a Sequel of short Songs and Rhapsodies, to be sung by himself for small earnings and good cheer, at Festivals and other days of Merriment; the *Iliad* he made for the men and the *Oddyseis* for the other sex. These loose Songs were not collected together, in the Form of an Epic Poem, til ... above 500 years later.[26]

Since there were no extant texts of the original short songs, it was necessary to postulate further that the songs were transmitted orally. Historical events fade from the memory of the people in a few generations unless they are committed to rhythm and rime. Whole epics could not survive orally; they are too long to be remembered; but short songs might be transmitted in this manner until in the course of time they are collected and written down in the form of an epic poem.

The standard theory, from 1795 on, was that expressed by F. A. Wolf in his *Prolegomena ad Homerum*: not only had the songs been transmitted orally, but even when they came to be written down there had been no deliberate revision of the materials. Thus no one man could fairly be called the author of the Homeric poems.

Germany's national epic, the *Nibelungenlied*, discovered in 1755, had consistently been compared to its own disadvantage with the classical epics. On the other hand, scholars had brought to light several puzzling aspects of the poem: in language and style it belonged to the twelfth or thirteenth century; its subject matter, however, was obviously much older; many of the names were historically identifiable, but the people to whom they belonged lived in widely separated historical periods. Since these same discrepancies had been noted apropos of the Homeric epics, it was inevitable that the Wolfian theory of epic origins should ultimately be applied to the *Nibelungenlied*. Karl Lachmann, in his famous book *Ueber die ursprüngliche Gestalt der Nibelungen Noth* (1816), transferred the theory in its entirety to the Germanic epic.

According to this theory, epic narratives of the primary sort represent a historical record preserved orally in short narrative lays or songs which later were amassed into cycles having no fixed form except by the accidental circumstance of their having been committed to writing at a particular time. This concept soon became solidly established. Imported into France by Fauriel about 1830, it arrived just in time to be applied to the *Chanson de Roland*, which was discovered in 1832.

The central event described in the *Chanson de Roland* was historical, a defeat of Charlemagne's rear-guard in the Pyrenees in 778. The epic itself in language and style belonged to the late eleventh century. The

---

[26] *Remarks upon a Late Discourse of Free-Thinking, in a Letter to N.N. by Philoeleutherus Lipsiensis*, in *The Works of Richard Bentley*, ed. Alex. Dayce (London, 1836-38), III, 304. Much earlier, the Alexandrian critics had arrived at similar theories about the Homeric epics.

relation between historical fact and epic poem was assumed to be an unbroken tradition from the eighth century through the eleventh, during which the story was handed down in short lyrico-epic poems, called *cantilènes* after 1835 when the term *cantilena* came to light in an early Latin text referring to songs of the people. According to Gaston Paris, these songs finally were brought together to form the extended poem that we known as the *Chanson de Roland*:

L'événement tragique qui fait le centre du *Roland* a dû susciter dès le moment même, des chants qui se répandirent très vite. Ces chants, probablement courts et pathétiques se sont transformés peu à peu et ont abouti au poème tout narratif et long de quatre mille vers qui a été rédigé vers la fin du XIe siècle.[27]

It was not long before all Old French narrative came to be seen in a similar light, even in cases where the subject matter was not historical. Writing of the Tristan legend, for example, Gaston Paris described its origins and development in accordance with the so-called *cantilènes* theory:

La première période de la vie de notre légende dut être caractérisée par des lais ou des courts poèmes épisodiques et surtout par des récits des conteurs de profession qui charmaient les réunions des jours de fête, se répandaient, essaim bourdonnant, de château en château, et comme les abeilles transportent le pollen sur les fleurs, dispersaient la matière épique qui devait être au loin féconde.[28]

Sometimes, in order to make the theory itself hold up against works whose structure seemed superficially strong, critics were obliged to perceive subtle discontinuities. The apparently logical dramatic structure of the Tristan legend, all the parts of which seemed logically interdependent, called for special treatment. One critic, speaking of Béroul's fragment, shrewdly noted:

Il suo poema, quantunque si possa dire costruito abbastanza solidamente, pure lascia scorgere ad ogni momento le connessure, la saldature dei pezzi che l'hanno formato; permette di comprendere come dai canti episodici sia sorto il poema biografico, dalla riunione dei *lais* sia uscita *l'histoire*.[29]

The Wolfian theory was both beautiful and coherent. It explained not only the conversion of fact into legend, but also the apparently haphazard structure of much medieval narrative. But the theory had its

---

[27]   G. Paris, *Extraits de la Chanson de Roland* (Paris, 1887), p. viii.
[28]   *Poèmes et légendes du moyen âge* (Paris, 1900), p. 147.
[29]   F. Novati, "Un nuovo ed un vecchio frammento del *Tristan* de Tommasso", *Studj di filologia romanza*, II (1887), 390.

drawbacks. One could hardly criticize it on the basis of there being no extant texts of the early songs, since these would necessarily and easily have been transmitted orally. Nor would they have been considered sufficiently important to be noted in contemporary historical works with any degree of detail; passing references had been found. The serious drawback was that when critics moved from general matters of theory to questions of detail, their unanimity disappeared.

In attempting to identify the historical prototype of Guillaume d'Orange, for example, critics came up with no less than sixteen different historical figures. There was also general disagreement about the division of particular poems into their original rhapsodic elements. Thus one day it occurred to Joseph Bédier to doubt the theory itself. He brought to light the numerous contradictions to which scholars had been led in their determined efforts to fit the poems to the theory, and he pointed out two essential facts: the *chansons de geste* appear for the first time in the late eleventh century; before that there is not a trace of any sort of epic activity, none, at least, that Bédier was unable to explain away. Secondly, he showed that many of the works scholars had alleged to be incoherent accumulations of short songs because a preconceived theory had made them seem so, showed a surprisingly strong structural unity when viewed without benefit of the theory.

There remained one problem. The *chansons de geste* frequently included accurate details from a distant past. How were these details transmitted to the epic poet? Bédier noted that many of the details were to be found in documents preserved in monasteries and churches, and even there the historical details were often mixed with pious propaganda in the form of legends about the ancient champions of the church. Moreover, these monasteries and churches turned out to be located along along the major pilgrim routes of the eleventh and twelfth centuries – the roads to Rome, Saint James of Compostela, and Jerusalem. Bédier concluded that the poet got his historical materials from monks and clerics along the road, who were happy to supply material that would appeal to the pilgrims. In return, the poet wrote songs glorifying local heroes – Roland on the road from Roncevaux to Blaye, Guillaume d'Orange in the neighborhood of Gellone – thereby attracting pilgrims to particular shrines and sanctuaries, and even holding them there by singing his songs daily in the shadow of the church. The arrangement was obviously profitable to church and poet alike.[30]

[30]   Bédier's theory, here much abbreviated, is developed with admirable erudition and subtlety through the four volumes of *Les Légendes épiques* (Paris, 1908-1913).

Bédier thus wiped out three centuries of hypothetical collective literary activity. The concept of the medieval author had to be revised accordingly: he was a man who conceived his work from beginning to end and shaped it in accordance with his notions of artistic form.[31] Bédier argued cogently for the structural unity of the *Chanson de Roland*, although he interrupted his analysis of the poem at the death of Roland, no doubt because he felt that it would be better not to be obliged to admit that the succeeding Baligant episode was rather awkwardly introduced.[32] He also brought his erudition and literary insight to bear on the structure of the hypothetical common source to all the known Tristan legends, showing that at the basis of this tradition there lay no series of tales sprung from the imagination of a crowd of individuals, but a single poem, a common source for the entire tradition. The *estoire* was no longer to be considered an assemblage of stories arbitrarily accumulated by a collector of *lais*, but a well thought-out work "où éclate superbement l'unité de création".[33]

The thirteenth-century prose romance, *La Mort le Roi Artu*, the last section of the Vulgate cycle of Arthurian romances, had been subjected to the disintegrating powers of the Wolfian theorists, even though its unity ought to have been evident at first glance.[34] Jean Frappier, after fully demonstrating the remarkable coherence of the work's structure, took the occasion to deliver a severe condemnation of the impenitent believers in gradual accumulation:

Cette opinion est un véritable contresens; elle provient d'esprits enfermés dans un système préconçu, toujours enclins à affirmer l'existence de formes perdues et primitives des oeuvres que nous possédons, mais peu aptes à dégager l'originalité de ces dernières. En réalité, la *Mort Artu* est tout à fait remarquable par l'adresse et la netteté de son plan d'ensemble, la force

---

[31]   Although this theory was generally accepted by medievalists in the beginning, there has been an insistent tendency to return to the notion of a continuous transmission of at least some of the legends in a poetic form from the ninth through the eleventh centuries. See especially R. Menéndez Pidal, *La Chanson de Roland y el neotradicionalismo* (Madrid, 1959). Whether Bédier is right or wrong need not concern us here. What I am concerned with is to show that because of Bédier it became necessary to abandon the traditional assumptions about the composition of the poems and to begin thinking about them as the products of conscious artistic intention.

[32]   *Les Légendes épiques*, III, 385-453.

[33]   *Le Roman de Tristan par Thomas*, ed. J. Bédier (Paris, 1902-1905), II, 175.

[34]   See, for example, E. Brugger, "Studien zur Merlinsaga", *Zeitschrift für französische Sprache und Literatur*, XXIX (1906), 95, and Jesse L. Weston, *The Legend of Sir Lancelot du Lac* (London, 1901), p. 145.

dramatique de son intrigue, et même par ce qu'il semble permis d'appeler son architecture secrète ou le développement de ses thèmes conducteurs.[35]

However, the matter was not quite so simple as it seemed. If there existed two or three medieval works whose structure might be seen as roughly conformable to the general idea of well-made narrative, the great majority resisted such a reduction very firmly indeed. In order to establish their artistic integrity against the Wolfians, it was necessary to seek out other principles of structure, not necessarily related to Aristotelian notions of structure, but in accordance with which a story might be built. The earliest important study of this kind is Ferdinand Lot's *Etude sur le Lancelot en prose* (1918).

The prose *Lancelot*, a voluminous romance of the thirteenth century, the central and lengthiest portion of the Vulgate cycle, crowded with incident and characters, had naturally been viewed as a haphazard compilation. Lot's careful study showed that, on the contrary, its structure was the result of studious and minute calculation: the writer sometimes prepared for events hundreds of pages in advance; furthermore, his narrative technique was that of *entrelacement* (Lot was the first the use the term in this connection), the same technique used by Boiardo and Ariosto. Finally, all the adventures, Lot demonstrated, were fitted into a rigid time-scheme of days and hours, so that the various pieces of the story agreed chronologically. This presupposed, of course, that the writer had set up a calendar beforehand, so that he might better find his way through the complexities of his work. The possibility that such a narrative could have resulted from the chance accumulation of originally separate stories had clearly to be rejected:

La théorie qui voit dans le *Lancelot* une collection de 'lais' ou d'historiettes, rassemblés, agglutinés par une nuée d'auteurs et de remanieurs, ne saurait subsister. Il est non seulement invraisemblable, mais organiquement impossible qu'un roman agencé de la façon que nous venons d'étudier soit dû à une pluralité d'auteurs. Le *Lancelot* est bâti avec des procédés, des 'ficelles', des trucs aussi conscients qu'une pièce de théâtre de Beaumarchais, de Scribe ou de Sardou, et il n'est pas un grand roman du XVIIIe ou du XIXe siècle qui soit aussi 'composé,' au bon comme au pire sens du terme.[36]

Eugene Vinaver recently established that Malory's *Morte Darthur*, far from being a helter-skelter accumulation of stories from French romances,[37] represents in fact a final phase in the development of nar-

---

[35]   *Etude sur la Mort le Roi Artu* (Paris, 1936), p. 347.
[36]   Ferdinand Lot, *Etude sur le Lancelot en prose* (Paris, 1918), p. 28.
[37]   As they had been described, for example, by Walter Scott in the introduction to his *Sir Tristrem*, 4th ed. (Edinburgh, 1819), p. lxxxi.

rative interlacing, perhaps the most important of all, for what Malory did was to unravel the complex web of stories he got from the Vulgate and post-Vulgate Arthurian romances and set them down as separate stories in single file. Thus from an extravagantly complex and unwieldy mass of carefully interwoven stories, Malory analyzed out a series of tales based on the principle of singleness that underlies the rhythmic structure of modern fiction.[38]

Another peculiarly medieval structural pattern, having no relation either to well-made story or to interlaced narrative, was revealed in three important studies published in 1936, when Tolkien, Kellermann, and Curtius all arrived, independently it would appear, at a notion of diptych narrative organization, in which the story is divided into two more or less symmetrical halves. Three important early medieval narratives were at that time so interpreted: *Beowulf*, *La Vie de Saint Alexis*, and Chrétien's *Conte du Graal*.

In the case of *Beowulf*, critics had long been of the opinion that its primary and most obvious structural flaw was its division into two loosely related parts held together only by the person of the hero. In the first part, Beowulf triumphs over Grendel and Grendel's dam in a reasonably coherent and well proportioned sequence. Then, at verse 2200, the writer skips over fifty years and presents the fatal conflict with the dragon. The second half, it had been generally assumed, was merely a late-conceived sequel not in any sense integral with the poet's original plan.[39] Tolkien argued that, on the contrary, the structure of the work as a whole was "simple and static, solid and strong":

We must dismiss the notion that *Beowulf* is a 'narrative poem,' that it intends to tell a tale sequentially . . . . The poem was not meant to advance, steadily or unsteadily. It is essentially a balance, an opposition of ends and beginnings. In its simplest terms it is a contrasted description of two moments in a great life, rising and setting: an elaboration of the ancient and intensely moving contrast between youth and age, first achievement and final death.[40]

Tolkien's view of the poem's structure has won the approval of such important scholars as R. W. Chambers, Kemp Malone, and Arthur Brodeur.[41] It bids fair to become an established 'fact' of English literary history.

[38] *The Works of Sir Thomas Malory*, ed. E. Vinaver (Oxford, 1947), I, xxix-lviii.
[39] See W. P. Ker, *Epic and Romance*, 2nd ed. (London, 1922), pp. 90, 117, 160-161; and Fr. Klaeber's introduction to his edition, *Beowulf and the Fight at Finnsburg*, 3rd ed. (Boston, 1950), pp. li, cvii.
[40] J. R. R. Tolkien, "Beowulf, the Monsters and the Critics", *Proceedings of the British Academy*, XXII (1936), 271-272.
[41] R. W. Chambers, *Man's Unconquerable Mind* (London, 1939), p. 68: "Toward the study of *Beowulf* as a work of art, Professor Tolkien has made a contribution

Ernst Curtius' perception of the structure of the eleventh-century *Vie de Saint Alexis* was remarkably similar. The poem's main structural peculiarity is that it goes on over nearly half the length of the poem with events occurring after the saint's death. Winkler had deplored this lopsided quality in the poem and had expressed his surprise that a work allegedly dealing with a saint's life should devote scarcely fifty of its one hundred twenty-five stanzas to that life.[42] Curtius corrected this view, pointing out that that author was not trying to write a biography in the usual sense of the word; he was trying rather to paint the saint's life in the form of a diptych, setting the imperfections and transitoriness of his earthly life over against the lasting glory of the world beyond, balancing the saint's earthly ordeals against his heavenly glorification, and that this concern was reflected in the poem's bipartite form.[43]

Finally, the same sort of solution came to be proposed with regard to Chrétien's unfinished romance, the *Conte du Graal*, which up to verse 4740 deals exclusively with the adventures of Perceval, his failure at the Grail Castle and his development from a foolish youth into a full-fledged member of the élite Arthurian company; the second half, another 4500 verses – except for the 300 devoted to Perceval's encounter with the hermit who instructs him in religion – are given over inexplicably to the entirely mundane adventures of Gawain, which to the superficial observer have nothing whatever to do with what has gone before. This sharp structural duality has seemed to many critics so egregious a flaw that they have refused to acknowledge Chrétien's responsibility for it. Hofer, for example, maintains that the Gawain material was added by an awkward continuator,[44] while De Riquer argues that the two sections were written by Chrétien as independent

---

of the utmost importance." Kemp Malone, *The Old English Period*, in *A Literary History of England*, general ed. Albert C. Baugh (New York, 1948), Bk. I, Pt. I, 64: "More striking is the originality of *Beowulf* in its structure . . . . The two main parts balance each other, exemplifying and contrasting the heroic life in youth and age." Arthur Brodeur, *The Art of Beowulf* (Berkeley, 1959), pp. 71-74.

[42]   E. Winkler, "Von der Kunst des Alexiusdichters", *Zeitschrift für romanische Philologie*, XLVIII (1927), 589.

[43]   Ernst Curtius, "Zur Interpretation des Alexiusliedes", *Zeitschrift für romanische Philologie*, LVI (1936), 124: "Der Dichter wollte . . . ein Diptychon malen, auf welchem das Erdendasein in seiner Unvollkommenheit und Vergänglichkeit . . . der *durable glorie* des Jenseits gegenübergestellt würde. Die eine Tafel zeigt des Alexius Bewährung, die andere seine Verklärung."

[44]   St. Hofer, *Chrétien de Troyes: Leben und Werke des altfranzösischen Epikers* (Graz-Köln, 1954), pp. 210-214.

romances, neither of which he finished, and that they were gracelessly yoked together after his death by an unscrupulous editor.[45]

The controversy is still in progress, but the majority of scholars appear to have decided in favor of the solution Kellermann proposed in 1936 to the effect that the adventures of Perceval and Gawain are to be viewed as two contrasting and deliberately juxtaposed tableaux, Gawain's adventures being purely mundane, those of Perceval informed by a contrasting ethical and religious spirit.[46]

In principle, if not in matters of detail, Frappier has taken a similar view. He sees in the first part of the story a sharp contrast between Perceval's rustic manners and Gawain's exquisite courtliness, while at the center the two stand at about the same level of worldly attainment; then their destinies diverge in favor of Perceval:

Perceval ... choisit de peiner à la quête du Graal; Gauvain se laisse entraîner dans un tourbillon d'aventures ... toutes mondaines. Dès lors, ils ne se situent plus au même niveau, et dans la composition organique du *Conte du Graal* le roman de Gauvain sert de contrepoint à celui de Perceval (contrepoint et non contraste appuyé).[47]

All the studies I have summarized from the recent period of criticism represent, I think, a significant advance over the earlier, Wolfian studies. Bédier, as I have already indicated, appears to have provided the initial impulse toward a more respectful view of the medieval writer. And even if he should turn out to be quite wrong about the origins of the epic, he rendered an important service in turning the attention of some scholars, at least, toward the study of the works themselves and away from the vain and sterile activity of reconstructing hypothetical earlier versions having whatever form the 'researcher' might care to endow them with.

I have the uncomfortable feeling, however, that some of the more recent scholars, intent or discovering design where none has been perceived before, have occasionally been led to implausible hypotheses of extraordinary refinement and complexity. If such studies are for the

---

[45] Martin de Riquer, "La composición de 'Li Contes del Graal' y el Guiromelant", *Boletín de la Real Academia de Buenas Letras de Barcelona*, XXVII (1957-58), 279-320.

[46] W. Kellermann, *Aufbaustil und Weltbild Chrestiens von Troyes im Percevalroman* ("Beiheft zur Zeitschrift für romanische Philologie", Vol. LXXXVIII, 1936), pp. 94-95: "In der Quest Gauvains versucht der Dichter ... ein Gegenbild der Percevalhandlung zu zeichnen. Er führt das rein weltliche Rittertum vor neben dem stark ethisch religiös unterstrichenen."

[47] J. Frappier, *Chrétien de Troyes* (Paris, 1957), p. 176.

most part difficult to accept without reservation, they merit at least some consideration here. As I see it, there are four groups of critics to be distinguished: some see, particularly in the romances, an intellectual structure based on symbolism; a second group rationalize structure in terms of 'interior form'; numerical systems of structure have been proposed by yet a third group; while a fourth sees complex patterns of design through motif duplication.

The possibility that much of the incoherence of medieval narrative is only an appearance concealing a secret design has tantalized some scholars – R. R. Bezzola and his students most particularly – into an attempt to penetrate that design by a systematic application of the symbolic lore of the Middle Ages, as we find it, for example, in the lapidaries and bestiaries, in Bible exegesis, and in Bernardus Silvestris' allegorization of Virgil's *Aeneid*. The assumption appears to be that the narrative data of a story can be explained fully once the conversion from concrete appearance to mystical reality has been effected. Things that originally seemed arbitrary, it is assumed – the color of a horse, the number of lines in an episode, and so on – will ultimately emerge as having been rigorously necessary within the superior symbolic framework.

While no one can seriously doubt that medieval man often engaged in the activity of interpreting symbols or even that he believed in some way that things would be absurd if their significance were limited by their function and place in the phenomenal world, still the problem of critically organizing a narrative line, with all its complexities and multiplicity of detail, in terms of a unified symbolic interpretation without any express invitation from the author – as we find, for example, in Dante[48] and in the *Queste del Saint Graal* – is one fraught with uncertainty, as Dante well knew: "Circum sensum mysticum dupliciter errare contingit: aut querendo ipsum ubi non est, aut accipiendo aliter quem accipi debeat."[49]

Symbols have a naturally static character; they tend to arrest the mind and invite it to ponder deep mysteries. When we find them in medieval literature – although we cannot always be sure whether the writer intended them – they function rather as ornament than as the

[48] See *Inferno*, ix, 61-63: "O voi ch'avete li 'ntelletti sani,/ mirate la dottrina che s'asconde/ sotto 'l velame de li versi strani."

[49] "With respect to the mystical meaning, errors may be committed in two ways: either by looking for it where it does not exist, or by interpreting it otherwise than it ought to be." *De Monarchia*, III, iv.

informing principle of a narrative development; their relation to structure thus appears incidental rather than fundamental.[50]

Interpretation by reference to interior or inner form may be seen as an analogous attempt to transpose the structural question from the simple plane of the disposition of narrative materials to an intellectual or poetic level. Narrative works, it is true, have, in addition to their manifest subject matter, poetic and philosophical implications. Themes and ideas may be developed in the course of the story. These proceed from the writer's mind, from his general outlook on life. Presumably, if his world view is profound and coherent, that coherence will ultimately be reflected even in matters of minor detail in the work of art that he produces. In some sense, therefore, even when there is no indication of logical coherence within the story itself, if the various episodes function to illustrate the coherent workings of the artist's mind, we may say that the work itself is coherent.[51]

This rather highly refined notion of structure forms the basis of Wilhelm Kellermann's study of the structure of Chrétien's *Conte du Graal*. Kellermann resolves the major structural problem of the romance, the lengthy development Chrétien gives to the adventures of Gawain in a story that seems properly to belong to Perceval, in terms of an ideological core around which the narrative is organized. He is not content simply to point out that the story is divided into two contrasting tableaux; he wishes to see this structure as a projection of Chrétien's preoccupation with a world view that has been called gradualism. For Chrétien, he feels, the problem at that point in his life was to reconcile religion and chivalric ideals. From a dualist point of view,

[50] Scholars who have studied the relation of symbolism and structure have often provided isolated insights of considerable value, but I find their notions of little real value when they are put forth as general theories of structure. It is hardly possible here to go into the matter in any detail, and in any case, the matter is not entirely germane. The most interesting discussions of the question may be found in D. Bethurum (ed.), *Critical Approaches to Medieval Literature* (New York, 1960); M. Bloomfield, "Symbolism in Medieval Literature", *Modern Philology*, LVI (1958), 73-81; J. Fourquet, "Littérature courtoise et théologique", *Etudes Germaniques*, XII (1957), 35-39; R. S. Loomis, "The Grail Story of Chrétien de Troyes as Ritual and Symbolism", *PMLA*, LXXI (1956), 84-92; J. Misrahi's review of R. R. Bezzola, *Le Sens de l'aventure et de l'amour*, in *Romance Philology*, IV (1950-51), 348-361; A. Micha's review in *Romance Philology*, XI (1957-58), 410-412, of S. Bayrav, *Symbolisme médiéval* (Paris, 1957).

[51] On the distinction between *Aufbau* and *innere Form*, see J. Fourquet, "La Structure du Parzival", in *Les Romans du Graal aux XIIe et XIIIe siècles*, p. 199. See also on interior form J. Hytier, "La Méthode de M. Leo Spitzer", *Romanic Review*, XLI (1950), 51-53.

which would have been characteristic of the eleventh and early twelfth centuries, religious conviction necessarily implies the forsaking of this world and all its vanities, including chivalric activity. Gradualism however makes it possible to retain high religious principles as well as chivalric ideals, since within this view the strict negation of this world is abandoned and everything is assumed to have some necessary place in God's plan.[52]

Gawain, therefore, as exemplar of chivalric behavior, is acceptable to God for having realized his own sort of perfection; yet he is not so high in the cosmic scale as Perceval, who, in addition to being a first-class knight, is also predestined to penetrate the sacred mysteries of the Grail. Perceval's development cannot be fully understood unless it is seen side by side with that of Gawain. The contrast implies a gradation at the critical level where knightly perfection shades into spirituality.[53]

It seems hardly questionable that for Chrétien chivalry and religion were compatible in just such terms, in the Conte du Graal at any rate. The danger of this kind of critical approach is that it tacitly assumes the priority of the philosophical conception as an organizing principle of the narrative. When Kellermann assures us that the story line of the Perceval is determined from within, he means not from within the story, but from within the Weltbild.[54] The events are not assumed to be linked to one another directly, but through an external center of philosophical reference.

It seems an obvious point that, although in reading the Conte du Graal one might legitimately be led to reflections about Chrétien's gradualistic view of the world, it is not by any means clear that such reflections in Chrétien's mind could have given rise to the story itself. Such a view could be offered as an 'explanation' of the structure of any of the numerous works of the twelfth and thirteenth centuries in which religion and chivalry manage to coexist. It seems somehow less strained to suppose that the bipartition of the story is at bottom a standard structural device of purely formal character, one that we find in many other medieval works, and that the conceptual aspect of structure is a secondary fact. Writers of well-made narrative are able to express widely differing philosophical outlooks without deviating from what has come to be accepted as standard structural form. Until we

---

[52]   See Gunther Müller, "Gradualismus", Deutsche Vierteljahrsschrift, II (1924), 681-720; H. DeBoor, Geschichte der deutschen Literatur, II (Munich, 1955), 13-19.
[53]   Kellermann, Aufbaustil und Weltbild, pp. 85-95, 231-232, and passim.
[54]   Ibid., p. 16.

know more precisely what sort of thing the medieval writer had in mind, there is a danger of simply rationalizing narrative form on the basis of what we already know about intellectual history, avoiding the basic problem of how the writers went about putting their stories together.

It has also been suggested that many of the peculiarities of medieval narrative are to be attributed to the writer's intention to write in accordance with a preestablished numerical scheme. Paul Zumthor writes, I know not on what evidence, that Chrétien habitually planned his stories in two or three parts, "équilibré dans le détail par un système numérique à la fois simple et conséquent".[55] If Chrétien actually used any such system it is apparently unknown to Frappier, who finds only "un certain esprit de géométrie qui apparaît dans l'étendue à peu près égale de tous ses romans".[56] It is true that for the most part Chrétien chose to write his romances to a length of approximately 7,000 verses and that there is a general tendency toward bipartition within them, but I find no evidence of a true numerical system.

The only medieval confirmation of any such tendency, with respect to narrative literature, is a passage occurring in the so-called *Suite du Merlin*, a fragment of a post-Vulgate Grail romance, in which the writer announces his intention of writing his story in three parts of equal length, specifying at exactly what point each begins and ends:

Et sacent tuit cil qui l'estoire mon signeur de Borron vaurront oïr comme il devise son livre en trois parties, l'une partie aussi grant comme l'autre, la premiere aussi grant comme la seconde, et la seconde aussi grant comme la tierche. Et la premiere partie fenist il au commenchement de ceste queste, et la seconde el commenchement dou Graal, et la tierche fenist il apriès la mort de Lancelot, a celui point meïsme qu'il devise de la mort le roi March.[57]

(And may all those who wish the hear *mon signeur de Borron's* story know that he divides his book into three parts, one part as big as another; the first as big as the second, the second as big as the third. And the first part ends at the beginning of this quest, and the second at the beginning of the Grail, and the third finishes after Lancelot's death just at the point where it relates the death of King Mark.)

The writer immediately adds however that he has chosen to do this only in order to guard against corruptions of his text in the hands of later writers, men who might unscrupulously choose to amplify or abbreviate his version of the story:

[55] *Histoire littéraire de la France médiévale* (Paris, 1954), p. 197.
[56] *Chrétien de Troyes*, p. 89.
[57] *Merlin: Roman en prose du XIIIe siècle*, ed. G. Paris (Paris, 1886), I, 280.

Et ceste chose amentoit en la fin dou premier livre, pour chou que ße l'Estoire dou Graal estoit corrompue par auchuns translatours qui après lui venissent, tout li sage houme qui meteroient lour entente a oïr et a escouter pourroient savoir se elle lour seroit baillie entiere ou corrompue, et connisteront bien combien il i faurroit.[58]

(And he mentions this thing at the end of the first book so that if the story of the Grail is broken up by later scribes, all wise men who could endeavor to hear and to listen could know whether they have been given the story in its complete form or in a corrupted state, and they will know how much is lacking.

For my part, I do not doubt that the medieval writer, who was much less bound by the natural length and coherence of his subject matter than is the modern writer, often arbitrarily decided in advance to write his story to a certain length and even perhaps decided to divide it into parts of approximately equal length. But I submit that this is not essentially different from deciding to write a three-act play or a long novel in our time. Jules Romains it would appear, decided to write *Les Hommes de bonne volonté* in twenty-seven volumes simply because twenty-seven is a mystic number, the cube of three; furthermore, counting the spaces between words, there are twenty-seven units in his title, and he wished to have a set printed with the title running the whole length of the series.[59] We have examples of similar intention in the *Vita Nuova* and the *Divine Comedy* of Dante, and in the *Amorosa Visione* and *Teseide* of Boccaccio.

The real disadvantage of this approach in analyzing structure is that it cannot tell us anything important about the actual business of organizing a story. Once the writer has decided to tell his story in three thousand lines or seven thousand, he still has to tell the story, and numbers in themselves are not likely to be of much help to him. The possibility that the symbolism of the numbers might provide to mysterious insight into the meaning of the story seems to me to be purely wishful thinking.[60] At best, it is no more than a conceit. In the case of the very clear numerical structure of Dante's *Divine Comedy*, for example, it is no doubt true that the poem is structurally equated with the universe and that the poet is following the example of the Creator, who worked in threes; but although this is so, it is not more than a

---

[58] *Ibid.*
[59] So, at any rate, he said in a lecture I attended in 1950 at the University of Lyons.
[60] See, however, E. Bulatkin, "The Arithmetic Structure of the Old-French *Vie de Saint Alexis*", *PMLA*, LXXV (1959), 495-502.

conceit, an external ornament, a principle of division which determined the order and the number of parts, but does not dictate the substance.[61]

The idea that the medieval writer sought to achieve certain effects of design by duplicating narrative motifs is of considerably greater interest. Since medieval stories frequently violate the principle of logical sequence, they tend under analysis to separate into event-clusters, or episodes, each having a satisfactory sort of narrative unity, however unrelated they may be to each other. The various episodes are often identifiable folklore motifs and thus seem to be, as it were, ready-made narrative pieces introduced into a loose structural frame. The notion that there might be some design in the manner of their introduction has inevitably struck some students, who feel that the writer achieved certain symmetrical effects by repeating or duplicating narrative motifs, very much as in the graphic arts or in music a figure is repeated in a rhythmic pattern. Of course, in narrative, the motif is never exactly the same. It cannot be. But the effect can sometimes come close to duplication. Sometimes the writer reverses or inverts the figure so that, for example, under similar circumstances the opposite action occurs, or the same action under contrary circumstances.

The structure of a narrative work may, within this view, be seen as depending on a pervasive system of correspondences between sets of episodes. The earliest attempt at this sort of structural analysis that I have found is that of Vinaver, who proposed the following triangular pattern for the Tristan story: [62]

La forêt de Morrois
Epreuves– – –Epreuves
Le mariage de Marc– – – – – –Le mariage de Tristan
Iseut reconnaît Tristan– – – – – – – – –Tristan fou
Combat contre le dragon– – – – – – – – –Dernier combat
Le cheveu d'or– – – – – – – – – – – –Le dernier message
Rivalen et Blanchefleur– – – – – – – – – – – –Le miracle des deux arbres

---

[61] For a very complex scheme of numerical analysis, see Hans Eggers, *Symmetrie und Proportion epischen Erzählens* (Klett, 1956). See J. Bumke's severe criticism of his method in *Euphorion*, LI (1957), 222-227.

[62] E. Vinaver, *Etude sur le Tristan en Prose* (Paris, 1925), p. 9: "C'est ainsi", he writes, "que les principaux leitmotifs du drame se développent sur une ligne symétrique à la montée et à la descente de l'action extérieure; il y a, entre eux, une *harmonia praedestinata*, comme dans tout organisme supérieure où le corps et l'âme se complètent et s'expliquent mutuellement." For a similar view of the structure of the *Nibelungenlied*, see Mary Thorp, "The Unity of the Nibelungenlied", *Journal of English and Germanic Philology*, XXXVI (1937), 478.

Fascinating as this notion is, we can readily see what its primary drawback must be: the critic, faced with a story composed of a multitude of narrative details, resolves the story into elements that fit the pattern he has chosen and disregards those that do not. The combat with the Morholt, one of the permanent features of the story, has no place in this scheme, and so it is left out. The episodes immediately preceding the life in the forest are subsumed under the general abstract heading "épreuves" while a minor, though necessary, detail, Tristan's final message to Iseut, assumes a structural importance far out of proportion to its place in the legend. Finally, I do not see exactly what correspondence exists between the story of Rivalen and Blanchefleur, Tristan's parents, and the miracle of the two trees. Vinaver simply asserts that at the end of the story, when the poet tells us that the two trees that sprang up from the tombs of the lovers intertwined their branches above the roof of the church that separated them, the story of the parents "revient à l'esprit aussitôt".[63] My personal experience does not confirm this assertion. If anything, the final event seems rather a symbolic recapitulation of the story as a whole.

There are further difficulties. Within this view, the Tristan story can take on a number of different forms. Arthur Witte, for example, who sees the impulse toward duplication as the central structural characteristic of the legend,[64] takes as his basic story a hypothetical version reconstructed by Friedrich Ranke using standard methods of motif analysis and comparison.[65] The vanity of examining the structure of a hypothetical romance need be noted here only in passing, for the illustration of the method is the point of central interest.

Ranke's *Ur-Tristan* tells the story as follows: Tristan fights the Morholt and is wounded by a poisoned lance. Despairing of recovery, he takes his harp and sails off without destination seeking only to die far from the company of men. He arrives at a strange island where a fairy, Morholt's sister, heals his wound and falls in love with him. But once he has recovered his health, he spurns her love and returns to Cornwall. There, Isolde, his uncle's wife, sees him one day and asks him to flee with her. He refuses and she retaliates by casting a spell over him such that his former friends find him ridiculous. Unable to bear their mockery he flees with Isolde into the forest, but he remains

---

[63]   Vinaver, p. 8.
[64]   "Der Aufbau der ältesten Tristandichtungen", *Zeitschrift für deutsches Altertum*, LXX (1933), 166.
[65]   F. Ranke, *Tristan und Isolde* (Munich, 1925), pp. 3 ff.

true to his uncle in refusing to have sexual relations with her. At night he lays his sword between them on the ground. Mark discovers them asleep one morning, recognizes the significance of the sword, replaces it with his own and departs. Tristan, upon awakening, finds his uncle's sword, is deeply moved, and wants to return home. Later, Isolde and he cross a stream on horseback and water splashes up onto her thigh. She says: "Thou, water, art bolder than the boldest of heroes." This taunt breaks his resistance and the two become lovers. Mark finds them again, this time without the sword between them. Tristan and Mark do battle and Tristan is mortally wounded. He calls Isolde to him and smothers her on his breast. They die together.

Ranke was troubled that even in its most primitive form, the story appeared to consist of two independent parts, the first an *immram* (*Schiffahrt*), the second an *aithed* (*Fluchterzählung*), the two held together only by the person of the hero.[66]

To establish the unity of the sequence, Witte proposed that the story reflected a precourtly warrior ethic within which love and women constitute serious threats to the warrior's integrity. Thus he finds it possible to see the fight with the Morholt and Tristan's subsequent involvement with the fairy as a prelude to the later involvement with Isolde. He sets up the structure of the story in the following way:[67]

    I. Tristan und die Fee: die Liebe wird dem Helden zum ersten Male gefährlich.
   II. Tristan und Isolde: die Liebe wird dem Helden zum zweiten Male gefährlich.
      A. Erster Angriff der Liebe.
         Treubruch um der äusseren Ehre willen.
         Marke findet die Liebenden zum ernsten Male.
      B. Zweiter Angriff der Liebe.
         Treubruch um der inneren Ehre willen.
         Marke findet die Liebenden zum zweiten Male.

That makes a very neat design, but again we can see that it is because the writer has very carefully selected what he considers to be the salient features of the narrative and arranged them under appropriately selected abstract headings. Motifs actually duplicated, like Mark's two-fold discovery of the lovers, can be included just as they appear in the story. Others require a high degree of abstraction: the two main sections of the story are seen as duplications only by virtue of the repetition of the moral implication that love threatens the hero.

[66]   Ranke, p. 6.
[67]   Witte, p. 165.

Bodo Mergell carries the matter considerably further. First, he divides the story into twelve units, for each of which there is another unit to which it corresponds. The whole can then be laid out in the form of a cross and described as a *Zentralkomposition*:[68]

12. Tristan, dying, smothers Isolde		
11. Wounded, calls to Isolde		
10. Tristan fights with Mark		

7. Isolde's mockery (bold water motif)	8. Tristan breaks faith with Mark	9. Second dis- covery by Mark
4. Isolde's love (the spell)	5. Flight to the forest, Tristan keeps faith	6. First dis- covery by Mark

3. Healed by the fairy		
2. Wounding and *immram*		
1. Tristan's fight with the Morholt		

The episodes correspond in the following way: 1 with 10, combat motif; 2 with 11, wound motif; 3 with 12, an inversion, healing and dying motif; 4 with 7, mockery motif; 5 with 8, an inversion, faith motif, and 6 with 9, discovery motif.

There is no need to criticize in detail this sort of analytical procedure. The main point is that almost anything in two different episodes may be used to constitute a correspondence. The flexibility of the criteria for determining such relations makes it possible to construct patterns of great intricacy and delicacy. It is difficult to imagine a story that could not be made to assume, using such methods, whatever structural form one might wish.

I feel, however, that while there are cases in medieval narrative in which the writer clearly uses motif duplications as part of a structural plan,[69] there is no case in which one can demonstrate so rigorous a system as that suggested by Mergell and Witte.

Duplication, after all, may arise in medieval story from causes having nothing to do with a concern for structural elegance. The meagerness of the story-teller's imagination, for example, may force him from time to time to revert to a motif he used earlier, changing enough details to disguise his ruse. Then too, as certain episodes were of a sort enduringly popular with audiences, writers may very well have used them over and over for that reason.

---

[68] B. Mergell, *Tristan und Isolde: Ursprung und Entwicklung der Tristansaga des Mittelalters* (Mainz, 1949), p. 14.
[69] *Cf. infra*, pp. 86-98.

Studies in medieval narrative structure, it would appear, have not yet taken any clear direction, nor have they proceeded along clearly established lines. The existence of patterns of bipartition and of interlacing seems to me to be quite solidly established, although there has been little in the way of general recognition of such patterns, even among medievalists. Neither method has been explored in detail, nor has there been any attempt to indicate a relation between the two.

Studies of symbolism, inner form, numerical composition, and patterned duplication seem to me to be subtle out of proportion to our present state of knowledge of the simple facts of narrative organization in the Middle Ages. A broader basis of study appears to be in order, one that crosses lines of genre, and, from time to time, even national boundaries, in an attempt to discern the common elements of narrative structure within the medieval tradition.

The materials involved are of course much too vast to be considered thoroughly in a work of this scope. For the most part I have concentrated on the Old French literature, and I think this concentration is defensible enough since this literature is germinal, providing both matter and form for the derivative literatures of Germany, Italy, England, and Spain. Within the Old French tradition, I follow what I feel to be the main line of development as represented in the important narrative works of the twelfth and thirteenth centuries: *La Vie de Saint Alexis, La Chanson de Roland, La Chanson de Guillaume,* the romances of Chrétien de Troyes, the *Roman de Renart,* and the prose romances of the thirteenth century, particularly the *Lancelot-Graal* and the *Tristan.* I have largely ignored the Tristan poems of the twelfth century, in spite of their great interest, because they exist only as fragments. I have also deliberately excluded all examples of 'pure' allegory, that is, those in which the actors are expressly indicated to be personified abstractions. Works of this sort – the *Roman de la Rose* and *Piers Plowman* are the prime examples – are clearly subject to structural principles of an entirely different sort from those of regular narrative and call for separate treatment.

As far as method is concerned, I have worked only within the simplest and most general categories, those, in fact, around which Tasso built his poetic theory: beginning, middle, and end; length; and unity. Of the three, length would appear on the surface to be the least appropriate to a study of literary form; yet it is, I believe, a matter of central importance, as I shall seek to demonstrate in the sequel.

I

THE QUESTION OF BEGINNING, MIDDLE, AND END

Although the medieval rhetoricians are in general primarily concerned with the problems of amplification and extension of the narrative line, they are not altogether indifferent to the question of how that line should begin and end. Geoffroi de Vinsauf is particularly concerned. He considers at some length the various ways of beginning and ending stories. Yet his treatment is so peculiar, so completely divorced from the problem as we should conceive it, that it offers virtually no practical insight into the structural habits of the medieval writer.

He outlines no less than nine ways of beginning a story: at the beginning, middle, or end; at any of these places preceded by a proverb; or finally at any of these places preceded by an exemplum, a moral tale.[1] When he takes up the important matter of beginning *in medias res*, however, and of the manner of moving from the middle back to the beginning, we realize that we are dealing with a theoretician who has no practical idea of what he is talking about. Anyone who has read Virgil, we might assume – and Geoffroi cites him frequently – knows exactly how this particular problem is to be solved:

> Most epic poets plunge 'in medias res'
> (Horace makes this the heroic turnpike road),
> And then your hero tells, whene'er you please,
> What went before — by way of episode,
> While seated after dinner at his ease.[2]

Geoffroi, however, simply tells us that when the time comes to move from the middle back to the beginning, we should do so by using a relative pronoun!

---

[1] *Documentum de arte versificandi*, I, 2 ff., printed in E. Faral, *Les Arts poétiques du XIIe et du XIIIe siècle* (Paris, 1923).
[2] Byron, *Don Juan*, I, vi.

Si principium artificiale sumptum fuerit amedio ... et ita recessum fuerit a naturali principio, continuandum est per nomina relativa, scilicet talia *qui, quae, quod*.[3]

He most helpfully provides an example of what he means. If, he tells us, we wish to write the story of how Minos sent his son Androgeus to Athens, where he was killed out of envy by Athenian youths, thus provoking a war between Minos and the King of Athens, we need not begin at the beginning by talking about Minos; we may indeed begin by talking about Androgeus, then, at a given point, return to the beginning by saying, "who, sent away to study, etc.":

Principium sumptum a medio ... tale est 'Androgei titulus, etc.' Sic continuandum:
> *Quem*, missum studiis, invasit livor Athenis,
> Cujus in exitium poena retorsit eas.[4]

It seems clear that in this case we have rather to do with the manner of beginning and ending the first sentence, doubtless a long periodic sentence. It would begin, according to Geoffroi's suggestion, with a summary treatment of Androgeus' character and upbringing; it would then turn, by means of a relative clause, to the reasons for his going to Athens, and in this manner come to grips with the main action. This sort of advice would obviously be worthless if one had it in mind to compose a story extending more than a few sentences in length.

It is therefore of considerably more interest, in this regard, to look at the twelfth-century adaptation of the *Aeneid* into the Old French *Roman d'Enéas*. Despite Virgil's authority in the matter of epic form, extolled time and again in the rhetoric manuals, the adaptor refused to begin *in medias res*. He saw exactly what Virgil had done and deliberately undid it. He abstracted the Trojan prehistory from Aeneas' discourse at Dido's court and prefixed it to the beginning in the form of a summary prologue some 800 verses long, with a corresponding abbreviation of Aeneas' recapitulation. He made another structural change by introducing at the end a lengthy love story, apparently of his own devising, in which he set forth the gradual awakening of Lavinia's love for Aeneas, and his for her, thus intertwining the conquest of Latium and the destiny of the lovers. Such deliberate alterations in the form of the story make it appear that the adaptor was following a structural pattern that had more weight in his mind than Virgil's

---

[3] *Documentum*, II, 2; Faral, p. 268.
[4] *Ibid.*, II, 3; Faral, p. 269.

example and Horace's precept. He seems to have looked at Virgil's masterpiece and said to himself: "This is a good enough story, but it has two structural weaknesses: it begins badly and it ends badly." And so he put the beginning at the beginning where he thought it belonged, and he saw to it that the end included not only a military and political victory, but also a romantic involvement ending in a happy marriage.

It may well be that the structural pattern the writer was working from in this case was that of bipartite narrative.[5] The story is made to assume the form of a diptych: there are two cycles of adventures, the first culminating in the affair with Dido, in which *amor* separates the hero from his destiny as founder of the Latin race, the second culminating in the affair with Lavinia, in which *amor* and destiny are brought into harmony. The two parts are separated by a descent into Hell, which bridges the gap between part one and part two, ending the first and setting the second in motion.

If this conjecture is correct, then the medieval adaptor simply saw the *Aeneid* as a faulty attempt at bipartite writing, a narrative form that appears to have been particularly widespread during the twelfth century and which has, of necessity, its own special sort of beginning, middle, and end. In this form the middle is relatively brief and functions mainly to bring the first part of the story to an end while setting the second part in motion. Therefore, while in well-made modern narrative the middle binds together the beginning and the end and thus stands ideally as the point of maximum logical continuity, in medieval narrative the middle is frequently a point of maximum logical discontinuity, a foggy area characterized often by a vagueness of motivation and by swiftness of transition. This seems the necessary result of the desire to organize narrative into diptych form.

The tendency may be noted as early as the writing of *Beowulf*. The very brevity of the transitional passage between the first and second parts suffices to make the writer's intention clear. At the end of the first part, Beowulf is still a young man, fresh from his glorious victory over Grendel's dam, while at the beginning of the second part he is already an old man, ready to end his fifty-year reign in a heroic sacrifice. The transitional verses read as follows:

Afterwards, in later days, it fell out through the tumult of battles thus. When Hygelac lay low and battle-blades were the death of Heardred, in spite of the sheltering shield, when the martial Scyldings, hardy war-wolves, sought him out among his conquering people and attacked the nephew of Hereric in

---

[5]   See R. R. Bezzola, *Le Sens de l'aventure et de l'amour*, pp. 84-85.

force – then after that, the spacious realm came into the hands of Beowulf. He ruled it for fifty winters — that was an aged king, a veteran guardian of his people — until in the dark nights a certain one began to have power — a dragon, who on an upland heath kept watch over the hoard, a high stone-barrow. Below there lay a path unknown to men.[6]

Clearly, if the poet had wanted to, he could have amplified this material considerably. He could have gone far toward bridging the gap between the two parts by telling of the heroic exploits of his hero during his fifty-year reign. It is not likely that he omitted them for want of any traditional basis, since he refers in lines 2354-96 to Beowulf's courageous stand in Frisia, his slaying of Daegrefn and his escape, his refusal of the crown, the aid to the young king Heardred, and his vengeance against the Swedish king Onela. All these matters he might have treated at length, but it would appear that his judgment as an artist impelled him to set up his story as a calculated balance, an opposition of beginning and end.[7]

The *Chanson de Roland* presents an analogous pattern. It tells a reasonably coherent story up to verse 2608, then very abruptly introduces a new narrative impulse that starts the story off again in a new direction. In the first part of the poem, Ganelon, out of hatred for his stepson Roland, betrays the rear-guard of Charlemagne's army to the pagans. Roland refuses to summon help from Charlemagne, not far off in the Pyrenees, feeling that such an appeal would be a disgrace to his family. At last, however, seeing that all is lost, he sounds his horn and dies gloriously. Then Charlemagne returns just in time to rout the pagan forces and bury the Christian dead. Up to this point everything is managed in reasonably strict accord with the requirements of well-made narrative. But now the writer introduces the so-called Baligant episode, almost as though he were beginning a new poem:

> Li emperere par sa grant poestet
> .vii. anz tuz plens ad en Espaigne estet;
> Prent i chastels a alquantes citez.
> Li reis Marsilie s'en purcacet asez:
> Al premer an fist ses brefs seiler,
> En Babilonie Baligant ad mandet,
> Ço est l'amiraill, le viel d'antiquitet,
> Tut survesquiet e Virgilie e Omer.
> En Sarraguce alt sucurre li ber,
> E, s'il nel fait, il guerpiat ses deus

---

[6] *Beowulf and the Finnsburg Fragment*, trans. John R. Clark Hall, rev. C. L. Wrenn (London, 1950), ll. 2200-14, p. 132.
[7] A. G. Brodeur, *The Art of Beowulf* (Berkeley, 1959), pp. 72-74.

> E tuz ses ydeles que il soelt adorer,
> Si recevrat seinte chrestientet,
> A Charlemagne se vuldrat acorder.
> E cil est loinz, si ad mult demuret.
> Mandet sa gent de .xl. regnez,
> Ses granz drodmunz en ad fait aprester,
> Eschiez e barges e galies e nefs;
> Suz Alixandre ad un port juste mer.
> Tut sun navilie i ad fait aprester.
> Ço est en mai, al premer jur d'ested.
> Tutes ses oz ad empeintes en mer.[8]

(The emperor in his great strength has been full seven years in Spain; he is taking castles there and many cities. King Marsile is very worried. In the first year he had letters sealed; he has sent word to Baligant at Babylon. He is the emir, the old man of ancient days, who has lived longer than Virgil and Homer. He has sent word to the baron that he should come to Saragossa to help him; and if he will not do it, Marsile will deny his gods and all the idols which he is used to worship; he will take holy Christianity and will be ready to make peace with Charlemagne. And Baligant is far away and he has made a long delay. He calls his people from forty kingdoms and has had his great warships made ready, his sailing boats and barges and galleys and ships. There is a port on the sea below Alexandria where he has had all his fleet made ready. It is in May, on the first day of summer. He has launched all his armies on the sea.)

The striking similarity between this laisse and that which begins the poem suggests insistently that the writer is, in a manner of speaking, beginning again at this point:

> Carles li reis, nostre emperere magnes,
> Set anz tuz pleins ad estet en Espaigne,
> Tresqu'en la mer conquist la tere altaigne.
> N'i ad castel ki devant lui remaigne,
> Mur ni citet n'i est remés a fraindre,
> Fors Sarraguce ki est en une muntaigne.
> Li reis Marsilie la tient, ki Deu nen aimet,
> Mahumet sert e Appolin recleimet.
> Nes poet guarder que mals ne l'i ateignet.
>
> (vv. 1-9)

(Charles the King, our great emperor, has been full seven years in Spain. He has taken the high land as far as the sea. There is no castle that still stands before him; there is no wall or city left for him to break, except Saragossa, which is on a mountain. King Marsile holds it, who does not love God; he serves Mohammed and confesses Apollin. There he cannot keep himself from the reach of trouble.)

---

[8]   *La Chanson de Roland*, ed. J. Bédier (Paris, 1922), vv. 2609-29. All subsequent references to the *Roland* will be to this edition.

At any rate, now that the writer has introduced Baligant, it is possible for him to resume the epic struggle between pagan and Christian. This time, however, we see the supreme representative of Christianity, in person, pitted against the supreme representative of pagandom, and the struggle thus acquires a symbolic flavor. Charlemagne, of course, defeats Baligant, for God is on the side of the Christians. Then he returns to France to punish the traitor Ganelon.

Nothing would have been easier than to introduce the summoning of Baligant at an earlier point in the narrative. Further mentions of the expectation of his arrival could equally well have been inserted along the way. And this is really all we should require in order to qualify the story as a generally coherent structure. The deliberate postponement of the Baligant material to the middle of the poem separates the two halves more sharply, accentuates the division into two roughly symmetrical and contrasting tableaux: Roland's struggle with Marsile, ending with the death of Roland, balanced by the struggle between Baligant and Charlemagne, ending with the death of Baligant, the whole tied together by the treason and punishment of Ganelon – an ABBA pattern of correspondences.[9]

Thus, in the case of both *Beowulf* and the *Chanson de Roland*, there is a form that may be described as having a beginning, middle, and end, but which in fact has two beginnings, two middles, and two ends. The central discontinuity that seems so clumsy to us appears to have served the medieval writer as a means to a particular esthetic end – it was, we may suppose, a special grace in story-telling.

Obviously, this sort of structure, where the story is extended beyond a point of logical discontinuity, partly for purposes of amplification and partly for purposes of symmetry, will lose much of its point if the balanced stories are proliferated into a series of episodes.

A story which resolves itself logically into a string of juxtaposed, mutually independent episodes, each of which makes a reasonably coherent short story, is happily called by French critics a *roman à tiroirs*, a phrase that makes us think of a chest of drawers which are explored one after the other. Usually a single hero serves to provide the elementary principle of unity in this sort of narrative. In English we have no comparable term; such stories are sometimes called episodic, which is not entirely appropriate since almost all stories can be resolved into episodes. We also refer to such stories as picaresque, since

[9] *Cf.* Pierre Le Gentil, *La Chanson de Roland* (Paris, 1955), p. 90, and J. Schwietering, *Die deutsche Dichtung des Mittelalters* (Potsdam, 1932), p. 104.

in Spanish stories of this type the hero is often a *picaro*, or rogue. The oldest story of this sort is that of the labors of Hercules, but perhaps the most widely known example of the genre is the French story of *Gil Blas* (1715) by Alain René Lesage. The moment Gil Blas comes to the end of one adventure the author sends him off on another. The person of the hero serves as the only real link between the various sections of the story. The parts might be reshuffled, added to or subtracted from, without detriment to the comprehensibility of the whole. Molière's plays *L'Etourdi* and *Les Fâcheux* are constructed in the same way. Other examples will occur to every reader: the Greek romances, the *Golden Ass*, and even to a certain degree the *Odyssey*. Frame stories, such as the *Canterbury Tales*, the *Decameron*, and the *Thousand and One Nights*, are a subspecies of *roman à tiroirs*, one incidentally not much in favor in the early Middle Ages, the only clear example being the *Roman des Sept Sages*, of which we have a Latin version titled *Dolopathos* written during the closing years of the twelfth century, and which was translated into Old French in 1210.

The structural pattern of such stories is basically repetitive and sequential, one event-cluster after another; it is not developmental. Such stories have not a single beginning, middle, and end; each episode has its own beginning, middle, and end. Structurally unimaginative, stories of this sort may nonetheless prove very effective in the reading, depending on the quality and arrangement of the episodes. For when we say that we can discard episodes or rearrange them at will, we are referring only to the matter of logical implication; we mean only that such operations would not introduce obscurities or contradictions into the narrative. They might, however, materially alter the impression the story makes on the reader's sensibility, for it is quite conceivable that an episode, without being logically necessary to the sequence of the story, may yet provide excitement, charm, poetry, and of course, variety.

It is sometimes assumed that the *roman à tiroirs* is a primitive narrative form from which modern fiction developed through the addition of a causative principle which organizes and unifies a simple chronological sequence.[10] In fact, however, this is by no means easy to prove, and the study of medieval narrative does not help to confirm this hypothesis. Some of the oldest narrative poems we have are quite logical in their structure: *Beowulf* and the *Chanson de Roland*, for example, show only one point of strong logical discontinuity – and in both cases

---

[10]   Wellek and Warren, *Theory of Literature* (New York, 1948), p. 222.

it appears to be deliberate. The purest examples of the *roman à tiroirs* occur in relatively late compilations like the *Roman d'Alexandre*, the *Roman de Renart*, and the cyclic prose *Tristan*, in all of which the structural principle appears to proceed from an encyclopedic impulse. There are relatively few examples of the genre in the early literature of France. However, the twelfth-century epic the *Couronnement Louis*[11] will serve to illustrate the technique. It falls readily into four quite independent episodes whose sequence is entirely arbitrary, the first alone being described by the title.

In the *Couronnement*, Charlemagne, old and weary, is about to retire and crown his fifteen-year-old son Louis at Aix-la-Chapelle. His son hesitates to take up the crown, and Charles is furious. A traitor, Anseïs of Orleans, offers to assume power as regent for a period of three years. The emperor is inclined to accept, but Guillaume d'Orange arrives, penetrates the traitor's designs, and strikes him dead with a single blow of his fist. He then takes up the crown and puts it on Louis' head by force.

II. Five years later, Guillaume gets permission to make a pilgrimage to Rome. There he learns that an army of Saracens, led by Galafré, has landed in Italy. At the head of the Pope's army, Guillaume meets the pagans. It is proposed that the matter by settled by a single combat between Guillaume and the pagan giant Corsolt. Guillaume triumphs, but in the course of the fight he gets the tip of his nose cut off, and thereafter he is to become known as Guillaume *al cort nez* (Shortnose). The Saracens fail to live up to their part of the bargain, and in a general engagement which follows they are soundly beaten. Galafré converts to Christianity and offers his daughter in marriage to Guillaume.

III. Guillaume is about to marry the girl when messengers arrive from France announcing that the barons of the realm are conspiring against Louis, trying to crown Richard of Normandy's son Acelin as king. Guillaume returns to France, puts down the rebellion, slays Acelin, and trims Richard's beard by way of admonition.

IV. Later, the Pope dies and Guy of Germany takes over the Holy City. Guillaume returns to Rome, slays Guy and throws his body into the Tiber, then crowns Louis king of Italy. A final laisse, forty-eight verses long, tells us hurriedly that new rebellions then broke out in France, that Guillaume returned to put them down, then married his sister to Louis.

[11]   *Le Couronnement de Louis*, ed. E. Langlois, *CFMA* (Paris, 1920).

Here we have an example of a writer who had two narrative strings to his bow: the story of Guillaume as defender of the Emperor, and that of Guillaume, defender of the Pope. He alternated the two in an ABAB pattern to avoid monotony, but he was able to introduce only a minimal amount of variation. He clearly had no interest in providing any logical basis for the sequence. It is purely chronological, held together only by the reappearance of certain central figures and themes, and if it has a point, the point is simply the greatness of Guillaume d'Orange. Of the four separate stories that compose the tale, none can lay claim more legitimately than any other to the position of beginning, middle, or end, except insofar as they are arranged in the sequence of time, and it would be possible to prefix other episodes to the beginning or to append still others to the end without detriment to the structure of the whole.

The same sort of structure may be seen in the fourteenth branch of the *Roman de Renart*,[12] a sequence of five unrelated episodes.

I. Renart and Tibert the cat steal into a cellar in search of food. Renart holds up the lid of a hopper while the cat goes in and drinks his fill from a container of milk. Then the cat maliciously knocks over the container so that there will be none left for Renart, trying the while to make it look like an accident. In retaliation, as the cat leaves the hopper, Renart 'accidentally' drops the heavy lid on the cat's tail. Then the two go to the henhouse, where Tibert advises Renart to attack the cock. The cock cries out and the farmer comes with his dogs. Tibert, foreseeing this result, has already fled. Renart barely escapes.

II. Fleeing from the dogs, Renart finds some sacramental wafers, which were dropped accidentally by a priest. He eats all but two, which he keeps in his mouth. He meets Primaut the wolf, Isengrin's brother, who asks what he has in his mouth. Renart lets him sample the wafers and suggests that they seek for more at a nearby minster. There, in addition to wafers, they find sacramental wine. Primaut gets drunk and is seized with an irresistible desire to sing vespers. Renart is charmed by the idea, tonsures the wolf, persuades him to ring the bells, and decks the wolf out in priest's vestments. Then Primaut climbs into the pulpit and begins to howl. Renart meanwhile sneaks out through the hole by which the two had entered, plugging it with earth after leaving. The priest, awakened by the bells, sees the wolf through a crack in the door and sounds the alarm. Primaut tries to get out through

---

[12]   *Le Roman de Renart*, ed. E. Martin (Strasbourg, 1882-1887), II, 109-139.

the hole, finds it plugged, and escapes only by crashing through a window, nearly breaking his neck. When he finds Renart, the fox convinces him that the priest must have plugged the hole.

III. Renart advises Primaut to pretend that he is dead and to lie down in the path of a cart driven by fish merchants, so that these merchants, hoping to profit by selling his hide, will throw him into the cart with the fish, which he will then be able to eat at his leisure. Renart had in fact successfully managed this maneuver in branch III. Primaut is not so lucky. He gets himself beaten and goes off with an empty belly.

IV. Renart now leads Primaut to a farm where salted hams are hanging in a shed. The two enter through a narrow opening and eat their fill. Renart manages to leave, but the wolf has eaten so much that he cannot squeeze through. Renart ties a rope around his neck and pulls, pinching him and causing him to yelp in pain. The noise arouses the farmer. Renart flees. Primaut fights with the farmer and manages, after being beaten, to escape with his life.

V. Renart now tells Primaut that he knows of a flock of geese guarded by only one man. Primaut goes after them and is badly torn up by two fierce dogs. He runs angrily back to the fox, strikes him in the face, tramples on him, but in the end, yielding to Renart's pleas, he agrees to swear eternal friendship. Renart wants the oath pronounced on the tomb of a saint nearby. It is in fact an animal trap, which is sprung when Primaut sets his foot on the spot indicated by Renart, who leaves him there in pain and goes home.

One is struck not only by the logical independence of the various episodes in this sequence, but more especially by their structural similarities. In three of them, the first, second, and fourth, the narrator follows the same plan: two animals in search of food break into a forbidden supply, engage in mutual trickery, and ultimately attract the attention of the owner. When the writer tries to vary his fare, as in the third episode, he is driven back on a motif from an earlier branch. He is at his best when he provides variations on his central theme. There is a certain artistry in all this, there is certainly humor in Primaut's continuing to come back for more punishment, but the author has evidently no interest in writing a continuous, organically developed narrative. None of the episodes may be considered as more legitimately a beginning, middle, or end than any other. Each is a separate unit.

We may distinguish another type of *roman à tiroirs*, in which there is both a beginning and an end, but the middle section is a series of drawers. The writer points early in the story to a terminal objective, then artfully delays its coming. The end is usually simple and easily foreseeable: a marriage, a military victory, the accomplishment of a quest, the reunion of separated lovers. In this sort of story there are minimally two fixed elements: the beginning and the end. The writer's task is to fill in the middle with exciting and various adventures. What he did in many cases was to sandwich a *roman à tiroirs* between the beginning and the end. The resulting structure is like an accordion, flexible in the middle and steady at both ends.

Examples of this structure are so numerous that we need only consider one classic case, Chrétien's *Chevalier de la Charrete*.[13] The initial situation is the abduction of Guenevere by Meleagant; the end it immediately puts in view is her rescue. Before Lancelot finds her, however, he must pass through dozens of adventures, a sort of obstacle course deliberately erected between him and his goal. The adventures are not logically related to one another, nor motivated in any usual sense, but Chrétien is a subtle enough artist to suggest an obscure and mysterious relation between them and the accomplishment of the quest, as though the obstacles were set out deliberately by some unknown person or persons in the story whose intent it was to test Lancelot's courage and devotion. One has the persistent feeling that Lancelot is being watched and his comportment duly noted and reported to the authorities, although in the end this feeling cannot by logically justified.

For example, in a famous episode, early in the tale, Lancelot's horse is killed and he is obliged to continue on foot. He meets a dwarf driving a cart, the kind in which prisoners were then exposed to public derision; the dwarf invites him to get into the cart, promising to lead him to the queen. Lancelot hesitates for a moment, then gets in. This has serious consequences later on, for when Lancelot finally rescues Guenevere she turns coldly from his presence and walks away. She explains later that it was because he had hesitated an instant before getting into the cart, and that for that moment at least, Lancelot was more concerned about himself than he was about Guenevere. This is one of the very few instances of intercomplication between the adventures and the frame of the story. But if we press the matter a little and ask how Guenevere knew about all this, we run into a blank wall. We may suppose that the dwarf told her, but under what circumstances and why? Was the dwarf sent by Guenevere? There is no such indica-

---

[13]   *Le Chevalier de la Charrete*, ed. M. Roques (Paris, 1958).

tion. Moreover, as a prisoner of Meleagant she was hardly in a position to manage such a maneuver. No explanations are offered.

Similarly, in another episode, Lancelot meets a beautiful maiden who offers to help him in his quest if he will consent to go to bed with her that night. He at first declines, then, realizing that he needs her help, he changes his mind. Before going to bed, the maiden suggests that Lancelot go outside and get some fresh air. When he returns, he finds her being attacked in her bedroom by a knight, while two other knights stand guard at the door, backed by four sergeants armed with axes. The maiden, her clothing torn off down to the navel, calls for help. Lancelot boldly steps in and begins to do battle with the attackers. After considerable spirited fighting, the maiden abruptly dismisses the men. The whole affair had been staged. At any rate, Lancelot now goes to bed with the girl, keeping his solemn word, but that is all he does. Once in bed, he turns his back on her and takes care not to touch her or to look at her. She then gets out of bed and goes to another room in order that he may sleep. The next day, she helps him along his way.

The whole episode looks as though it were some sort of test of Lancelot's capacity for sexual fidelity, presumably arranged by Guenevere. But how could Guenevere, who was herself a prisoner, have found such a willing and available accomplice? Chrétien offers no explanations. He is unconcerned to provide a logical substructure for the story. Although a few summary explanations at the end would have sufficed for the purpose, Chrétien preferred to mystify. To the degree that the various episodes in his romance remain logically unrelated to the main story and to one another, they constitute a sort of internal *roman à tiroirs*. Clearly, Chrétien could have used more or fewer adventures in his series without disturbing the structure of his story, which, it will be noticed, affords a conveniently flexible frame in which to insert episodes. In its simplest form, the story contains only two events, the abduction and the rescue. Everything else is episode.

The idea that a story may be thought of as a loose framework holding together a series of episodes is not peculiar to the Middle Ages. Aristotle's discussion of the art of narrative shows that he thought in much the same terms. The first thing, he tells us, that a writer must do is to make a plot outline in general terms, which he may then amplify with episodes:

His story, whether already made or of his own making, he should first simplify and reduce to a universal form, before proceeding to lengthen it out by the insertion of episodes. . . . One must mind, however, that the episodes are appropriate. . . . In plays the episodes are short; in epic poetry they serve to lengthen out the poem. The argument of the *Odyssey* is not a long one. A certain man has been abroad for many years; Poseidon is ever on the watch for him, and he is all alone. Matters at home have come to this, that his substance is being wasted and his son's death plotted by the suitors to his wife. Then he arrives there himself after his grievous sufferings, reveals himself, and falls on his enemies; and the end is his salvation and their death. This being all that is proper to the *Odyssey*, everything else in it is episode.[14]

It is only Aristotle's general insistence on a sequence governed by probability or necessity that makes his conception – and ours – different from that of the medieval writer in this respect. The difference, of course, is not to be minimized.

At any rate, we have so far distinguished two sorts of *roman à tiroirs*. The first is an indeterminate string of episodes, none of which functions either as an end or as a beginning. A second sort has the episodes sandwiched between a clearly defined beginning and end. There is yet a third sort to be found in medieval story, a simple series of unrelated episodes that is nonetheless provided with a beginning, an initial impulse that calls into play the series of episodes of which the story is composed, but which leads nowhere, or, it may be, only to an arbitrarily designated conclusion. The eleventh branch of the *Roman de Renart* has this form.[15]

The story opens on a grave situation. All of Renart's family are suffering from hunger pangs. His wife, Hermeline, is pregnant and fears that she will lose her child. Renart goes off on a search for food. If we keep this initial situation in mind, we shall only fatigue ourselves needlessly: the author has by this time forgotten it. Renart meets Ysengrin, fleeing from a crowd of *vileins*. The two run together until Ysengrin gets tired and lies down to sleep beside a tree. Renart decides to play a trick on him by tying him to the tree. A *vilein* happens along, sees the wolf at a disadvantage, fights him but soon gives up. Renart then frees his companion. The wolf, not suspecting Renart's role in all this, thanks him and invites him to dinner. Renart then goes off on a series of adventures, tries unsuccessfully to pull a similar trick on Roenel the mastiff, whom he also finds beside a tree, eats four young birds, then, surprised by the parents, fights with them and barely manages to survive. Found unconscious by a passing knight, he is carried off, but manages again to escape. He tricks a mother sparrow into letting him

[14] *Poetics,* 17. 1455b (Bywater's translation).
[15] *Le Roman de Renart*, ed. Martin, I, 390-484.

administer medical aid to her nine young ones, eats them, and tells the mother they are now permanently out of harm's reach. The mother retaliates by enlisting the services of a large dog, Morhout, who tears Renart with his teeth and claws and leaves him for dead. Ysengrin finds Renart and cares for him at his home. The convalescence lasts nearly a month (v. 1482), and eventually Renart is restored to health. Then the writer begins a long mock *chanson de geste*, a struggle between the Saracen animals – camels, lizards, and so on – and the Christian animals. Renart is made regent during the Emperor's absence, betrays his overlord, and by forging letters manages to establish himself as emperor and hushband of the lioness. Noble eventually returns and regains control over his empire. He forgives Renart's treason upon being reminded that Renart had once saved his life. So the branch ends. We never find out whether Hermeline lost her child.

The early thirteenth-century epic *Girart de Vienne*[16] has a similarly curious structure. It begins, more or less, with the departure of the four sons of Garin de Monglane in search of fame and fortune. Milon strikes out for Italy, Hernault for Beaulande, Girart and Renier for Charlemagne's court. After a period of devoted service to the emperor, Renier is rewarded with the duchy of Gennes, Girart with that of Vienne. After a period of married life, Girart is one day visited by a young, headstrong fellow, with whom he almost comes to blows. But upon learning that this is Aymeri, son of his brother Hernault, he opens his arms, and uncle and nephew embrace.

In time Aymeri is bored living with his uncle and he too goes to Charlemagne's court. There he learns that the Empress Galienne had many years before humiliated his uncle Girart without his knowing it, by sticking out her toe – she and the emperor were in bed at the time – at the moment when Girart knelt to kiss the emperor's foot as a gesture of homage. Aymeri flies back to Vienne in a rage and tells Girart of his disgrace; whereupon Girart summons the clan and declares war on Charles.

After a long indecisive battle, it is proposed that the matter be settled by a single combat between Roland and Olivier, Roland being Charles's nephew and Olivier Girart's. To complicate matters, Roland is in love with Alda, Olivier's sister. But the duel is terminated by divine intervention, and Roland and Olivier swear eternal friendship. The main struggle goes on, however, until Charlemagne is captured by

16   *Girart de Vienne*, ed. G. F. Yeandle (New York, 1950).

Girart, who yields to a generous impulse and pardons the Emperor, who in turn pardons him. The marriage of Roland and Alda would then have brought the poem to a close except for the arrival of a messenger announcing a Saracen invasion.

The *trouvère* began in this case with a story of the four sons of Garin, quickly dropped the first two, then a third, switched the focus of the story onto Aymeri, worked up an epic struggle to pull the family together again, then shifted his focus once more, this time to Roland and Olivier, whose struggle came to nothing, finally brought the war to a close, and nearly ended with the marriage of Roland and Alda. It was no doubt of such epics as this that Léon Gautier wrote:

> Sauf de bien rares exceptions, nos épiques des tout premiers temps ne songent même pas à faire le plan de leurs poèmes. Ce que nous appelons la composition leur est généralement inconnue. Ce sont des improvisateurs ou des enfants. Il marchent devant eux sans savoir où ils vont ni quelles seront les étapes de leur route. A l'aventure ils vont à l'aventure. Si l'on pouvait comparer leurs chansons à un délit (certains critiques ont été jusque-là) on ne saurait en tout cas les accuser de préméditation.[17]

Indeed, it does not appear as though the *trouvère* in this case had any clear notion of where he was going. But the composition of the poem is not so absurd as it looks. The important roles given to Aymeri de Narbonne and to Roland and Olivier, which seem so strangely out of place, are in fact determined by the fact that *Girart de Vienne* belongs to an epic cycle, a series of poems of considerable length, in which it immediately precedes the epic *Aymeri de Narbonne*, which begins on the way back from Roncevaux, site of the famous battle described in the *Chanson de Roland*. Thus the writer was in a sense writing a double prelude, first to the *Chanson de Roland*, which is why he introduced Roland, Olivier, and Alda, and second to the epic *Aymeri de Narbonne*, which no doubt was already in existence.[18]

In fact the matter of beginning, middle, and end is considerably altered when we begin to look, not at individual epics and romances of the Middle Ages, but at whole cycles.

[17] *Histoire de langue et de la littérature française*, general ed. L. Petit de Julleville, I, Pt. 1, 132.

[18] Neither epic can be dated with any certainty. Both are from the first quarter of the thirteenth century. The assumption that *Girart de Vienne* was written later is based on the general knowledge we have of the usual rule in the composition of epic cycles, which, as Frappier notes, "a procédé presque régulièrement à rebours de la chronologie . . . . Les fils ont engendré les pères". *Les Chansons de geste du cycle de Guillaume d'Orange* (Paris, 1955), I, 63.

A large part of medieval narrative exists in cyclic form. The manuscripts, that is, contain not one, but a series of stories, epics, and romances, revolving around a single hero (King Arthur, Renart) or a family of heroes (Guillaume d'Orange and his uncles and nephews, Charlemagne and his kin). They are of massive construction; one cyclic manuscript of the Guillaume cycle contains no less than eighteen epics, making some 80,000 lines in all; the Vulgate cycle of Arthurian prose romances takes up 2,800 pages of close print in Sommer's edition.[19]

We know many of these stories today in separate editions, partly because the task of editing and printing, or even reading, an entire cycle is scarcely inviting. It is nonetheless important to remember that the authors of these cycles – in most cases there were several – were not in fact concerned with the problem of writing a whole narrative, but with adding on to an already existing narrative corpus. The content and structure of such stories is therefore in large part determined by their position in a narrative series.

For example, the Old French epic *La Chevalerie Vivien* is known to us in nine cyclic manuscripts, the largest of which (B1) contains seventeen others. In eight of the nine, it occurs between the *Enfances Vivien*, which relates the adventures of the hero's childhood and young manhood – a standard feature of the epic cycles – and *Aliscans*, which tells the story of the battle in which Vivien lost his life. The story of his *chevalerie* is therefore part of a biographical sequence, and this in turn accounts for the story's major structural peculiarity, which is that it ends *in medias res*.

On the occasion of his being dubbed knight by his uncle Guillaume d'Orange, Vivien takes an oath never to retreat before the pagans by so much as a full foot of earth (*plein piet de terre*). Guillaume tries to persuade him to retract so foolhardy a vow, but without success. Vivien goes into Spain with ten thousand knights, newly dubbed, and wreaks havoc. One day he and his men massacre a group of pagan merchants and send their corpses in defiance to King Deramed at Cordova, after which the Christian knights camp near the sea at a field called Aliscans, awaiting Deramed's response. Deramed embattles an enormous army. Vivien and his cousin Girard see the formidable fleet approach. Girard advises sending for help from Guillaume, but Vivien will not hear of it; such an appeal might be construed as an indication of cowardice. Later, after most of his men have been killed in the unequal struggle, Vivien

---

[19] *The Vulgate Version of the Arthurian Romances*, ed. H. Sommer, 8 vols. (Washington, 1908-1916).

reconsiders and sends Girard after Guillaume.[20] When the latter arrives
with twenty thousand men, things are going badly for Vivien. His horse
has been killed and he himself is badly wounded, but he goes on fighting in a blind rage. He meets his uncle in the melee, recognizes him
briefly and is separated from him. Here the story abruptly ends, in the
middle of an undecided battle.

If we simply read this epic in Terracher's edition (Paris, 1923), without being aware that the battle continues into and through the next
poem of the series, *Aliscans*, we are likely to arrive at the conclusion
that the writer had a curious notion of how a story should end. We
should be wrong, but no more wrong than in admiring the *Aliscans* for
beginning *in medias res* in accordance with the classic formula.

Writers of three centuries, of widely differing tastes and talents, all
contributed to the elaboration of the macroepic we know as the *geste*,
or cycle, of Guillaume d'Orange, which was famous in the Middle Ages
as the *geste* of Garin de Monglane, Guillaume's great-grandfather.[21]

It is not clear in any detail how such cycles came to be established.
Obviously the idea of such a development could hardly have been
present from the beginning. What apparently happened was that the
earliest epic of the cycle – probably the *Chanson de Guillaume*[22] –

---

[20]   An obvious echo of the *Chanson de Roland*. See E. Hoepffner, "Les Rapports
littéraires entre les premières chansons de geste", *Studj Medievali*, IV (1931), 233-
258.

[21]   The *chansons de geste* are traditionally grouped into three major cycles: the
cycle of Charlemagne, the cycle of Doön de Mayence (the unruly vassal cycle), and
the cycle of Garin de Monglane. The division dates back to a thirteenth-century
trouvère, Bertrand de Bar-sur-Aube:

> N'ot que trois gestes en France la garnie,
> Ne cuit que ja nus de ce me desdie.
> Des rois de France est la plus seignorie,
> Et l'autre aprés, bien est droiz que jeu die,
> Fu de Doön a la barbe florie
>
> . . . .
> La tierce geste qui molt fist a prisier,
> Fu de Garin de Monglenne au vis fier.
>
> (*Girart de Vienne*, ed. Yeandle, vv. 11-15; 46-47.)

[22]   The problem of the origins of the cycle has been much debated. General
critical opinion tends toward the view that the *Chanson de Guillaume* was the
earliest. It does not appear in any of the cyclic manuscripts, its place being occupied
by *La Chevalerie Vivien* and *Aliscans*. We have only a poor manuscript from the
middle of the thirteenth century, unknown in recent times until 1903. Its importance lies in the fact that it is an Anglo-Norman copy, and the Anglo-Normans
often preserved older versions of epics which in France were modernized and
adapted to the changing tastes of the day. The Oxford *Roland* and the eleventh-
century text of the *Vie de Saint Alexis* are other precious legacies of Anglo-

was very successful and suggested to other *trouvères* the possibility of exploiting Guillaume's current popularity by composing epics purporting to relate to other periods in the great hero's life. Some of them extended the story backwards to tell of his activity as a young warrior (*Le Couronnement de Louis, La Prise d'Orange, Le Charroi de Nîmes*), or the events of his childhood (*Les Enfances Guillaume*); some reached farther back to recount the exploits of Guillaume's father, Aymeri de Narbonne, his grandfather, Renier de Gennes, and his great-grandfather, Garin de Monglane; others contributed lateral extensions dealing with the deeds of brothers, uncles, nephews and cousins.

When enough of these were in circulation to suggest the possibility of their being grouped together in a single manuscript, someone was there to receive the suggestion. This cyclic rehandler, or perhaps a group of rehandlers, put the epics together in a roughly chronological order, sometimes filled in gaps and provided transitional material, and in the case of epics whose language was so archaic as to be difficult to understand, rewrote the whole thing in a contemporary idiom, frequently substituting rime for assonance to satisfy later tastes. He thus produced a composite work, which in a sense was his own creation, the structural unit of which was the epic poem. However, since in the beginning there had been no thought of grouping the stories together, nor any thought of making each part fit neatly into a predetermined plan, there are gaps and inconsistencies, not only in matters of factual detail,[23] but also in the manner and tone of presentation. The earlier poems of the cycle are spare and muscular, charged with heroic and religious tone; the later ones, under the influence of the increasingly popular courtly romances, are refined and prolix, amorous and secular. If we imagine in juxtaposition the *Chanson de Roland*, Pulci's *Morgante Maggiore*, and Dumas' *Three Musketeers* we shall have a fair notion of the heterogeneous character of the whole.[24]

The strict application of the principle of beginning, middle, and end, to such constructions would be fairly meaningless. Aristotle's notion of

---

Norman conservatism. See Maurice Delbouille, *Sur la genèse de la Chanson de Roland* (Brussels, 1954), p. 31.

[23] One example should suffice: in *Aliscans* and in *Foucon de Candie*, Vivien is the son of Guillaume's sister and is brought up in early childhood by Guillaume's wife, Guiborc, while in the *Enfances Vivien, Chevalerie Vivien*, and *Aymeri de Narbonne*, Vivien is the son of Guillaume's brother, Garin d'Anseüne; his mother is the daughter of Naismes de Bavière, and he is brought up by his parents. See Frappier, I, 58.

[24] Frappier, I, 40.

the beginning as that which has nothing before it, is negated with each successive extension to a more remote ancestor. The 'story' at any point in its development has distressingly elastic dimensions. There always remains the possibility of adding on to either end or of interpolating from within, for the story of Guillaume d'Orange is coextensive with his *geste*, that is, his family, which can be as large as the *trouvère* cares to make it, since beyond a certain point historical accuracy does not come into question.

Within the cycle as a whole, the various epics function in somewhat the same way as chapters in a novel. It is possible to locate the beginnings and endings of particular actions, but these do not necessarily correspond to the division into epic chapters. As we have seen, the *Chevalerie Vivien* ends *in medias res*, and the peculiar ending of *Girart de Vienne* is the result of its being in part at least a prelude to *Aymeri de Narbonne*. In five of the cyclic manuscripts the *Moniage Guillaume*, the story of Guillaume's retirement to a monastery and later to a hermitage, closes the cycle, and it may be said by virtue of its position and content to constitute an end.

In the fifteenth century, the process of consolidation and extension was carried to its final phase, the 'translation' – *translaté de vieille rime* is the usual expression – of the entire corpus into continuous 'derimed' prose. Two such manuscripts have come down to us in French and one in Italian, *I Nerbonesi*, which comprises fifteen of the epics of the cycle.[25]

The case of the Guillaume cycle is typical of the epic cycles in general. It offers us, in the words of Gaston Paris, "le spécimen le plus complet de la formation et de l'évolution, à moitié spontanées, à moitié factices, d'un grand cycle épique",[26] which is to say that, within the cyclic manuscripts, there exists an elementary principle of design, or rather of order, the idea, very much alive in medieval times, of genealogy. It gives the cycles a principle of sequence, without giving an initial or terminal principle. If we compare two typical manuscripts we shall see that while one may have more or fewer poems than another, the poems they contain in common appear in the same order. Manuscripts B1 and A4 of the Guillaume cycle, for example, contain the following poems in the following order:[27]

---

[25]   See H. Suchier (ed.), *Les Narbonnais* (Paris, 1898), II, xxiii-xxxvi.

[26]   *La Littérature française du moyen âge: XIe-XIVe siècles* (Paris, 1888), p. 62.

[27]   See Frappier, I, 42. There were, of course, cases where the chronology was not clear: *Les Narbonnais* and the *Enfances Guillaume* coincide temporally and the exact chronological position of the *Siege de Barbastre*, *Guibert d'Andrenas*,

B1
Garin de Monglane
Girard de Vienne
Aymeri de Narbonne
Les Narbonnais   A4
Enfances Guillaume   Enfances Guillaume
Couronnement Louis   Couronnement Louis
Charroi de Nîmes   Charroi de Nîmes
Prise d'Orange   Prise d'Orange
Enfances Vivien   Enfances Vivien
Chevalerie Vivien   Chevalerie Vivien
Aliscans   Aliscans
Bataille Loquifer   Bataille Loquifer
Moniage Rainouart   Moniage Rainouart
Moniage Guillaume   Moniage Guillaume
Siege de Barbastre
Guibert d'Andrenas
Mort Aymeri de Narbonne
Foucon de Candie

The *chansons de geste* were not alone in being subjected to cyclic organization and extension. The same mania that drove the *trouvères* to assemble works relating to Guillaume d'Orange, Charlemagne, and the unruly vassals into vast compilations, first in verse, then in prose, also presided over the formation of the animal epic, *Le Roman de Renart*, and the vulgate cycle of Arthurian romances. The three groups taken as a whole serve to define the range of styles in cyclic composition: sequence in the Guillaume cycle is based on chronology and genealogy; the *Roman de Renart*, while lacking in a sequential principle, has a sort of beginning and end; the vulgate cycle has a beginning, middle, and end of sorts and an intricately worked out sequential plan. Ferdinand Lot has held that the major part of the vulgate cycle must therefore have been written by one man over a fairly short period.

The shortest of the cycles we are considering is that of Renart, a compilation of relatively short, independent animal poems, called 'branches' during the Middle Ages. The branches vary in length from less than a hundred to more than 3,000 verses, and there are twenty-six branches in all. They may be said to group around a central theme, the conflict of the wolf and the fox, although this conflict is more

_____

and the *Mort Aymeri* is not indicated by any details in the stories themselves. *Cf.* Duncan McMillan, "Les *Enfances Guillaume* et les *Narbonnais* dans les mss. du grand cycle", *Romania*, LXIV (1938), 313-327; and M. Delbouille, "Le système des *Incidences*", *Revue Belge de Philologie et d'Histoire*, VI (1927), 617-641.

evident in some branches than in others. The order in which they appear in the various manuscripts varies considerably. The numbering which scholars now use is based on the order of the branches in Ernest Martin's edition, which for the first eleven is approximately that of ms. 20,043 of the Bibliothèque Nationale.

This cycle might fairly be described as a *cycle à tiroirs*. A comparison of the manuscripts illustrates the principle of the *roman à tiroirs*, namely that the parts may be interchanged or discarded without materially affecting the whole. It differs, however, from the usual *chanson de geste* cycle in that beginning and end are relatively fixed. Of the fifteen manuscripts, eleven begin with Branch I, three with Branch II, and one with Branch XXIV. Branch XXIV, however, is a late composition presenting, in the manner of the *chansons de geste*, an account of the *Enfances Renart*, designed to form a new first chapter of the whole. Six manuscripts end with Branch XI, five others with Branch XVII. Branch XVII is again a later composition; its subject is the *Mort de Renart*, and it was designed to close the cycle. One manuscript ends at Branch VIII, which tells of the death of Ysengrin. As for the order of branches normally located within the cycle, a glance at the structure of three manuscripts selected at random will indicate how much variety there might be:[28]

A: I, II, III, IV, V, Va, VI, VII, VIII, XII, IX, XIV, XIII, X, XI
C: II (1-22), XXIV, II (1025 ss.), Va (257-288), III, II (23-468; 665-842), XV (1-364), XIV, Va (289 ss.), I, XVI, XV (365 ss.), XX, XXI, II (843-1024), XVIII, XIX, II (469-664), V, IV, VII VIII, VI, XXII, IX, X, XI, XVII
D: I, VII, VIII, IV, V, Va, XII, II (1-842), XV, II (843 ss.), III, VI, IX, XIV, XIII, X, XI (1-3189), XVI (94 ss.)

Some of the branches, we see, can be left out entirely; some can be interchanged with others; some, like Branch II, can be split up into pieces and redistributed through the work.

The persistent presence of Branch I at the beginning seems to be due to its popularity, for the most elementary chronological consideration would put it after Branch II, on which it depends. In the last episode of Branch II, Hersent, Ysengrin's wife, chases Renart into his lair, but gets stuck at the entrance, which is not large enough for her. Renart goes out by another exit, comes up behind her, and takes advantage of her helpless situation by raping her. Ysengrin arrives in time

---

[28] The contents of the manuscripts are charted by E. Martin, *Le Roman de Renart*, III, vi.

to see this indignity being inflicted on his wife. This event is the core of the dispute at the beginning of Branch I, which in fact starts off with a direct allusion to it. The poet tells us that Pierre de Saint Cloud, author of Branch II, forgot to tell the best part of the story, the judgment of Renart at the court of Noble the Lion, where he was accused of the "grant fornicacion envers Dame Hersent la love":

> Perrot, qui son engin et s'art
> Mist en vers fere de Renart
> Et d'Isengrin son cher compere,
> Lessa le meus de sa matere:
> Car il entroblia le plet
> Et le jugement qui fu fet
> En la cort Noble le lion
> De la grant fornicacion
> Que Renart fist, qui toz maus cove,
> Envers dame Hersent la love.
>   (I, 1-10)

It is difficult to understand why those who compiled the cyclic manuscripts should in this case have been so careful to invert the normal chronological order of the branches. None of the manuscripts begins with the sequence II, I. Still, in a general way, it is clear that this matter belongs at the beginning of the cycle. The most general theme of the romance, as we have noted, is the conflict of the fox and the wolf. What we have here is the origin of the quarrel.

It looks, therefore, as though the compilers of the *Roman de Renart* attempted in some measure to make up for the haphazard quality of the middle branches by providing a clear notion of beginning and end. In the Guillaume d'Orange cycle, on the other hand, chronology and genealogy (of which there is no question in the *Renart*), controlled the sequence through the middle, but permitted indefinite extensions at either end.

The period of poetic activity during which the *Roman de Renart* was composed extends from about 1174 to 1250, a much briefer time-span than we noted in the case of the cycle of Guillaume d'Orange, which extended from the eleventh through the fourteenth centuries. An even briefer time-span than that of the *Renart*, however, sufficed for the composition of the most extensive narrative work of the thirteenth century, the vulgate cycle of Arthurian romances. This could not have been begun before the late 1180's, when Chrétien wrote his *Conte du Graal*, and it was apparently completed by 1230.

This cycle, one of the most popular and influential works of the

Middle Ages, is made up of five symmetrically arranged romances in the following order: *L'Estoire del Saint Graal*, an account of the early history of the Grail; *Merlin*, an extended prose version of Robert de Borron's poem treating of the early history of King Arthur; the *Lancelot* proper, a vast central structure filled with carefully interlaced adventures; the *Queste del Saint Graal*, an interlaced romance recounting the accomplishment of the quest of the Holy Grail by Lancelot's son, Galahad; and *La Mort le Roi Artu*, which recounts the fall of the Arthurian kingdom and the death of Arthur, substantially in accordance with the account of Geoffrey of Monmouth. Of these the first two are generally looked upon as later additions. The original corpus – *Lancelot, Queste, Mort Artu* – the last two elements of which are respectively Grail matter and Arthurian chronicle, was apparently balanced at the beginning by the addition of the *Estoire* (Grail matter), and the *Merlin* (Arthurian chronicle), so that the whole eventually assumed the form: A: Grail, B: Chronicle, C: Lancelot, A': Grail, B': Chronicle. Two narrative lines are intertwined here, the beginning and the end of the Grail matter, and the beginning and end of the history of Arthur. The knot that holds these two narratives together is the conception of Galahad as the son of Lancelot. The man who had that particular idea may be said to have created the cycle, which is thus seen to have a genealogical basis which reflects a deep poetic intention, that of presenting the passage from the old chivalric dispensation, as represented in the mundane exploits of Lancelot, to the deeply spiritual conception of chivalry we find in the *Queste del Saint Graal*.

All the elements form a fairly unified structure, bound together by preparations and prognostications on the one hand, and by backward references on the other. In all this diversity, the cycle yet presents a high degree of unity, and this unity has long been considered one of the most enigmatic problems of medieval literature.[29] How many people had a hand in composing this enormous structure? How did they manage to keep the structure of the whole so consistently in mind? Ferdinand Lot feels that the concluding trilogy must have been conceived and written by one man.[30] Pauphilet explains the cohesion of the parts as due to the patching of later redactors and interpolators, the creation of a multitude of bridges at a late date to hold the disparate elements together.[31] Frappier believes that a single man, an 'architect', planned

[29]   A. Pauphilet, *Le Legs du moyen âge*, p. 214.
[30]   *Etude sur le Lancelot en prose*, p. 64 and *passim*.
[31]   Pauphilet, pp. 212-217.

the concluding trilogy, and that a limited number of other authors followed his blueprint.[32]

The mystery of the composition of the vulgate cycle is not, for the purposes of the study, a particularly pressing matter. It is important to realize that someone appears to have consciously worked out the problem of relating the beginning to the end, or rather the beginnings to the ends. But the middle remains a vast welter of carefully intertwined adventures which only occasionally bear on the beginning and end.

In summary it seems to me that all the problems that arise in connection with the application of the principle of beginning, middle, and end, in diptych narrative, in the *roman à tiroirs*, and in the cyclic literature, all stem from the same root: in every case we are faced with a multiplicity where we should like to see unity. There is, in general, more material than we need. Somehow this multiplicity must derive from a fundamental impulse on the part of the medieval writer toward increased length, an impulse counterbalanced in part by a concern for symmetry and balance in the diptych narrative, controlled and yet furthered by the technique of narrative interlacing, yet fundamentally an impulse to amplify. An examination of this tendency toward amplification, and its further consequences will therefore be the theme of the next chapter.

---

[32] Frappier, *Etude sur la Mort le Roi Artu*, pp. 122-146.

II

THE QUESTION OF LENGTH

In our day we are scarcely disposed to think better of a story simply because it is long. It is therefore a little puzzling for us to find Aristotle saying that the longer a story is, consistent with total comprehensibility, the better it is:

Beauty is a matter of size and order, and therefore impossible either (1) in a very minute creature, since our perception becomes indistinct as it approaches instantaneity; or (2) in a creature of vast size – one, say, 1,000 miles long – as in that case, instead of the object being seen all at once, the unity and wholeness of it is lost to the beholder. . . . The limit, however, set by the actual nature of the thing is this: the longer the story, consistently with its being comprehensible as a whole, the finer it is by reason of its magnitude.[1]

Length is, for us, a secondary consideration at best. But when we come to consider the narratives of the Middle Ages, we must be prepared to see the matter in a different light, for, in general, it would appear, medieval man saw the lengthening process as the very heart and soul of the writer's craft. The writer's job, after all, was not to make up stories. He found them: he was a *trouvère*. If, by chance, he did happen to make up a story of his own, he usually began by saying that he had found it in an old Latin book. His real job was to amplify the matter he had found, to give it fullness and magnitude.[2] At least one writer was known proudly to sign his name after the designation *amplificavit*.[3]

---

[1] *Poetics* 7. 1450b-1451a (Bywater's translation).
[2] *Cf.* E. Faral, *Les Arts poétiques du XIIe et du XIIIe siècle*, p. 61: "L'amplification est la grande chose: elle est la principale fonction de l'écrivain." See also E. Curtius: "Sah der mittelalterliche Dichter seine Hauptaufgabe in der Erweiterung und Aufgestaltung des gegebenen Stoffes." "Zur Interpretation des Alexiusliedes", *Zeitschrift für romanische Philologie*, LVI (1936), 124.
[3] A. Bates (ed.), *Le Roman de vrai amour et Le Pleur de sainte âme* (Ann Arbor, 1958), pp. 20-21.

It is not surprising, in consequence, to find that whenever two or more manuscripts exist for a single story, the later ones tend to be the more extensive. A writer simply would not be doing his job if he left a story no longer than it was when he found it. The eleventh-century version of the *Vie de Saint Alexis*, for example, contains 625 verses, the twelfth-century version 1,356; Benoît de Sainte-Maure, working from Dares' sparse and dry summary of the Trojan War, about thirty pages of Latin prose, left it a full-blown romance of 30,000 octosyllables; the *Chanson de Guillaume* contains 3,554 verses, while *Aliscans*, a later rehandling of the same material, runs 8,500 verses. *Ogier le Danois* in its thirteenth-century form is a fair-sized epic of 10,000 verses, but in its fourteenth century transcription it attains a length of 25,000 verses. *Huon de Bordeaux* in its oldest form has 10,000 verses, while the later Turin manuscript has 30,000. Finally, Marie's *Lai du Fresne*, only 534 verses long, furnishes the plot outline for *Galeran de Bretagne*, a romance of 7,812 verses. Examples could be multiplied indefinitely: this is a commonplace of medieval literature.

Inevitably the impulse to amplify had structural consequences. It is self-evident that short stories will generally be more coherent than long ones, for the simple reason that there is less physical space in which to be diffuse or digressive. The short stories of the Middle Ages accordingly tend generally to approximate the form of well-made narrative. However, since there was a premium on length, serious narrative artists generally avoided the shorter genres. The fabliaux are typical. Unpretentious and straightforward, they are intended to amuse, not to impress the connoisseur. The usual thing is to recount without loss of time some stratagem by which the ubiquitous clerk and the young wife deceive the stupid husband. The motives of the several participants are generally clear and consistent, and the events are made to succeed one another in a reasonably logical way.[4]

Similarly, many troubadour *vidas* and *razos* have a simple, logical structure.[5] But, as we should expect, such stories can hardly be said to have constituted a serious and respectable narrative genre; they were

---

[4] The structural similarity of the *fabliaux* and the short story in our time is argued by M. W. Hart in "Narrative Techniques of Fabliau and Prose Tale", *PMLA*, XXIII (1908), 329-374, and in "The Narrative Art of the Fabliaux", in *Anniversary Papers to George Lyman Kittredge* (Boston, 1913), pp. 209-216.

[5] The *vidas* are usually short biographical notices about the troubadours. They pretend to historicity, but in most cases it is clear that they are fictions based on the writers' poems. The *razos*, on the other hand, purport to give the stories behind particular poems, to give a narrative explanation of the sometimes obscure lyrics.

rather a narrative adjunct to the elevated lyric genre. They were written partly to maintain the reputations of the poets of an earlier day, and partly to explain the obscurities of the poems. Both motives are evident in the most famous of these pieces, the *vida* of the twelfth-century troubadour Jaufré Rudel:

Jaufre Rudels de Blaia si fo mout gentils hom, e fo princes de Blaia. Et enamoret se de la comtessa de Tripol, ses vezer, per lo ben qu'el n'auzi dire als pelerins que venguen d'Antiocha; e fetz de leis mains vers ab bons sons, ab paubres moz. E per voluntat de leis vezer, el se croset, e mes se en mar, E pres lo malautia en la nau, e fo condug a Tripol en un alberc per mort. E fo fait saber a la comtessa, et ella venc ad el, al son leit, e pres lo entre sos braz. E saup qu'ella era la comtessa, a mantenent recobret l'auzir e·l flairar e lauzet Dieu que l'avia la vida sostenguda tro qu'el l'agues vista. Et enaissi el mori entre sos braz. Et ella lo fez a gran honor sepellir en la maison del Temple. E pois, en aquel dia, ella se rendet morga per la dolor qu'ella ac de la mort de lui.[6]

(Jaufre Rudel of Blaye was a man of very noble birth, and he was prince of Blaye. And he fell in love with the Countess of Tripoli, without seeing her, for the good things he had heard about her from the pilgrims who came back from Antioch; and he wrote many songs about her, with good melodies and poor words. And desiring to see her, he took the cross and put out to sea. And sickness took him on the boat, and he was taken to an inn in Tripoli, as though dead. And it was made known to the Countess; and she came to him, to his bed, and she took him in her arms. And he knew that it was the Countess, and he recovered his smell and hearing, and he praised God that he had sustained his life until he had seen her. And thereupon he died in her arms. And she had him buried with great honor in the house of the Templars. And then, on that day, she became a nun, for the sadness she felt at his death.)

The story is, of course, pure fiction. Its writer, probably a thirteenth-century *jongleur*, knew considerably less about the historical Jaufré than we do. He put this story together by assembling from Jaufré's poems a number of suggestive details: references to an *amor de lonh* or *amor de terra lonhdana*, and an allusion to his going on a crusade.[7] Thus, as is the case for most of the troubadour *vidas*, the poems themselves furnished the matter for the stories that purport to explain the poems.[8]

---

[6]   Jean Boutière and A.-H. Schutz (eds.), *Biographies des Troubadours* (Toulouse, 1950), pp. 202-203.

[7]   See the lyrics numbered I, II, V, and VI in *Les Chansons de Jaufré Rudel*, ed. Alfred Jeanroy, 2nd ed. (Paris, 1924). See also Gaston Paris, "Jaufré Rudel", *Revue Historique*, LIII (1893), 225-260.

[8]   See A. Jeanroy, *La Poésie lyrique des troubadours* (Toulouse, 1934), I, 109-127; Stanislaw Stronski, *Le Troubadour Foulquet de Marseille* (Cracow, 1910), pp. vii-

Since the purpose of the story was at least in part explanatory, its structure is logical and coherent. The writer wastes no time on frivolous embellishment or elegant digression; and since such stories were apparently recited by a *jongleur* as a narrative preface to a series of lyrics, it would appear natural that he should tell them quickly and get on to the songs themselves.[9]

Of course, mere length cannot always be an accurate index to narrative cohesiveness. Some of the longer epics, like the *Chanson de Roland* (4002 vv.) and *Raoul de Cambrai* (5555 vv.) hold together much better than some of the shorter ones: the *Pèlerinage de Charlemagne* (870 vv.) and the *Couronnement de Louis* (2695 vv.) are conspicuously incoherent by comparison.[10]

Still, it remains true that, in general, the longer a story is, the more its structure tends to be episodic and digressive. But this is only part of the picture. The medieval writer amplified his work in many ways, all of which are of considerable interest from the point of view of their structural consequences.

As I see it, there are two preliminary classifications to be made: rhetorical and material amplifications. In the first case, the writer tells the story, essentially as he heard it or read it, reproducing the events in the same sequence, but he tells it in greater detail. He describes people and places, reports long conversations, and in general eschews the use of narrative summary. The resulting structure tends to be long, and often dull; it is usual for the medieval writer to amplify all his nar-

---

xi; and *La Légende amoureuse de Bertrand de Born* (Paris, 1914), p. 89: "Ce sont les poésies mêmes du troubadour qui formèrent le point de départ. Les chansons amoureuses contiennent toujours des motifs littéraires qui peuvent être pris pour des allusions à la réalité vécue. C'est ainsi que notre biographe les considérait, en se proposant de les expliquer."

[9] See A.-H. Schutz, "Were the *Vidas* and *Razos* Recited?", *Studies in Philology*, XXIII (1939), 565-570. It is worth noting that this combination of song and story may be viewed as an early form of the *chant-fable*, exploited in several important narratives of the thirteenth century, notably the *Roman de la Violette*, the *Castelain de Couci*, and *Aucassin et Nicolette*. For a complete list see D. Buffum's edition of the *Roman de la Violette* (Paris, 1928), p. lxxxiii.

[10] J. Rychner, *La Chanson de geste: Essai sur l'art épique des jongleurs* (Geneva, 1955), pp. 37 ff. In this regard it is worth noting that even some of the very short troubadour *vidas* are mere collections of pseudo-biographical *disjecta membra*. That of Guillaume IX, for example, reads as follows: "Lo coms de Peitieus si fo uns dels majors cortes del mon e dels majors trichadors de dompnas e bons cavalliers d'armas e larcs de dompnejar, e saup ben trobar e cantar. E ac un fill, que ac per moiller la duquessa de Normandia, don ac una filla que fo moiller del rei Enric d'Engleterra, maire del rei jove e d'en Richard e del comte Jaufre de Bretaigne." (Boutière and Schutz, p. 83.)

rative data without stopping to consider the advantages of selective expansion, of developing only the dramatic portions and of summarizing intermediate matter of only secondary importance in the progress of the story.[11] Material amplifications, on the other hand, result from the introduction of new narrative matter, either by interpolation from within or by adding to either end. Here the structural consequences are more drastic, producing such narrative oddities as, for example, the genealogical diptych.

RHETORICAL AMPLIFICATION. The medieval treatises on poetics are our main source of knowledge about the theoretical bases of the literature. They derive, for the most part, from Latin sources: Horace's *Ars poetica*, Cicero's *De inventione*, and, most importantly, the *Rhetorica ad Herennium*, which the medieval writers accepted as Cicero's.

Of course, the word *amplificatio* did not, for the classical writers, have anything to do with the lengthening of a narrative. On the contrary, its application seems to have been strictly limited to the manner of presenting an idea, giving it grandeur and magnitude, exalting its importance, or heightening its effect.[12] But the rules for amplification, originally intended to give fullness to an exposition, were ultimately applied to narrative and came to mean spinning out the story, lengthening, widening, and heightening, stuffing it out with the full complement of rhetorical devices.

The medieval treatises of poetics are best understood, it seems to me, as attempts to apply to the writing of imaginative literature precepts originally designed for use in persuasive oratory. The transference was facilitated by an ambiguity already present in classical times: the main part of an oration was traditionally called the *narratio*, a term meaning simply an orderly presentation of the facts of a case. Such a *narratio* might or might not be what we would call narrative. In a criminal case, for example, the narration of the facts might well turn out to be a good story; however, in most cases, the *narratio* was purely expository in character. The classical writers were perfectly aware of the ambiguity of the term. The writer of the *Ad Herennium*, for example, distinguishes three types of *narratio*, although the third, he freely admits, has nothing to do with judicial oratory. Nevertheless, he goes on to describe it in considerable detail:

[11]   Faral, *Les Arts poétiques*, p. 77.
[12]   See Quintilian *Inst.* viii. 4; Aristotle *Rhetoric* i. 9. 1468a; Faral, p. 61; Curtius, p. 492.

There are three types of *narratio*. It is one type when we set forth the facts and turn every detail to our advantage so as to win the victory, and this kind appertains to the causes on which a decision is to be rendered. There is another type which often enters into our speech as a means of winning belief or incriminating our adversary or effecting a transition or setting the stage for something. The third type is not used in a case actually pleaded in court, yet affords us convenient practice for handling the first two types more advantageously in actual cases. Of such narratives there are two types: one based on facts, the other on persons.

The kind based on the exposition of the facts (*negotiorum expositio*) presents three forms: legendary (*fabula*), historical (*historia*), and realistic (*argumentum*). The legendary tale comprises events neither true nor probable, like those transmitted by the tragedies. The historical narrative is an account of exploits actually performed (*res gesta*), but removed in time from the recollection of our age. Realistic narrative recounts imaginary events (*argumentum est ficta res*), which yet could have occurred, like the plots of comedies (*argumenta comoediarum*). A narrative style based on the persons should present a lively style and diverse traits of character, such as austerity and gentleness, hope and fear, distrust and desire, hypocrisy and compassion, and the vicissitudes of life, such as a reversal of fortune (*fortunae commutatio*), unexpected disaster, sudden joy, and a happy outcome.[13]

In view of the emphasis given here to fictional narrative, we need not be surprised that the medieval theorists were able to transfer the theory of rhetoric to that of poetics.[14]

We can see evidence of the transference in several places in the medieval poetics. Geoffroi de Vinsauf, for example, suggests that if the writer wishes to begin his story at the beginning, in this case the story of Minos and Scylla (Ovid, *Metamorphoses*, VII-VIII), he might begin by praising Minos:

Sumitur etiam naturale principium quando materiam initiamur a laude Minois, immorando circa laudem ejus; sed iste modus tractantis est, non narrantis. Narratio namque juxta doctrinam Tulii in *Rhetoricis* debet esse brevis et delucida.[15]

(A story is taken up at its natural beginning if we start it by praising Minos, dwelling on his praise. But this is a form of amplification, not of narration. For narration, according to Tully's doctrine in the *Rhetorica*, ought to be brief and lucid.)

Praise of Minos, he seems to be saying, is not a form of narration,

13   [Cicero] *Rhetorica ad Herennium*, i. 8. The translation is based on that of H. Caplan in the Loeb Classical Library series (Cambridge, Mass., 1954).
14   Scholars have taken general note of this transference. See Ernst Curtius, *European Literature and the Latin Middle Ages*, pp. 489 ff.; E. Vinaver (ed.), *The Works of Sir Thomas Malory* (Oxford, 1947), I, lxiv.
15   *Documentum*, I, 3; Faral, p. 266.

but of amplification. I take *modus tractantis* to mean a way of stretching out the subject. The reason he alleges is that Cicero specifies brevity and clarity as the essential qualities of narration. The passage to which he is probably referring occurs in the *Ad Herennium* (i. 9) immediately after the passage cited above. After describing *narratio* in its literary meaning, the writer directs his attention specifically to its oratorical meaning, and says that the statement of facts in a case should be characterized by brevity, lucidity and plausibility:

How we should handle that type of *narratio* which pertains to actual cases (*illud quod ad veritatem pertinet*) I am about to explain.
  A *narratio* should have three qualities: brevity, lucidity, and plausibility.

Geoffroi may have failed to perceive that the writer of the *Ad Herennium* had shifted from one meaning to another, and although a major part of Geoffroi's treatise is given over to the procedure of amplification, by which he clearly means the lengthening of the story,[16] he here acknowledges Cicero as authority that narration should be brief and to the point. He manages to avoid the contradictory implications of his position by positing a puzzling distinction between *modus tractantis* and *modus narrantis*.

Faral, surprised at the extensive treatment given to apostrophe as a means of amplification, a category which seems hardly appropriate, suggests that the medieval theoreticians were thinking about the passage in the *Ad Herennium* (iv. 15), where the writer describes *exclamatio:*

Exclamatio serves to reinforce the expression of pain or indignation by addressing a man, a city, a place, or some sort of object.

The writer adds that this sort of ornament is used only when the grandeur of the subject requires it, an obvious question of decorum, since it would bring ridicule on the orator if he were to abuse such a figure. However, the Latin expression the writer uses here: "hac exornatione utemur ... cum rei magnitudo postulare videbitur", may have been interpreted wrongly. By *rei magnitudo*, Faral suggests, the medieval theoretician may have understood 'ampleur de développement', which would explain why apostrophe was made to figure among the instruments of amplification, as a device for lengthening a narrative rather than a means for moving an audience.[17]

---

[16] See *Documentum*, II, 3, 11, 17 and *passim*.
[17] Faral, p. 71.

The confusion of oratory and imaginative literature is carried to its ultimate point in Jean de Garlande's *Poetria*, in which the writer holds that a literary work divides into six parts: *exordium, narratio, partitio, confirmatio, confutatio,* and *conclusio.*[18] However, in a more generalized form, *exordium, narratio, conclusio,* the formula can and did apply to literary composition. Many medieval stories begin with some sort of general observation, proverb or exemplum, pass into the story proper, and conclude with some general statement pointing up the moral of the work. This is the formula we find in Matthieu de Vendome's *Ars versificatoria,* and, with some modifications, in Geoffroi de Vinsauf's *Documentum.*[19]

The consequences of this confusion as they appear in actual narrative practice are extremely interesting, since of the devices usually recommended for purposes of amplification – *descriptio, circumlocutio, prosopopoeia, apostrophatio (sic), digressio, expolitio,* and *interpretatio* – only *descriptio* would appear to apply with any degree of generality to narrative art. The others could be of only limited use. Still, there are indications that the medieval story-tellers found some surprising uses for them.

Digressions, for example, clearly have their place in oratory: for purposes of clarification, to shed light from another source on the matter in question, and so on. But what is their place in narrative art? With our relatively refined notions of unity and coherence, we are perhaps too readily inclined to consider as a digression anything that does not contribute directly to the progress of a story; but the medieval writer would scarcely have been inclined to see the matter in this way. For him, digression would have implied a much more drastic movement, a shift from one branch of the story to another. The procedure is defined as follows in Geoffroi de Vinsauf (*Documentum,* II, 17):

Digressio ... ampliat et decorat materiam. Fit autem digressio duobus modis, sed pluribus ex causis. Unus modus digressionis est quando digredimur in materia ad aliam partem materiae; alius modus quando digredimur ad aliud extra materiam.

That is, we may digress in one of two ways: either to another part of the same subject, or to another subject altogether. We may, I think, see an early example of the first in the eleventh-century *Vie de Saint Alexis.* The situation is this: Alexis, only son and heir of a wealthy Roman family, married the daughter of another wealthy Roman, but on his wedding night he realized that wedded bliss was not for him, left his bride, and sailed far away to Edessa; there he gave to the poor the little money he had left, exchanged his rich clothes for beggar's raiment, and sat down outside a shrine to the Holy Virgin. At this point the writer finds it necessary to return to the family, who were very upset by his sudden disappearance and instituted a world-wide search for him. The writer accomplishes the shift of focus by suddenly breaking into the story in his own person and saying: "Now I shall return to the father and mother":

> Or revendrai al pedre et a la medre,
> Et a la 'spose qui sole fut remese:
> Quant il ço sovrent qued il fuiz s'en eret,
> Ço fut granz dols qued il en demenerent,
> Et granz deplainz par tote la contrede.[20]

(Now I shall return to the father and to the mother, and to the spouse who had remained alone; when they knew that he had fled, they mourned greatly, and great was the lamenting through all the country.)

The writer has in effect moved from one part of the story to another, but he has remained within the same subject. This sort of transition, in which the writer announces that he is going to stop talking about one thing and turn to something else, is, however, most characteristic of the thirteenth-century technique of interlaced narrative, as we find it particularly in the vulgate version of the Arthurian romances, where it is common for the writer to carry forward several story lines simultaneously, moving from one sequence to another, and then back to the matter left in suspense. Each shift is marked by the use of the formula: "Ores laisse li contes a parler de . . . et retorne a parler de . . .", the next division beginning: "Ores dist li contes que . . .". A decorated capital usually appears at this point to indicate further the break in the narrative thread. Thus, once all the several stories have been set in motion, each shift marks a digression *extra materiam* relative to the previous episode, and a return *in materia* to an earlier sequence. It is possible that the technique stems at least in part from a purely mechanical application of the counsels of the rhetoric manuals relative to *digressio*.[21]

---

[20]   *La Vie de Saint Alexis*, eds. G. Paris and L. Pannier (Paris, 1887), vv. 101-105, p. 144. All subsequent line and page references to the *Vie de Saint Alexis* will be to this edition.
[21]   Vinaver suggested this possibility in his introduction (pp. li-liii) to the *Works of Thomas Malory*, offering in support of it the ambiguity surrounding the word *narratio* (lxiv), and Faral's statement that "l'enseignement des arts poétiques, qui

Of course, story-tellers frequently find it necessary to move from one part of their subject to another: Homer moves from earth to Mount Olympus and back again; Thucydides interlaces his narrative in order to present in chronological parallel the action in the different theatres of the Peloponnesian War; Villehardouin finds it necessary to do the same sort of thing. It is one way of solving the problem of presenting simultaneous actions. However, its gratuitously developed and extended use in prose romance may well derive its status as a legitimate artistic procedure from the authority of the rhetoric manuals.

The case of the figures *interpretatio* and *expolitio* is similarly interesting. The distinction between the two is slight enough in the classical rhetoric books, and practically nonexistent in the medieval treatises. The *Ad Herennium* defines *interpretatio* as follows (iv. 28):

Interpretatio is the figure which does not duplicate the same word by repeating it, but replaces the word by another of the same meaning, as follows: 'You have torn the republic from its roots; you have demolished the foundations of the state.'

Expolitio is somewhat more complicated. The orator, wishing to dwell on a single idea at some length, refines it and varies it by changing the tone of his voice, by stating his idea in different words, or by turning the thought differently (iv. 42):

Expolitio consists in dwelling on the same topic and yet seeming to say something ever new.... There are three ways of varying the expression: by words, by tone of voice, and by turn of thought.

The writer adds that *expolitio* lends force and distinction to a speech, and that "multo maxime per eam exercemur ad elocutionis facultatem" (iv. 44); that is, it is one of our most important means of developing skill in style. This high recommendation may account in some measure for the prominence with which the device figures in the medieval treatises.

At any rate, both *interpretatio* and *expolitio* reduce in the poetics to the same general formula: *eandem rem dicere, sed commutate.*[22] Geoffroi de Vinsauf, in his treatise *Poetria Nova* (III, 220 ff.) discusses and illustrates these procedures:

> ... Si facis amplum
> Hoc primo procede gradu: sententia sit
> Unica, non uno veniat contenta paratu,

---

ne brille pas par l'envergure de ses conceptions, paraît avoir agi précisément par ce qu'il contenait de plus superficiel et de plus mécanique" (*Les Arts poétiques*, p. 60).
[22] Faral, p. 63.

> Sed variet vestes et mutatoria sumat;
> Sed verbis aliis praesumpta resume; repone
> Pluribus in clausis unum, multiplice forma
> Dissimuletur idem; varius sit et tamen idem.[23]

(. . . If you amplify, proceed first in this way: If the thought is simple, let it not be content to appear in one form, but let it change its vestment and take on a variety of appearances; take up what you have already said, but in different words; put one thing into several clauses; let the same thing be concealed in a variety of forms; be various and yet remain the same.)

Keeping these prescriptions in mind, if we look at the *Vie de Saint Alexis* and notice how the writer treats one of the most dramatic moments of the poem, Alexis' farewell to his bride, we shall see that he has followed the prescription quite closely:

> Quant en la chambre furent tot sol remes,
> Danz Alexis la prist ad apeler;
> La mortel vide li prist molt a blasmer,
> De la celeste li mostret veritet,
> Mais lui ert tart qued il s'en fust alez.
>
> 'Oz mei, pulcele: celui tien ad espos
> qui nos redenst de son sanc precios.
> En icest siecle nen at parfite amor;
> La vide est fraile, n'i at durable honor,
> Cest ledice revert a grant tristor.
>
> (vv. 61-70)

(When they were all alone in the room, Lord Alexis began to speak to her; mortal life he began to criticize severely to her; of the heavenly life he showed her the truth; but much he wished that he were gone from there. 'Hear me, maiden, take him for spouse who redeemed us with his precious blood. In this world there is no perfect love; life is frail, nor is there lasting honor: this joy becomes great sorrow.)

In the first of these two *laisses*, the writer says that Alexis began to speak to his bride, criticized this mortal life, showed the truth of the heavenly one, and wished that he had already left. The second recapitulates the same matter, but in the form of direct discourse.

We find the same sort of thing occurring in almost all the early *chansons de geste*. A famous example appears in the *Chanson de Roland* at the moment when Oliver, aware of the overwhelming numbers of the pagan army, pleads with Roland to summon back Charlemagne and the army by sounding his horn:

---

[23] Faral, p. 204. In the *Documentum* (II, xxix) we find: "Est interpretatio color quando eamdem sententiam per diversas clausulas interpretamur." In the *Summa de coloribus rhetoricis* (Faral, p. 235): "Interpretatio est quando eadem oratio diversis verbis explicatur."

Dist Oliver: 'Paien unt grant esforz;
De noz Franceis m'i semblet aveir mult poi.
Cumpaign Rollant, kar sunez vostre corn,
Si l'orrat Carles, si returnerat l'ost.'
Respunt Rollant, 'Je fereie que fols.
En dulce France en perdreie mun los.
Sempres ferrai de Durendal granz colps;
Sanglant en ert li branz entresqu'a l'or.
Felun paien mar i vindrent as porz.
Jo vos plevis, tuz sunt jugez a mort.' AOI

'Cumpainz Rollant, l'olifan car sunez,
Si l'orrat Carles, ferat l'ost returner,
Sucurrat nos li reis od sun barnet.'
Respunt Rollant, 'Ne placet Damnedeu
Que mi parent pur mei seient blasmet
Ne France dulce je cheet en viltet.
Einz i ferrai de Durendal asez,
Ma bone espee que ai ceint al costet:
Tut en verrez le brant ensanglantet.
Felun paien mar i sunt asemblez.
Jo vos plevis, tuz sunt a mort livrez.'

'Cumpainz Rollant, sunez vostre olifan,
Si l'orrat Carles, ki est as porz passant.
Jo vos plevis, ja returnerunt Franc.'
'Ne placet Deu,' ço li respunt Rollant,
'Que ço seit dit de nul hume vivant,
Ne pur paien, que ja seie cornant.
Ja n'en avrunt reproece mi parent.
Quant je serai en la bataille grant
E jo ferrai e mil colps e .vii. cenz,
De Durendal verrez l'acer sanglent.
Franceis sunt bon, si ferrunt vassalment.
Ja cil d'Espaigne n'avrunt de mort garant.
(vv. 1049-1092)

(Oliver says: 'The pagans are strong in number: of our French there are but few, it seems to me. Friend Roland, please sound your horn. Charles will hear it and the army will return.' Roland answers: 'That would be madness! In sweet France I would lose my reputation. I shall now strike great blows with Durendal: its blade will be bloody to the gold of the hilt. The evil pagans came to the pass to die. I assure you that all are marked for death.'

'Friend Roland, please sound your horn. Charles will hear it and make the army return; the King and his barons will come back to help us.' Roland answers: 'God forbid that through my fault my family should incur blame, and sweet France fall into humiliation. Rather will I strike great blows with Durendal, my good sword that I wear at my side. You will see its blade all bloodied. The pagans are here met to die. I assure you, they are destined to perish.'

'Friend Roland, sound your horn. Charles will hear it going through the pass; I assure you that they will return.' 'God forbid,' Roland answers him, 'that any man be able to say that I sounded my horn for fear of the pagans. My family will never be reproached for that. When I am in the thick of battle, I shall strike a thousand and seven hundred blows, and you will see the steel of Durendal covered with blood. The French are good men and will strike valiantly. The Spanish will not escape from death.')

The technical procedure in question here, *laisses similaires* they are customarily called, is used with striking effectiveness, lending a sense of urgency and intensity to the situation. We are not disturbed by the repetitions, since they are dramatically realistic, Roland and Oliver both stubbornly clinging to their points of view.[24]

The device is, however, often used with less effectiveness. When the writer describes a completed action or a series of completed actions in one *laisse*, then in the following *laisse* returns to the same starting point and goes through the same matter with variations, the effect is extremely confusing for the modern reader, and must have been so even for the medieval audience. Narratives, after all, are chronologically arranged and we are not prepared for chronological regression to matters that have already been told. An extremely interesting example of this occurs in *Aliscans*, one of the finest epics of the cycle of Guillaume d'Orange. The situation is this: Guillaume, after considerable valiant fighting at Aliscans, loses the last of his men and fights his way through the pagan forces in an attempt to return to Orange to gather reinforcements. While crossing the battlefield, he comes accidentally upon the body of his dear nephew Vivien, lying beside a pond, covered with horrible wounds. In laisse XXII, he finds his nephew:

> Per devers destre s'est li quens regardés:
> Viviën voit gesir desor un gués,
> Desous un arbre k'est foillus et ramés.
> Par mi le cors ot .xv. plaies tés,
> De la menor morust uns amirés,
> Tos ot les bras et les flans decopés.
> Li quens le voit, molt en est esfraés.
> De grant dolor est li quens tressüés.[25]

---

[24] The reader will also notice that the presentation has a musical quality in its repetition of themes. This aspect of *laisses similaires* has been closely studied by Rychner in *La Chanson de geste*, pp. 68-125.

[25] *Aliscans*, eds. E. Weinbeck, W. Hartnacke, and P. Rasch (Halle, 1903), vv. 686 ff. Further line references will be to this edition. The text is conveniently available, however, in Bartsch and Wiese, *Chrestomathie de l'ancien français*, 12th ed. (Leipzig, 1927), pp. 56 ff.

(The count looked to the right, sees Vivien lying beside a ford, under a tree with its leaves and branches. Upon his body there were fifteen wounds, such that the least of them would have caused the death of an emir. His arms and sides were mutilated. The count sees him, is struck with fear; he breaks into a sweat in his great anguish.)

The following *laisse* begins as though this had not yet happened:

> Li quens Guillaumes ot molt le cuer dolant,
> Molt fu iriés et plains de mautalent.
> Vivën vit gesir sor un estanc,
> Desos un arbre foillu et verdoiant.
> A la fontaine, dont li dois sont corant,
> Le quens Guillaumes vint cele part poignant,
> Par grant dolor a regardé l'enfant,
> La ou il gist desor l'erbe en l'Archant,
> Ses blanches mains sor son pis en croisant.
> Tot ot le cors et le hauberc sanglant
> Et le viaire sos l'elme flanboiant;
> Et la cervele li chiet as iex devant.
>   (vv. 693 ff.)

(Count William's heart was charged with pain, he was wrathful and full of anger. He saw Vivien lying beside a pond, beneath a green and leafy tree. Count William spurred toward the spring with flowing conduits (?). Greatly grieved he looked on the young man, there where he lay on the field at Archant, his white hands crossed on his breast, his body and hauberk covered with blood, his face inflamed under his helm, and his brains fallen over his eyes.)

The writer here takes pains to introduce the scene again, but he develops – a clear use of *expolitio* – the description of Vivien's wounds. William then delivers an extended lament, a new element, which is taken up for further development in the *laisses* that follow. However, the very next *laisse* begins again with the discovery of Vivien's body:

> Li quens Guillaume fu iriés et dolans:
> Vivën voit, ki gisoit tos sanglans,
> Plus souëf flaire ke baumes ne encens,
> Sor sa poitrine tenoit ses mains croisans,
> Li sans li ist par ambedeus les flans,
> Par mi le cors ot .xv. plaies grans;
> De la menor morust uns amirans.
> 'Niés Vivën,' dist Guillaumes li frans,
> 'Mar fu vos cors, ke tant par ert vaillans.
>   (vv. 722 ff.)

(Count William was wrathful and grieved; he sees Vivien, who lay covered with blood, smelling more sweetly than balm or incense, his hands crossed on his breast, the blood flowed from both his sides. On his body were fifteen wounds, the least of which would have killed an emir. 'Nephew Vivien,' said William the noble, 'how pitiful your body, which was once so valiant.)

At this point in the story fifty-five verses have elapsed since the time when Guillaume originally saw Vivien, but the writer makes it happen again. He also repeats, almost word for word, that from the least of Vivien's wounds an emir would have died. William begins again the lament he delivered in the second of these *laisses*, but this time its length is doubled (vv. 758-80). The next three *laisses* (vv. 781-894) contain the same lamentation extended and developed at leisure.

Now it seems clear that the writer fully intended to develop his story in this curious way, amplifying and polishing one theme, then another, setting the stage separately for each development. It seems equally clear that what we have here is an application of the counsels of the rhetoric manuals apropos of *interpretatio* and *expolitio*. That its use entailed a narrative regression seems not to have bothered the writer, who is in no particular hurry to get on with his story. His task, as he sees it, is learnedly to amplify his matter. Indeed, if we compare the matter as it appears in *Aliscans* with the same matter in the earlier *Chanson de Guillaume*, from which it derives, we see that the earlier version devotes a total of 102 verses to the subject, the later version 275.[26]

This quite unusual way of telling a story, breaking the narrative thread and reversing chronology in order to introduce variations on matter already recounted, is a recurrent feature of the *chanson de geste*. It is quite interesting to note that something very much like this also occurs in *Beowulf*, at the point where the writer describes Grendel's approach to the high hall, where Beowulf waits for him:

> Cōm on wanre niht
> scriðan sceadugenga.   Sceotend swāfon,
> þā paet hornreced   healdan scoldon,
> ealle būton ānum.   þaet waes yldum cūþ,
> þaet hīe ne mōste,   þa Metod nolde,
> se scynscaþa   under sceadu bregdan;—
> ac hē waeccende   wraþum on andan

---

[26] See the *Chanson de Guillaume,* ed. Duncan McMillan (Paris, 1949-50), I, 82-85. In this version, there is also use of the device of *laisses similaires*: Laisse CXXXI tells how William found his nephew, briefly describes the wounds, and gives a short version of the lament. Laisse CXXXII extends the lament. Laisse CXXXIII describes again how William found his nephew near the spring, describes the wounds, and gives a longer version of the lament. It is curious to note that the place where Vivien is found is called variously *estanc, gué,* and *fontaine,* words not synonymous but apparently so used here to introduce variety.

bād bolgenmōd　　　beadwa geþinges.
　　Ðā cōm of more　　　under misthleoþum
Grendel gongan,　　　godes yrre baer;
mynte se mānscaða　　　manna cynnes
sumne besyrwan　　　in sele þām hēan.
Wod under wolcnum　　　tō þaes þe hē winreced,
goldsele gumena　　　gearwost wisse
faēttum fāhne.[27]

(The creature of the shadows came stalking in the dusky night. The liegemen who had to guard that gabled hall slept – all except one. It was known to men that the demon foe could not drag them to the shades below when the Creator did not will it. But he, fiercely watching for the foe, awaited in swelling rage the ordeal of battle.

Then came Grendel, advancing from the moor under the misty slopes; God's anger rested on him. The wicked foe thought to take by treachery one of the race of men in the high hall; he strode beneath the clouds until he came to where he could very clearly discern the wine-building, the gold-hall of men, gleaming with plated gold.)

Clearly, the writer chose here to present two aspects of the monster's approach: first, the situation in the hall and Beowulf's attitude; second, returning to the same starting point, the progress of Grendel himself toward the high hall. The effect is cubistic and cumulative.

　Faral chooses to explain the recurrence of *laisses similaires* in the *chanson de geste* in terms of the rather special requirements imposed by oral presentation. The audience, assembled in the open air, easily distracted by the various peripheral noises of the public square, might very well miss some important point of the poem, and so "il fallait . . . remédier aux défaillances de son attention, lui fournir la possibilité de rattraper ce qui . . . lui avait échappé. La répétition des laisses répondait à cette nécessité".[28] Rychner similarly compares the *jongleurs* to sports announcers, who are obliged by the shifting character of the radio audience to sum up the situation repeatedly, bringing new listeners abreast of the action.[29] But while all this is clear enough, it is hard to see why the *chansons* in their written form should reproduce a procedure a *jongleur* would use at his discretion during a performance. There would be no need to repeat if the audience remained stable and distractions minimal, and there would certainly be no possibility of predicting when the audience would shift, therefore no valid reason for

---

[27]　Klaeber's ed., vv. 702-716. The translation is Clark Hall's.
[28]　E. Faral, *La Chanson de Roland: Etude et analyse* (Paris, 1932), p. 270. *Cf.* also E. Auerbach, *Mimesis* (Princeton, 1953), p. 105.
[29]　J. Rychner, *La Chanson de geste*, p. 51. See also pp. 68-125.

including the *laisses similaires* in the written version. In fact, considering the work involved in transcribing some of the very long *laisses
similaires* (such as those in *Aliscans*), one would expect just the contrary, a short form of the narrative, which could be developed and
refined at the *jongleur's* discretion. Furthermore, the procedure tends
to be used at points in the story that constitute lyric peaks, moments of
moral beauty, rather than at moments when the development of the
plot has to be understood. All in all, it appears reasonable that the
inclusion of these repetitions in the manuscripts argues for their having
been considered stylistic elegances, which in turn would call for some
basis in the rhetorical tradition.[30]

The *laisses similaires* do not occur in the French romances. Since
these are written in prose or in rimed couplets, they could not, of
course, present a strophic phenomenon. Still, it is worth noting that
there is nothing that even remotely corresponds to it. Repetitions of
one sort or another, yes, but nothing quite like this. Chrétien, for
example, describes the events at the Grail Castle, and later on he has
Perceval describe the same events to his cousin. But there is no violation of chronology here. I suspect that the romancers perceived the
awkwardness of the device and declined on that ground to use it. However, its use had apparently become traditional in the *chansons de
geste*, and it continued to be used with increasing refinement. Furthermore, while the *chansons de geste* rarely exploit the narrative possibilities of surprise, the main source of narrative interest in the romances is
the unexpected. The writer's task is continually to pique the reader's
curiosity and to lead him on by holding back explanatory matter. The
chansons de geste, on the other hand, fully exploit the dramatic value
of particularly impressive moments, dwelling on them to magnify their
beauty. Thus repetitions of the sort we have seen are much more suitable to the epic than to the romantic genre.

What we have so far discussed under the heading of rhetorical
amplification – the relation I have suggested of interlaced narrative to
the figure *digressio*, and that of *laisses similaires* to the figures *interpretatio* and *expolitio* – are essentially narrative peculiarities, appearing
to stem, on the one hand, from the confusion of the techniques of narrative fiction and those of oratory, and on the other from a shift in
meaning of the word *amplificatio* from the idea of expansion to that of
elongation.

---

[30]   For further discussion see Werner Mulertt, *Laissenverbindung und Laissen-
wiederholung in der Chansons de Geste* (*Romanistische Arbeiten*, VII, 1918).

However, the usual thing was much more simple and obvious: the general idea was simply to make a story longer and more effective by providing more in the way of circumstantial detail. In this connection it hardly seems likely that the elementary recommendation of the rhetorical manuals were of much practical use. Geoffroi's counsels on description, for example, are so highly generalized as to be of relatively little value to a working writer:

Descriptiones dilatant materiam. Cum enim haec brevis sententia dicenda sit: Iste mulier est pulchra, ponatur descriptio pulchritudinis suae et fiet brevitas illa diffusa.[31]

The writers generally proceeded in a simple way, amplifying as they went along, accumulating details around the action. Their practice can be briefly illustrated by comparing two versions of the same event in the *Vie de Saint Alexis*, one as it appears in the eleventh-century text, the other in its expanded fourteenth-century form. The matter recounted is Alexis' reaction upon finding himself alone with his bride on his wedding night. It is at this point that his vocation to sainthood crystallizes in his mind. This is, therefore, an important, indeed, a crucial moment. The eleventh-century version is relatively swift:

> Com veit le lit, esguardat la pucele,
> Donc li remembret de son seinor celeste,
> Que plus at chier que tot aveir terrestre:
> 'E, Deus,' dist il, 'com forz pechiez m'apresset!
> S'or ne m'en fui, mout criem que ne t'en perde.'[32]

(When he sees the bed, he looked at the maiden, then he remembers his heavenly lord, whom he holds more dear than any earthly good. 'O Lord,' he said, 'how strongly sin presses upon me! If I do not flee now, I greatly fear that I shall lose thee.')

The same matter in the fourteenth-century text has undergone considerable expansion:

> Adonquez regarda Alexis sa moulier
>
> Qui en son lit estoit couchiée toute nue:
> Mout la vit blanche et tendre, bienfait et parcreüe.
> Lors ne sout il que fere, puis dist: 'Vierge asolue,
> Ne soufrez que fache euvre dont m'ame soit perdue.'
>
> Alexis vit la chambre qui estoit bien parée
> Et persut la pucele vermelle et coulourée;

---

[31] *Documentum*, II, 3. Faral, p. 271.
[32] *La Vie de Saint Alexis*, eds. Paris and Pannier, vv. 56-60, p. 142.

> Adont li remembra et li vint en pensée
> Que la joie du monde n'avoit point de durée;
>
> Et puis li ressouvint comme li dous Jhesus
> Vout en povreté nestre, puis soufri que pendus
> Fust en la sainte crois tout descaus et tout nus;
> Lors s'est l'enfant en crois contre terre estendus,
>
> Puis dist: 'Dous Jhesus Christ, bien sai, se me couchoie
> Avec ceste pucele, que m'i deliteroie,
> Et vostre dous service de tous poins delairoie.
> Je seroie trop fol si pur lie vous lesoie.[33]

(Then Alexis looked at his wife, who lay all naked in his bed; he saw her very white and tender, well proportioned and fully developed. Then he did not know what to do, and he said: 'Holy Virgin, do not let me do a deed for which I might lose my soul.'

Alexis saw the room, which was well decorated, and he saw the pink-fleshed maiden; then he remembered and it came to his mind that the joy of this world was not lasting.

And then he remembered how sweet Jesus chose to be born in poverty and allowed himself to be hung unclothed and unshod on the cross; then the child [Alexis] stretched himself out on the floor in the form of a cross.

Then he said: 'Sweet Jesus Christ, I know well that if I go to bed with this maiden I shall sin and abandon your sweet service in every way. It would be madness to leave you for [earthly] joy.')

Thus from a single stanza the writer has made four. To be sure, the replacement of assonance by rime accounts in part for the extension, since it necessitates a certain amount of line padding (*Adont li re-nembra et li vint en pensée*), but in general it is the increase in circumstantial detail that is noteworthy. The fourteenth-century writer does not undertake a detailed or systematic description of the maiden's beauty. He chooses rather to present those details which presumably would have struck Alexis himself: she lies naked on the bed; she is white, tender, physically well developed; the writer rather awkwardly begins the next stanza as though he were going to describe the room itself, but he wisely abandons this digression and returns to the maiden, whose flesh now becomes more highly colored (*vermelle et coulourée*). And when Alexis thinks of his savior, the writer tells us quite particularly what passes through his mind; a number of concrete details present themselves, in contrast to the present situation: Christ's poverty, the richly decorated room; Christ's ascetic nakedness, the maiden's voluptuous nudity; Christ nailed to the cross, the maiden lying in a soft

[33]   *Ibid.*, pp. 349-350.

bed. All these details serve to sharpen Alexis' dilemma and to force his resolution. This sort of amplification has, without doubt, a certain artistic value.

By way of contrast, the twelfth- and thirteenth-century versions both contain at this point in the story a striking example of ineffective amplification in the form of an interminable discourse on the virtue of chastity addressed by Alexis to his bewildered bride. The result of this is that while in the eleventh-century text twenty lines serve to present the whole scene, from Alexis' entrance into the bedroom to his exit, the twelfth-century text runs to 203 verses and the thirteenth-century text to 239. The fourteenth-century writer wisely cut out this extended discourse and reduced the matter to 76 verses.[34]

One of the most remarkable examples of rhetorical amplification is Benoît de Sainte-Maure's *Roman de Troie*, a romance of 30,000 lines. The first twenty-four thousand lines reproduce the events of the Trojan War substantially as they appear in Dares' resume, which, as I have said, takes up a scant forty pages or so in Latin prose. The amplification is so extensive that scholars have in general refused to believe that Benoît was using the text of Dares as we know it today. There must have been, it is argued, a much fuller version, which we know only in an abbreviated form.[35] Benoît himself tends to confirm this idea by assuring us – rather conventionally – that he is following the Latin text to the letter, putting in nothing more than a 'bon dit' now and then:

> Le latin suivrai et la letre:
> Nule autre rien n'i voudrai metre
> Si ainsi non com truis escrit.
> Ne di mie qu'aucun bon dit
> N'i mete, se faire le sai,
> Mais la matiere en ensuivrai.
>
> (vv. 135-40)

But until we find more rigorous evidence for the existence of a more extensive text of Dares' *Historia de excidio Troiae*, we shall have to

---

[34] All four texts may be consulted in the edition of Gaston Paris and Léopold Pannier, already cited. The passages in question are on pp. 141-142, 225-231, 282-289, and 349-353. There are of course many other medieval versions of the Alexis legend; these four, however, are very closely related. The twelfth-century writer obviously had the eleventh-century text before him; he reproduces almost every line of it. The thirteenth-century rimed version is clearly based on the twelfth-century version and served in its turn as the basis for the fourteenth-century text. See G. Paris' discussion of the mss., pp. 2-7.

[35] See Léopold Constans, in *Histoire de la langue et de la littérature française*, general ed. Petit de Julleville, I, 204-214.

admit at least the possibility that Benoît was entirely responsible for this massive expansion, and that he accomplished it almost exclusively by rhetorical means. The sequence of events is virtually the same as we have it in Dares, but it is amplified by detailed descriptions, long conversations and speeches, and, now and again, by short substantive amplifications, such as the story of Troilus and Briseïda, which is grafted onto the main narrative line in eight separate sections, amounting in all to something over a thousand lines of new matter.[36]

Once the medieval writer decided to amplify his story by adding more narrative matter, he could proceed in any number of ways. Of these, it seems to me that there is some advantage in distinguishing two main categories: amplifications of logical and those of nonlogical character. Logical amplifications would be those in which we can detect a desire to explain, to motivate, to elucidate, or to rationalize, while nonlogical amplifications – usually by repetitions or free association of narrative motifs – remain permanently separable from the main story line and appear to derive only from the desire to amplify. Of course, the line of distinction is often hard to draw, since what seemed logical to the medieval writer sometimes seems fantastic to us, and nonlogical additions may occasionally be shown to have structural functions susceptible of rational analysis. Still, in the interests of clarity, it seems advantageous to maintain the distinction whenever we can.

THE PRINCIPLE OF FREE ASSOCIATION. It stands to reason that in the absence of strict logical control over a narrative sequence, some form of association would from time to time dictate the development of an episodic sequence. It is hazardous to imagine that we can accurately reconstruct any such sequence over so vast an expanse of time, particularly in view of our general uncertainty about the exact nature of the source materials any given writer may have had available to him. Still, there are cases where the matter seems tolerably clear.

It is, and always has been, the business of the professional story-teller to have at his command a considerable stock of stories. This stock is the basis of his craft, his 'elements of production'.[37] It is understandable that in the practice of his craft the story-teller will change the elements that make up his repertory, add to them, or combine them

---

[36] *Le Roman de Troie*, ed. Léopold Constans, 6 vols.; *SATF* (Paris, 1904-1912). The passages I refer to are vv. 13065-13120, 13261-13866, 14268-14352, 15001-15186, 15617-15658, 20057-20118, 20193-203-40, 20666-20682.
[37] *Cf.* C. M. Bowra, *Heroic Poetry* (London, 1952), p. 221.

in various ways. Thus, in composing an episodic sequence, it would seem inevitable that some of these narrative threads should associate themselves through the relation of details and that these associations should in some measure determine the flow and development of the story.

In the case of Chrétien de Troyes, we are generally obliged to reconstruct his sources hypothetically, but there occurs in *Yvain* an episodic sequence the sources of which seem quite clear and the development of which appears to stem from an associative process.

The second half of *Yvain* consists of an extended series of episodes, a sort of terminal *roman à tiroirs*. The first half of the story is coherent and unified. It looks as though here Chrétien amplified a short narrative *lai*, by adding to the story of Yvain a tale of rehabilitation through a series of trials in the course of which the hero comes to be associated with a lion and thus is called the *chevalier au lion*. Since there is no logical reason why the conjunction of knight and lion should occur, and in all likelihood no traditional or historical basis for it, the explanation must lie elsewhere than in reason.

In the first part of the story, Yvain wins chivalric esteem and a lovely bride by defeating Esclados the Red, defender of the magic fountain, and by marrying his widow Laudine. His friend Gawain, however, persuades him that his marriage will lead him to a decline in chivalric dynamism and that he will do well to leave his wife temporarily and devote himself to jousting and other knightly exercises. Though reluctant to leave his lovely bride, Yvain gets permission from her to be gone for a year and a day. Since he overstays his leave, he is visited one day at court by his wife's messenger, who roundly denounces him before his fellows and takes away his ring. Shame and grief unhinge his mind, and he flees stark mad, into the forest, where he lives naked and wild. He kills wild animals and eats their raw flesh (vv. 2824-26), thus becoming something of a wild animal himself. One day, however, he meets a hermit, who realizes that he is insane and generously puts out bread and water for him. In gratitude, Yvain hunts wild game for the hermit and lays it at his door (vv. 2829-2875). Up to this point the story has developed in accordance at least with a principle of moderate probability, once we accept the notion that loss of love can drive a man to madness and thus reduce him to a state of semi-bestiality. But the development is suggestive: Yvain is behaving toward the hermit like a grateful animal, and the *locus classicus* of this motif is, of course, the story of Androcles and the Lion. In the following episode, Yvain is restored to sanity thanks to the ministrations of the Dame de Noroison, who has a magic ointment for just such purposes. The hero gratefully responds by defending her from her enemy, the Count Allier, who covets her land and her person. During the combat, Chrétien notes that Yvain fights like a lion:

> Tot autressi antr'aus se fiert
> Con li lïons antre les dains.
> (vv. 3203-04)

This is certainly not an unusual comparison, but it is significant in this context, for in the next episode, Yvain comes upon a snake and a lion engaged in a mortal struggle. After a moment of hesitation, Yvain decides to aid the lion. He kills the snake, and to his surprise, the lion, instead of turning on him, kneels in gratitude. The two now go off together and the lion kills game for his new friend.

This is not at all the story as we know it from Aulus Gellius (*Attic Nights*, V, xiv), but the general movement is the same. The man helps the lion, and the lion becomes his friend, travels with him, and kills game for him to eat.

The general dependence seems clear. The presence of the snake in the story would appear to derive from another well known story by a process of association, in this case a story of animal ingratitude. It occurs in Petrus Alfonsis' *Disciplina Clericalis*, which was translated into Old French just about the time Chrétien was working on *Yvain*, under the title *Le Chastoiement d'un père à son fils:*

> Uns hons par un bois trespassoit
> Et el chemin, que il erroit,
> Trova un serpent mout blechié,
> Que pastor avoient lïé:
> O broches cleufichiés estoit,
> Si que movoir ne se puet.
> Li bons hons, quant il l'esguarda,
> Pité en ot, sil deslïa.
> Pour escaufer, par bone foi,
> Le mist sous ses dras prés de soi.
> Dés que li serpens escaufa,
> De sa nature li membra;
> Tot environ a l'omme chaint,
> E griément blechié et estraint.
> 'Avoi,' dist li hons, 'tu as tort.
> Ja t'ai garanti de mort,
> Et tu me vels geter de vie.'
> 'Che fu,' dist li serpens, 'folie

Que de moi presis nule cure,
Car faire m'estuet ma nature.' [38]

(A man was passing through a wood, and on the road that he was travelling he found a serpent badly wounded, tied by shepherds: he was fastened down with stakes so that he could not move. The good man, when he saw him, had pity and released him. To warm him up, in good faith, he put him under his shirt near him. As soon as the serpent was warmed, he remembered his nature; he coiled all around the man and squeezed him and grievously wounded him. 'Oh,' said the man, 'you do wrong. I just saved you from death and you wish to end my life.' 'It was madness,' said the snake, 'to take any care for me, for my nature makes me do this.')

Thus, we may conjecture, just as the two complementary motifs of gratitude and ingratitude became entwined in Chrétien's mind, the lion and the snake appeared in his story engaged in struggle. And I dare say that Yvain's momentary fear that the lion might turn against him owes something to the snake story.

However, the most interesting development is in the next episode, in which Yvain and his lion happen to pass by the castle where Yvain's wife lives. Remembering former bliss in present woe, he is overcome by grief and falls into a swoon, accidentally cutting himself as he falls. The lion, seeing him lying on the ground with blood on his neck, mistakenly assumes that his friend is dead and tries, rather clumsily, to commit suicide by propping Yvain's sword against a stump and running against it. Yvain revives in time to stop him. Then, through a crack in the wall, he hears a woman lamenting. It is Lunete, his wife's servant, who had saved his life in an earlier episode and helped him win the hand of her lady. She has been accused of treason for advising her lady to marry Yvain and is to be burned at the stake on the following day unless she finds a champion to defend her against her accuser, the seneschal, and his two brothers. Yvain promises to be there as her champion.

It seems clear that Chrétien, once he got hold of the lion, was led by association to another classical story about a lion, the story of Pyramus and Thisbe. Two elements in the story make the association almost a certainty: first, the attempted suicide based on a false appearance, and second, the conversation through a crack in the wall. [39]

Ultimately, of course, it does not matter whether it was Chrétien or a predecessor who originally devised this sequence, but in the absence of

[38] Text from Bartsch and Wiese, *Chrestomathie de l'ancien français*, pp. 183-184.
[39] *Yvain*, ed. Foerster, v. 3567. Frappier notes the concurrence in detail between the two stories, *Chrétien de Troyes*, p. 158.

direct evidence to the contrary, we may assume that Chrétien is responsible. There is much to be said about the manner of the adaptation, about the control Chrétien exercised in working into the fabric of his story such essentially disparate elements of production, but my concern here is only to indicate how narrative motifs may derive from a simple associative process to produce such curiously irrational sequences as the one we find in *Yvain*.

THE PRINCIPLE OF REPETITION. Frequently we find that in a medieval story the narrative is amplified by repetitions of narrative motifs. There is no difficulty in understanding how this happens. The writer arrives at the end of an episode, and, having nothing special in mind except to expand the story or else to delay the end, he simply puts in another episode of the sort he has just told, since its narrative structure is still present in his mind and all he has to do is to change a few details. This sort of amplification hardly excites our admiration, but it does achieve the desired end with a minimum of effort.

The *Roman de Renart* is full of examples of this sort of amplification. In Branch XI, which we have already cited, Renart goes off in search of food and soon meets Ysengrin. The two run together for a while; then Ysengrin tires and lies down to sleep beside an oak tree. Renart maliciously ties him to the tree and withdraws. A *vilein* happens by, sees the wolf at a disadvantage, and attacks him. In spite of his handicap, however, Ysengrin has the better of the fight and the *vilein* goes on his way. Renart then rushes up and unties the wolf, who thanks him for this kindness and invites him to dinner.

In the next episode, Renart finds his enemy, Roenel the mastiff, lying at the foot of a tree, badly beaten from an encounter with a *vilein*. He is conscious but has not enough strength to move. Renart takes a rope and prepares to hang him but is interrupted by the arrival of King Noble and his company. Renart flees. The King asks Roenel who is responsible for his battered condition and the mastiff accuses Renart. Renart, meanwhile, has gone off on other adventures.

It is easy enough to see that the two adventures are formally repetitive. The elements of the first situation – the tree, the rope, the prostrate animal, the *vilein*, and the fox – all appear in the second, transposed and reorganized into a variant. Renart succeeds in his first trick and fails in the second. The episodes mirror one another, but it seems to me that it would be foolish to argue that the writer had it in mind to compose a miniature narrative diptych here. He wanted simply to expand his story, and since it had as yet no particular direction, he just varied the narrative data of the first episode.

A somewhat more artistic example of this procedure occurs in Branch I. The various animals, except for Renart, assemble at Noble's court and accuse Renart of disturbing the recently proclaimed peace of the animal world. Noble is inclined to consider most of the charges flimsy, but then arrive Chantecler and Dame Pinte bearing the dead body of the latter's sister Dame Copée, recently murdered by Renart. Noble is furious and dispatches Brun the bear to summon Renart to court for trial and judgment. Renart easily tricks the bear by playing on his appetite for honey: he leads him to a partly split tree wedged open by a woodman, he gets the bear to put his nose into the opening to look for honey that is supposed to be there, then removes the wedges. Brun comes back to court with a mutilated nose, and Noble is infuriated that his messenger should have been so treated. He sends Tibert the cat on the same mission. The results are the same, but in this case Renart tricks the cat by playing on his appetite for mice and leads him into a snare. When Tibert returns, Noble is doubly enraged and sends Grimbert the badger after Renart. This time Renart is brought to judgment and sentenced to be hanged, but he escapes his punishment by making a show of repentance.

Clearly, from a strictly logical point of view, the three successive summonses might have been reduced to one. The story pattern requires an accusation, a summons, and a judgment. The writer chose to amplify by tripling the summons. It is worth noting that each of the first two summonses functions dramatically to bring the story to a climax. Noble, already enraged by the murder of Dame Copée, is goaded into greater and greater fury by Renart's treatment of his emissaries. The movement of such a narrative clearly merits praise, especially when we compare it with another story, in which, as we have seen, the episodic movement is anticlimactic, the *Chanson de Guillaume*.

This story may be analyzed into a pattern of four juxtaposed battles. In the first, Vivien is mortally wounded, but he sends for help at last from his uncle Guillaume, who arrives with reinforcements. When his troops are all killed, Guillaume returns to the castle for more. They too fall before the superior numbers of the pagans, and Guillaume again escapes. He goes to the court of the Emperor Louis and gets another army together, among them the pagan giant Reneward, kitchen steward to the Emperor, who at last helps the Christians to victory.

The *trouvère*, in this case, clearly realized that he could not hope to pass off on his audience so monotonous a structure without introducing new elements of variety into each unit. Thus the first battle is dominated by Vivien's sublime heroism; the second introduces Guichard and Girart, both nephews of Guillaume's wife Guiborc, whose deaths are presented in a symmetrical contrast, with Girart dying a noble Christian death, and Guichard denying his faith at the last moment; the third battle sees the introduction of yet another center of narrative interest in the person of Guillaume's fifteen-year-old nephew Guiot, wise beyond his years, who comments perceptively on the action, like a proper *puer senex*; and the final battle features the heroic-comic activities of Reneward, whose Herculean strength carries the day for Christianity.

The principle of composition is a varied repetition of the theme of battle, and the design is technically comic, since it begins badly and ends well. But as the variations appear in a declining order, descending from Vivien's heroic sacrifice to Reneward's clownish feats of strength, the impression is that the writer began with a legitimate inspiration, but that his desire to amplify led him into more and more trivial extensions as his inspiration ran out. Bédier's judgment of the poem as a whole is severe:

L'épopée, jusque-là si belle du pathétique de la défaite, s'achève en une sorte de boufonnerie héroïque, et sainte chrétienté est sauvée par la massue d'une sorte de butor, Rainouart. . . . Ce qu'il choque en nous, ce n'est pas tant notre instinct classique de l'unité de ton et de la distinction des genres. C'est un sentiment plus profond: on eût aimé que celui qui a communié Vivien mourant [Guillaume] fût aussi son vengeur, et que Guillaume dès qu'apparaît le bon géant Rainouart, ne fût pas tout à fait rejeté à l'arrière-plan.[40]

Varied repetition appears to function most effectively as a principle of structure when it is supported by a climactic movement. Even in the absence of a logical progression in his story, the narrator can manage to engage the attention of the reader more and more deeply by making each adventure more serious or more intense than the preceding one. In the absence of a device of this sort, repetition palls.

The three great crises of Beowulf are so arranged: the fight with Grendel, the struggle with Grendel's dam, and the combat with the dragon are varied repetitions of the same narrative motif in a sequence of graded difficulty. The hero's struggle with Grendel is fairly short and easy. Once Beowulf seizes him, the monster struggles only to escape. The second combat, that with Grendel's dam, ends in a triumph

---

[40]   J. Bédier, *Les Légendes épiques*, I, 196-197.

for the hero only by a sort of miracle: Beowulf must fight the hag on her own ground; he must dive into the mere and gain the submarine cavern; in the battle the sword that Unferth gave him fails him; he stumbles and falls; it is only at the very last moment that he catches sight of the marvelous sword with which he manages to cut off the monster's head. The third combat, long afterward, is fatal to Beowulf: he wins victory only at the cost of his own life.[41] The pattern, as in the parodic case of Renart in the first branch, is tragic – two victories and a heroic defeat. This is clearly more effective than the comic pattern of the sequence in the *Chanson de Guillaume*: three defeats followed by an easy victory.

The principle of repetition is, of course, susceptible of much refinement, since the repeated elements can be organized into fairly complex patterns. An interesting example of such refinement may be seen in the extended sequence that makes up the second half of Chrétien's *Erec*.

The narrative situation from which the sequence departs can be summed up in a few words. Erec, in the first part of the story, passes through a series of well concatenated adventures, not in any sense a *roman à tiroirs*, in which he takes revenge on the knight Yder for an offense to Queen Guenevere. In the course of the action, he falls in love with the daughter of a poor vavassour and takes her back with him to Arthur's court, where she is admired by all. They marry and afterward Erec becomes so engrossed with his beautiful wife that he abandons chivalric activity and spends most of his time in bed with her. One morning, he finds out that the whole court is talking about his *recreance*. He is greatly distressed and, determined to rebuild his reputation, he has two horses saddled and leaves with Enide in quest of adventure. There follow ten episodes, logically unrelated, which present themselves as though they were being fed into an assembly line. But this sequence, arbitrary though it seems to us, is not so in reality. It is carefully controlled by a concern to produce a structure of patterned repetition, graded and varied in a fairly mechanical way. The episodes occur in the following order:

1. An encounter with three brigands, who covet Erec's wife and his other belongings. Erec takes on all three and defeats them.
2. An encounter with five brigands. Similar motives, same result.
3. Count Galoin invites Erec and Enide to his château and attempts to seduce Enide. She outwits him, warns Erec, and they flee together. Erec wounds the count and some of his men.

---

[41] *Cf.* Fr. Klaeber (ed.), *Beowulf*, p. liii.

4. Erec encounters Guivret le Petit, King of the Irish, a dwarf of extra-
    ordinary impetuosity and bellicose temper. After a difficult set-to, Erec
    triumphs and wins Guivret's admiration and friendship.

5. Weak from his encounter with Guivret, wounded in several places,
    Erec comes accidentally to Arthur's court, where he convalesces. Arthur
    heals his wounds with a salve he got from his sister Morgain. After a
    brief stay, Erec sets out again.

6. Erec hears a maiden cry out for help. Her beloved has been carried off
    by two giants. Erec goes after them, does battle with both, frees the
    captive knight, and returns, but he is so badly wounded that he falls
    from his horse as though dead. Enide laments.

7. She is heard by the Count Oringle di Limors, who takes both of them
    to his castle. Assuming Erec to be dead, he forces Enide to marry him.
    When she refuses to eat at the wedding table, he strikes her in the face.
    At the sound of her cry, Erec is startled into consciousness, gets up,
    draws his sword, and kills the count, whose retainers, thinking that Erec
    has risen from the dead, flee in terror.

8. Erec now has a second encounter with Guivret, who has heard that his
    friend is in trouble. They fail to recognize one another in the darkness
    of night, and Guivret attacks, nearly killing Erec, who is still weak
    from his encounter with the giants. Enide rushes to Erec's aid and
    admonishes Guivret for attacking a wounded man. Guivret is distressed
    to learn that he has injured his friend, apologizes, and takes the pair
    to his castle.

9. Erec is nursed back to health by Guivret's two sisters. Once recovered,
    he sets out with Enide and hears of a fearful adventure called the *Joie
    de la Cour*. He determines to undertake it.

10. In the final adventure, which we are given to understand is extremely
    perilous, Erec enters an enchanted orchard, surrounded by a wall of
    air. At its center lies a beautiful maiden asleep in the shade of a syca-
    more. Around her is a picket fence, each picket but one capped with the
    skull belonging to an earlier victim. On the last there hangs a horn.
    A gigantic warrior named Mabonagrain appears and does battle with
    Erec, who ultimately triumphs. He discovers in subsequent conversation
    with his opponent that he has just liberated him from the service of the
    demoiselle du verger, who had held him in thrall. She, in turn, is re-
    vealed to be Enide's cousin. She is distressed at no longer having
    Mabonagrain at her service, but she comes finally to realize that she
    may be happier in her love now that she is obliged to relinquish her
    tyranny over her beloved. Erec blows the horn and there is general re-
    joicing at the outcome of the adventure. Then he and Enide return to
    his father's kingdom, where Erec, because of his father's death, is
    crowned king in a grand ceremony.

In this series, aimless as it seems at first glance, it is noteworthy that
there are two combats with brigands, two occasions on which Enide is
exposed to the amorous advances of malevolent noblemen, two encounters with Guivret le Petit, two convalescences, and two occasions

on which Erec fights with gigantic opponents. What is more, within
each pair of events, the second is more serious, more intense. The final
adventure, in keeping with the principle of gradation, is the most
perilous of all.

The principle of repetition can be summed up for this series as
though it were a rhyme scheme: AABCDEBCDE, corresponding to
episodes one through ten. The first two episodes are the least impressive of the series, for the second repeats the first in every detail except
for the number of brigands, which is increased from three to five.

Chrétien shows an obvious concern with episodic contrasts, as distinguished from variety. Erec is made to occupy the center of the stage
in the encounters with Guivret, the giants and the brigands, while Enide
moves into the foreground in the episodes involving the Counts Galoin
and de Limors. Scenes of convalescence and rest intervene between
scenes of violence. Furthermore, Erec's opponents are contrasted in
terms of their physical size: Guivret is a dwarf, Mobonagrain a giant.

Finally, the last major episode, the *Joie de la Cour* adventure, is
considerably more than a simple repetition in a graded series. Much
more extensively developed than the rest, and hardly reducible to a
simple conflict with a large opponent, it contains a restatement, or recapitulation, of the courtly theme of the story: in liberating Mabona-
grain from his slavish service to the *demoiselle du verger*, Erec sym-
bolically repeats his own liberation from uxoriousness. Thus it is no
accident that Enide and the *demoiselle du verger* should turn out to be
cousins: they are related from a conceptual point of view.

We may well wonder whether the medieval audiences could have
appreciated this sort of artistry, which admittedly does not leap to the
eye. It is a concealed artistry that works unobtrusively on the sensibility
of the audience, in a way quite analogous to the use of theme and variation in music, or as the number-scheme in Dante's *Vita Nuova* gives
form to the piece without obtruding itself on the mind of the reader.
Chrétien evidently sought to avoid monotony by varying his narrative
elements, using the intervening material to provide contrast. But to
avoid the opposite pitfall of confusion, he supported the story with
repetitions and restatements. The main thing, however, is that Chrétien
apparently found it convenient, in the absence of logical sequence, to
construct this story in a fairly geometrical way.

I have so far treated repetition as though it were essentially a device
for amplification and only secondarily a principle of structural design.
But the matter is not so clear. Even in some of the earliest examples of

vernacular narrative, we find repetitions whose justification appears to be almost exclusively a matter of design and poetic effect. Repetitions of narrative motifs may be used as a sort of narrative equivalent to rime. For an example, we may turn to the eleventh-century *Vie de Saint Alexis*, which we have already compared in part to the fourteenth-century version. The story is this: after Alexis left his bride and family to take up the ascetic life, he spent seventeen years of unrelenting poverty in far-off Alsis (Edessa). There an *imagene*, an icon in the temple near the place where he customarily sat collecting alms, spoke out miraculously, requesting that the Man of God be brought to the temple because he was near the kingdom of Heaven. The miracle made Alexis a local hero and he found himself plagued by worshippers. To protect his humility, he was obliged to flee. The boat he took was blown off its course to Rome, where Alexis now went to live under the stairs in his family's house, unrecognized, and humiliated by his former servants, who amused themselves by pouring dishwater on his head. After seventeen years of patient travail, he died. But during the week preceding his death, a voice had sounded in the sanctuary instructing the people of Rome to seek out the Man of God or perish by being swallowed up by the earth. The Pope himself and the Emperors of East and West joined in the search. The voice directed them to the house of Alexis' father, who could not imagine who the Man of God might be. But Alexis was finally found, not long dead, with the written story of his life clutched in his hand. Pope and Emperors knelt to pray, the family and bride lamented his death. His body, richly dressed and put in a marble bier studded with diamonds was carried across the city through a throng of frenzied admirers to the church of St. Boniface, where after being honored for seven days, it was laid to rest.

There are three main turning points in this story, and they are all, in a sense, repetitions of one another. The first is Alexis' flight from his home on his wedding night, after which he renounces power, wealth and sensual pleasure to espouse the ascetic life. The second turning point is at Alsis (Edessa) after he has been designated by the icon as a holy man. Now he flees to escape veneration as a saint. The third turning point is his death, his final withdrawal from the world. At this point he is about to be found by the Pope and Emperors, who would do him honor and beg him to save the city from impending catastrophe. This also he avoids by dying in the nick of time.

It is noteworthy that the events are spaced so that the second occurs seventeen years after the first, the third seventeen years after the second. Intertwined with this motif, which we might designate as 'a flight from glory', there is a corollary 'nonrecognition' motif. Nobody recognizes Alexis. The first failure occurs when Alexis' father sends out messengers to look for his vanished son. Two of them actually get to Edessa, walk right by him, even give him a few coins, but they do not recognize him. Seventeen years later, at Edessa, when the icon sends the sacristan out to bring Alexis into the temple, the sacristan is unable to pick out Alexis from the many beggars outside the church. He has to return to get more specific indications.

As far as the development of the narrative line is concerned, this incident is entirely useless. The sacristan finally finds Alexis, who as a result becomes an object of public veneration, and it is this in turn that motivates his flight. The fact that the sacristan did not recognize him immediately, although it contributes nothing to the narrative development, is there as a thematically interesting repetition of an earlier motif. The same motif dominates Alexis' stay in Rome. There he meets his father on the street and is not recognized; then for seventeen years he lives under the stairs in his father's house in full view of his family and servants without once being recognized. Finally even when the voice in the sanctuary sends the Pope and the Emperors to the father's house, no one in the household can guess who the Man of God may be.

Both motifs, flight from glory and nonrecognition, are thematically rich, and they are set up so that each repetition carries a more intense moral significance.

A more automatic sort of repetition may be seen in the threefold lamentation of Alexis' family. The first occurs immediately after his flight from home. It is quite brief:

> Ço dist li pedre: 'Chiers filz, com t'ai perdut!'
> Respont la medre: 'Lasse, qu'est devenuz?'
> Ço dist la 'spose: 'Pechiez le m'at tolut.
> Amis, bels sire, si poi vos ai out!
> Or suis si graime que ne pois estre plus.'
> (vv. 106-10)

(The father said: 'Dear son, I have lost indeed.' The mother responded: 'Alas, what has become of him?' The wife said: 'Sin took him from me. Friend, handsome lord, I had you with me so short a time. Now I am so sad that I can no longer endure.')

The second lamentation occurs when the messengers return to say that they have been unable to find Alexis. It extends over five full stanzas (vv. 126-50); the father delivers the first, the mother the next three, his abandoned wife the last. The lamentation is considerably more intense, but it is as nothing in comparison with the final repetition of the motif, which occurs upon the discovery of Alexis' corpse. There the family, in standard order, father, mother, and wife, deliver themselves of a lament that fills no less than twenty-three stanzas (vv. 386-490).

It seems tolerably clear that for the writer of the *Alexis* these repeated motifs arranged in a climactic order functioned as unifying devices. It is not simply a matter of their location at points of structural importance, as turning points within the narrative; there are also stylistic reasons for supposing that the writer took special care to see that these motifs stood out in sharp relief. This becomes evident when we compare the Latin and Old-French versions of some of the scenes.

In the first expression of the 'nonrecognition' motif, for example, the poet took extraordinary pains to make sure that the audience would not miss his point, and thus prepared for the later variations of the theme. In the Latin version the text simply says that when the messengers sent by Alexis' father got to Edessa, "viderunt eum inter ceteros pauperos sedentem and dantes ei eleemosynam discesserunt, quia non cognoverunt eum".[42] But the vernacular poet wrote:

> Donc prent li pedre de ses meilors serjanz;
> Par moltes terres fait querre son enfant.
> Jusqu'en Alsis en vindrent dui edrant;
> Iloc troverent dan Alexis sedant,
> Mai*s n'en conurent* son vis ne son semblant.
>
> Si at li enfes sa tendre charn mudede,
> *Nel reconurent* li dui serjant son pedre.
> A lui medisme ont l'almosne donede;
> Il la receut come li altre fredre.
> *Nel reconurent*, sempres s'en retornerent.
>
> *Nel reconurent ne ne l'ont enterciet.*
> Danz Alexis en lodet Deu del ciel
> D'icez son sers cui il est almosniers.
> Il fut lor sire, or est lor provendiers;
> Ne vos sai dire com il s'en firet liez.
>   (vv. 111-25; italics mine)

The writer plays insistently on the fact that Alexis was not recognized, but this event has practically nothing in the way of narrative consequence: he was not seen and therefore nothing happened. In a purely

---

[42] The Latin text on which the eleventh-century version is based is printed in J. M. Meunier's edition, *La Vie de Saint Alexis* (Paris, 1933), pp. 11-17. The passage cited above is on p. 13.

narrative sense, the scene is useless to the further development of the
story. Nor is the scene exploited for its dramatic value. There is no
attempt to develop suspense: Alexis does not even express concern lest
he be recognized. The messengers are not made to come gradually
closer and closer, then to everyone's relief pass on. Not at all. They
simply find him sitting there and do not recognize him.

The second instance of nonrecognition is less striking, but the intent
is the same. In the Latin text, the sacristan sent out to bring Alexis
into the sanctuary fails to recognize him and has to return for more
information. The icon tells him that the man he seeks is sitting outside
near the entrance:

Exiensque paramonarius quaesivit eum et non cognovit et reversus intro
coepit precari omnipotentis Dei clementiam ut ostenderet eum illi. Iterum
imago ait: 'Ille qui sedet foris in ostio ipse est.'[43]

Here is the vernacular version:

> Ço dist l'imagene: 'Fai l'home Deu venir!
> Quer il at Deu bien ed a gret servit,
> Ed il est dignes d'entrer en paradis.'
> Cil vait, sil quiert, mais il *nel set choisir,*
> Icel saint home de cui l'imagene dist.
>
> Revint li costre a l'imagene el mostier
> 'Certes,' dist il, *'ne sai cui entercier.'*
> Respont l'imagene: 'Ço'st cil qui lez l'us siet;
> Pres est de Deu e del regne del ciel;
> Par nule guise ne s'en volt esloinier.'
>   (vv. 171-180; italics mine)

(The icon said: 'Bring me the Man of God, for he has served God well and
is worthy to enter into Paradise. He went, he sought, but he could not find
him, that holy man of whom the icon spoke. The sacristan went back into
the minster: 'Indeed,' he said, 'I cannot recognize him.' The icon answers:
'It is he who sits by the door. He is near to God and the Kingdom of
Heaven. In no way will he withdraw from it.)

In this case the writer first tells us that the sacristan is unable to recognize Alexis; then he has the sacristan tell the icon that he cannot
recognize him. The Latin text, on the contrary, manages by a sort of
periphrasis to avoid repeating the motif: "Coepit precari . . . ut ostenderet eum illi."[44]

---

[43] Meunier's edition, p. 13.

[44] This detail, incidentally, although it figures in the Latin version, is absent from
the original Syrian life (fifth century) as well as from the four later Greek versions
(sixth through ninth centuries). See Meunier's introduction, pp. 2-17, for the
development of the legend. Its appearance for the first time in the tenth-century

All these instances of nonrecognition prepare, of course, for the second half of the story, which is a glorious pageant of recognition and acclaim, occurring in the capital of the Christian world, presided over by the Pope and Emperors. The development is similar to the use of anagnorisis in classical tragedy and epic.

Finally, in addition to the pattern of repetition, there is in the *Alexis* a didactically oriented pattern of complementary correspondences such that events of the first part of the story are reflected and fulfilled in the second. Ascetic anonymity dominates the first part; general recognition the second. Alexis abandons his bride at the beginning of the story, rejoins her in Heaven at the end (a feature not in the Latin *vita*). He abandons his rich clothes for beggar's raiment at Edessa, but is magnificently clothed for the procession across the city. His mother drapes his room with rags and tears away all its decorations, but his bier is of marble studded with precious stones.

The *Chanson de Roland*, certainly the most artfully constructed of the *chansons de geste*, contains some extraordinary examples of repetition with inversion. This is all the more remarkable in that the *Roland*, at least up to the Baligant episode, has a fairly tight logical structure that appears to derive from the poet's desire to rationalize a defeat. Events follow one another in such a way that incident and character interact to produce an inexorable movement toward the catastrophe at Roncevaux. The specific elements that the writer chose to present in this sequence reveal a conscious attempt to organize the action into complementary scenes. For example, when the Franks assemble to choose an emissary to treat with the pagans, Roland nominates his stepfather Ganelon, who turns on him in fury and accuses him of sending him to his death. He accepts the mission, but upon taking leave of Charlemagne, he urges the king to watch over his son, whom he does not expect to see again. Charlemagne accuses him of being fainthearted and tells him to go on his way. Ganelon goes to Marsile, arranges the treason, and promises that Roland will be chief of the rearguard. When the ranks again assemble to choose the leader of the rearguard, Ganelon not unexpectedly names Roland. Roland thanks his stepfather and gladly accepts the dangerous post. When Charlemagne offers him half the army for the rearguard, he proudly declines and accepts only twenty thousand men.

Latin life suggests that the Latin writer was himself working with a view to duplicating a particularly appealing feature of the story.

It is, of course, perfectly clear that the second scene is a logical development from the first. It is quite as clear that the second is an inverted image of the first, a similar situation with the roles reversed: Roland names Ganelon for a dangerous mission; then Ganelon names Roland: Ganelon responds with anger and fear; Roland responds with an ironic expression of thanks to his stepfather and with obvious relish for the dangers of the situation. Ganelon had dropped the glove given him as a symbol of office by Charlemagne; Roland asks for the bow and refers back to the incident of the glove. These pivotal scenes, essential in determining the course of the story and in portraying the characters of the two major figures, are thus made symmetrically to balance one another.

Such a balance is not likely to have occurred accidentally. The contrast is explicit in the incidents and the dialogue. There is a similar example of balanced events just a little further on, and here the artistic intent is even more clear. When Olivier sees that the pagan forces are overwhelmingly superior in numbers, he advises Roland to sound his horn and call Charlemagne back. Roland refuses, since in the presence of his stepfather he had haughtily refused to accept half of Charlemagne's army. Thus he can hardly call for help at the first sign of danger. Roland and Olivier quarrel through three *laisses similaires* (cited above, p. 73); Roland remains adamant. However, when only sixty French soldiers remain alive and Roland realizes that many a brave man will never look on *douce France* again, he perceives that fighting against insuperable odds is not quite the delicious game he had thought it to be. He discusses the matter with Olivier, who has no solution to propose except to die valiantly. But Roland has an idea: why not sound his horn and have Charles return with the army? Olivier furiously rejects this suggestion and reminds Roland that when he, Olivier, suggested it in the first place, Roland did not deign to listen, and that as a result of this reckless irresponsibility (*legerie*) the French have died. It would be an insult to them to call back the Emperor now. Here again, it is clear that we are dealing with two scenes involving a psychological chiasmus, but the second scene cannot be said to be entirely necessary to the logical structure of the story. Bishop Turpin intervenes and settles their quarrel, advising Roland to blow his horn in order that Charlemagne may return and avenge their death and give them honorable burial.[45] Thus Olivier's opposition really comes to

---

[45]   The passages I refer to occur in *laisses* 19-23 (Ganelon's nomination), 58-62 (Roland's nomination): 83-85 (Roland's refusal), 129-131 (Olivier's refusal). The

naught. The scene is there for its structural and moral beauty. It balances the earlier scene and it further develops the contrast between the characters of Roland and Olivier.

Repetition, therefore, may serve several ends in the composition of medieval narrative. Fundamentally an instrument of amplification, it may also serve as a principle of thematic recurrence or as a way of balancing one part of a story against another: Even in the composition of logically developed narrative it may dictate the choice of scenes and the manner of their presentation. In any case, it is important to distinguish between the use of repetition as a substitute for narrative imagination and its use as a principle of poetic design.

Logical Amplifications. We often hear that medieval man, because of his peculiar view of the world, tended to be rather indifferent to notions of cause and effect, preferring symbolic relations to causal ones. When he came to consider how one thing proceeded from another he fell back on naïve notions of procreation or ramification. A tree or a pedigree sufficed to indicate the relation of cause and effect. Law was understood by reference to an *arbor de origine juris et legum*, and so on.[46] As might be expected, some rather fanciful explanations of this aspect of medieval thought have been put forward and applied to the composition of narrative.[47] Most such attempts to deny a sense of logic to medieval man seem wide of the mark. We can find a common-sense idea of logical motivation in much of medieval literature.

---

artifice which appears in these reversals suggests strongly that many of the combinations of narrative motifs are extensions of rhetorical procedures: here is an example of chiasmus (or *commutatio* as the rhetoric manuals call it) transported to a narrative plane. Episodic repetitions may be viewed in the same light: *eandem rem dicere, sed commutate.* And, as I have mentioned, interlaced narrative may derive in part from the figure *digressio* as defined in the manuals. Of course, we need not assume that the *trouvères* were generally in direct touch with the Latin rhetorical tradition; yet some of them unquestionably were and could easily have transmitted it to others, either by precept or example.

[46] See J. Huizinga, *The Waning of the Middle Ages*, p. 202 ff.

[47] Kellermann, for example, in *Aufbaustil und Weltbild* (p. 85), seeking to understand why in courtly romance so little of the incident is determined by psychology, that is, by logical motivation, writes as follows: "Das System dieser Welt . . . trägt den Mensch nicht an der Spitze, sondern enthält ihn als Glied . . . . Seiner Aktivität sind Grenzen gesetzt. Er ist tief in dieser Welttotalität verhaftet, kann sich nicht von ihr losmachen oder sich trotzbietend gegenüberstellen. Er ist untragisch und undramatisch. Die Unfähigkeit des Mittelalters zu wahrhaft dramatischen Schöpfungen erklärt sich von hier aus . . . . Der Reichtum an seelischen Beobachtungen und Motivationen, den das Mittelalter in seiner erzählenden Literatur ausbreitet, ist ungeheuer . . . . Die Welt aber einzig vom Seelischen her erklären zu wollen, war ihr unvorstellbar."

The real difference is that in time we have developed a highly refined notion of logical sequence in narrative. We require that causation operate steadily and persistently over the entire narrative line and that there be no breaks in the logical thread, no coincidence, no *deus ex machina solutions*. We do not, however, delude ourselves into supposing that this is a reflection of what life really is. It is for this reason that Walter Scott could distinguish as follows between REAL and FICTITIOUS narrative:

The most marked distinction between a real and a fictitious narrative is that the former, in reference to the remote causes of the events it relates, is obscure, . . . whereas in the latter case it is part of the author's duty to . . . account for everything.[48]

The *Chanson de Roland*, for example, owes its basic structure to the writer's concern logically to explain one of the more inglorious episodes in Charlemagne's career. The defeat at Roncevaux was the result of Ganelon's treason, which in turn was motivated by Ganelon's hatred for Roland. Roland's refusal to sound the horn and call back the army was due to his pride, and so on. However, if we look for the remote causes we run into difficulty. The reason for the mutual hatred of Roland and Ganelon is only hinted at briefly toward the end of the poem. There had apparently been some quarrel between them about money and property (*Rollant me forfist en or e en aveir*, v. 3758). But the exact difficulty is at no time made clear. Perhaps the audience was supposed to know without being told.

As to courtly romance, we need not be surprised that adventures crop up without any rational explanation or connection, one after another, in a long series. It is the very nature of adventure to crop up unexpectedly and even inexplicable. And this sort of thing is not without parallel in modern literature.

Still, my major concern here is not with logic as a principle of structure, but as a means of amplification. More precisely, I am concerned to show how certain episodes in medieval narrative owe their creation to the writer's desire to explain, or at least to exploit the narrative potentialities of explanation.

William of Orange's nose is a case in point. From the surname *Naso* applied by Bernard de Septimanie to William's son, there is reason to believe that a remarkable nose was a hereditary trait of the historical

---

[48]   Cited in Wellek and Warren, *Theory of Literature* (New York, 1948), p. 225.

family of the Count of Toulouse.[49] There are two eleventh-century Latin documents, the so-called *Nota Emilianense* and the *faux diplôme de Saint-Yrieix*, which refer respectively to *Guillelmus Curbinasus*, and *Ghigelmo alcorbinatas*. There is no hesitation about identifying both with the hero of the epic legend, *Guillaume al corb nez*.[50] Since, however, we are here concerned with orally transmitted legend, and since apparently neither final *b* nor *t* was sounded before a consonant, the name gradually assumed an alternative form, *Guillaume al cort nez*, William Shortnose. This version of Guillaume's name evidently suggested to a *trouvère* the possibility of an accidental cause for the nose-shortening, and so he wrote an extended episode in the *Couronnement Louis*, in which Guillaume, defending the Holy City against a Saracen army, fights with a giant called Corsolt, who manages before being vanquished to cut off the tip of William's nose. Upon being asked how he feels after the battle, William proudly declares that his nose has been shortened but that his glory will thereby be extended. Thereupon he baptizes himself *Guillaume al cort nés:*

> ... mon nés ai un pou acorcié;
> Ben sai mes nons en sera alongiez.'
> Li cuens meïsmes s'est iluec baptiziez:
> 'Des ore mais, qui mei aime et tient chier,
> Trestuit m'apelent, Franceis et Berruier,
> Conte Guillelme al Cort Nés le guerrier.' [51]

(I have shortened my nose a bit, but I know well that my fame will be extended.' Thereupon the count baptized himself: 'From now on, those who love me and hold me dear, may they all call me, the French and the Berrichons, Count William Shortnose the warrior.')

The explanatory impulse is similarly evident in the troubadour *razos*. The word *razo* itself (from Latin *rationem*) sufficiently indicates that these short narratives were intended as *explications de texte*. The reason why such explanatory pieces were felt to be necessary is clear enough: the troubadours often went out of their way to write difficult and obscure poetry; the hermetic style (*trobar clus*) was felt to be particularly high style; it appealed to a small exclusive group of initiates. Still, there are always people who like to know clearly what poetry is

---

[49]   F. Lot, "Etudes sur les légendes épiques françaises: 4", *Romania*, LIII (1927), 462, n. 3.
[50]   J. Frappier, *Les Chansons de geste du cycle de Guillaume d'Orange*, I, 90.
[51]   *Le Couronnement Louis*, ed. Ernest Langlois (Paris, 1925), vv. 1157-64. No one seriously questions the fact that the name preceded the story, rather than vice-versa.

about, and one of the common ways of doing this is to relate the poem
to the writer's biography. Some of the narratives that derive from this
practice are quite remarkable indeed, much more full and lively than
they would need to be to serve their explanatory purpose. The case of
the *razo* relating to Richard de Berbezilh's song "Atressi cum l'orifans"
is a remarkable example of the genre.

To understand the story, we must first try to place ourselves in the
position of a thirteenth-century *jongleur* puzzling over the first stanza
of that song:

> Atressi com l'orifans,
> Que, can chai, no·s pot levar,
> Tro que l'autre ab lor cridar,
> De lor votz lo levon sus,
> Et ieu vuelh segre aquel us,
> Quar mos mesfagz es tan greus e pesanz
> Que si la cortz del Puey e lo bobanz
> E l'adregz pretz dels leials amadors
> No·m relevon, ia mais no serai sors,
> Que denhesson per me clamar merce
> Lai on preiars ni razos no·m val re.[52]

(Just as the elephant, who when he falls, cannot rise up, until the others,
with their outcry, raise him up with their voices, I too will follow that custom, for my misdeed is so grave and heavy that if the court of Le Puy and
the pomp and the right esteem of loyal lovers do not raise me up, then I shall
never recover, unless they deign to ask in my name where neither prayers
nor reasons have availed me anything.)

He would have understood the comparison with the elephant, for
that was part of the bestiary tradition: an elephant could not get up
once he fell down, since he was supposed to have no joints in his legs.
The bestiary story, of course, was intended to reflect the state of the
fallen sinner who without God's grace cannot rise again. But there is
no way of understanding from the poem itself just what that grave
misdeed was that caused Richard to fall into disgrace. Nor is it at all
clear how it happens that the loyal lovers at the court of Le Puy should
be so bound up with his personal fate that only their testimony of
confidence in his worth will suffice to get him out of his trouble. The
razo undertakes to explain all this and it succeeds remarkably well.
The story is interesting enough to be cited in full:

Ben avetz entendut qi fo Richhautz de Berbesiu, e com s'enamoret de la
molher de Jaufre de Tonay, q'era bella e gentils e joves; e volia li ben outra

---

[52] Text from Carl Appel, *Altprovenzalische Chrestomathie*, 6th ed. (Leipzig,
1930), p. 70.

mesura, e apellava la 'Mielz-de-dompna,' et ella li volia ben cortesamen. E Ricchautz la pregava q'ella li degues far plaser d'amor, e clamava li merce. Et la dompna li respondet q'ella volia volentier far li plazer d'aitan qe li fos honor, et dis a Ricchaut qe s'el li volges lo ben q'el dixia, q'el non deuria voler q'ella l'en dixes plus ne plus li fezes con ella li fazia ni dizis.

Et aisi estan et duran la lor amor, una dompna d'aqella encontrada, castellana d'un ric castel, si mandet per Ricchautz si s'en anet ad ella. Et la dompna li comencet a dir con ella se fasia gran meravilha de so q'el fasia, qe tan lonjamen avia amada la soa dompna, et ella no·l avia fait null plazer endreit d'amor; e dis q'en Ricchautz era tal hom de la soa persona e si valentz qe totas las bonas dompnas li deurion far volentier plazer, et qe, se Ricchautz se volia partir de la soa dompna, q'ella li faria plaser, d'aitan com el volgues comander, et disen autresi q'ella era plus bella dompna e plus alta qe non era aqella en qi el s'entendia.

Et avenc aisi qe Ricchautz, per las granz promessas q'ella li fazia, qe·ll dis q'el s'em partria. Et la dompna li comanda q'el anes penre comjat d'ella, e dis qe nul plazer li faria s'ella non saubes q'el s'en fos partiz. E Ricchautz se parti e venc se a sa dompna en q'el s'entendia; e comenset li a dir com ell l'avia amada sobre totas las autras dompnas del mon, e mais qe si meseis, e com ella no li volia aver fach nul plaser d'amor, q'el s'en volia partir de leis. Et ella en fo trista e marrida, e comenset a pregar Ricchautz qe non se degues partir d'ella, et se ella per temps passat non li avia fach plazer, q'ella li volia far ara. Et Ricchautz respondet q'el si volia partir al pus tost; et enaisi s'en partir d'ella.

Et pois, qant el ne fo partiz, el se venc a la dompna qe·l n'avia fait partir, e dis li com el avia fait lo sieu comandamen e com li clamava merce q'ella li degues complir tot so q'ella li ac promes. Et la dompna li respondet q'el non era hom qe neguna dompna li degues ni far ni dir plazer, q'el era lo plus fals hom del mon, qant el era partiz de sa dompna, q'era si bella e si gais e qe·l volia tant de be, per ditz d'aucune autra dompna, et si com era partiz d'ella, si se partria d'autra. Et Ricchautz, qant auzi so q'ella dizia, si fo lo plus trist hom del mon e·l plus dolenz qe mais fos; et parti se, e volc tornar a merce de l'autra dompna de prima; ne aqella no·l volc retener; don ell, per tristessa q'el ac, si s'en anet en un boschage e fetz se faire una maison e reclus se dinz, disen q'el non eisseria mais de laienz, tro q'el non trobes merce de sa dompna; per q'el dis in una soa chanson: 'Mielz-de-dompna, don sui fugitz dos ans.'

Et pois las bonas dompnas e·ill cavalier d'aqellas encontradas, vezen lo gran dampnage de Ricchaut, qe fu aisi perduz, si venguan la on Ricchautz era recluz, e pregero lo q'el se degues partir e issir fora; et Ricchautz disia q'el non se partria mais tro qe sa dompna li perdones. E las dompnas e·l cavalier s'en venguen a la dompna e pregero la q'ella li degues perdonar: e la dompna lor respondet q'ella no·n faria ren, tro qe .c. dompnas et .c. chavalier, li qual s'amesson tuit per amor, non venguesson tuith denant leis, mans jontas, de genolhos, clamar li merce, q'ella li degues perdonar; et pois ella li perdonaria, se il aqest faisian. La novella venc a Ricchaut, don ell fetz aquesta chanson qe ditz

Atresi com l'olifans
Qe, can chai, no·s pod levar, . . .

Et qant las dompnas et li cavalier ausiren qe podis trobar merce ab sa
dompna, se .c. dompnas e .c. chavalier qe s'amesson per amor, anassen
clamar merce a la dompna de Ricchaut q'ella li perdones, e ella li perdonaria, las dompnas e·l chavalier s'assembleron tuit et anneron e clameron
merce as ella per Ricchaut; e la dompna li perdonet.[53]

(You have of course heard about Richard de Berbesilh and how he fell in
love with the wife of Geoffrey de Tonay, who was beautiful and of
gentle birth and young, and he loved her beyond measure, and called her
Better-than-Lady, and she loved him in the discreet courtly way. And
Richard begged her to give herself to him and to take pity on him. And the
lady answered that she would willingly give him pleasure so far as honor
permitted, and she said to Richart that if he loved as he said he did, he ought
not to wish her to say or to do more than she was doing or saying. And this
was the situation between them when a lady of the region, mistress of a rich
castle, sent for Richart. And Richart went to her. And the lady began to tell
him how she marveled that he had for so long loved his lady without her
giving him pleasure, and she said that Sir Richart was so good looking and
so worthy that all good ladies should be willing to give him pleasure, and
she said that if Richart wished to leave his lady, she herself would give him
pleasure, as much as he should ask, saying as well that she was more
beautiful and of higher birth than she to whom he aspired. And so it happened that Richart, because of the great promises she made him, said that
he would leave his lady. And the lady commanded him to go and take leave
of her, and said that she would give him no pleasure until she knew that he
had left her. And Richart went to his lady and told her how he had loved
her above all other ladies in the world, and that she had not seen fit to give
him pleasure, and that therefore he wished to leave her. She was saddened
and disturbed and began to ask Richart not to leave her, and she said that if
in the past she had not given him pleasure, she would do so now. And
Richart said that he wished to leave as soon as possible. And so he left her.
And then, when he had left, he went to the lady who had caused him to
leave her and said that he had done her commandment and he asked her to
do what she had promised. And the lady answered saying he was such a man
that no lady should give him pleasure, either in word or deed, that he was
the most faithless man in the world, for he had left his lady, who was so
beautiful and gay and who loved him so much, according to some other
ladies, and if he left her, he would just as well leave another. And when
Richart heard what she said, he was the saddest man in the world and the
most doleful. And he went back to ask pity of the first lady, but she would
not have him back; and he, because of his sadness, withdrew to a wood and
had a house made and took refuge inside, saying that he would never come
out until he had found forgiveness from his lady, since he writes in one of
his songs: 'Better-than-Lady, from whom I fled two years ago.' And then the

---

53 Text from Boutière and Schutz, *Biographies*, pp. 311-314.

good ladies and the knights of the region, seeing the great suffering of Richart and how lost he was, went where he stayed and begged him to come out. And Richart said that he would not until his lady pardoned him. And the ladies and the knights went to her and asked her to pardon him. And the lady answered that she would not unless 100 ladies and 100 knights, all true lovers, should come before her, hands joined, and on bended knee, to ask her to forgive him, and that then she would forgive him if they did that. The news came to Richart who then wrote the song that says: 'Just as the elephant, etc. . . .' And when the ladies and the knights heard that he might be pardoned by his lady if 100 knights and 100 ladies who were true lovers went to ask her forgiveness, the ladies and knights assembled and went to her and asked for forgiveness for Richart; and the lady pardoned him.)

The structure of this charming story is clearly that of well-made narrative. There is a beginning, middle and end, and for the most part the motivation is logical. Character and incident interact to propel the story forward to its climax and resolution. But when we inquire into the remote causes for the action, it does not hold up too well. Why, we wonder, did the second lady start all this trouble? How did she know that Richart had not enjoyed his lady's physical person? Even if he had, of course, the courtly code would oblige him strenuously to conceal the fact. And how does it happen that in an affair presumably secret and hardly likely to be appreciated by the husband, Jaufré de Tonay, no less than two hundred others should be obliged to intervene to save the affair? These questions, matters of secondary reflection, we must keep down lest they interfere with our appreciation of the subtle artistry of the story, whose primary explanatory impulse imposes a logical structure on the narrative.

If we imagine now a story-teller looking over a series of poems attributed to a particular poet and envisioning the possibility of writing a romance such that every poem, instead of having a story to itself, will fit into one long story, we can begin to see the value of this technique as a source of narrative inspiration. There are *razos* in which two and even three poems figure. Why not even more? In any case, this is partly what appears to have happened in the case of the *Roman du Castelain de Couci*,[54] a late thirteenth-century romance some 8,000 verses in length.

The writer, who is often referred to for convenience as Jakemès or Jakemon, a name resulting from an acrostic at the end of the story, saved himself a good bit of trouble by borrowing the general frame-

---

[54] *Le Roman du Castelain de Couci et de la Dame de Fayel*, eds. J. E. Matzke and Maurice Delbouille, *SATF* (Paris, 1936). Line references will be to this edition.

work of his narrative, its beginning, middle, and end, from the *vida* of Guillem de Cabestanh. The Provençal biographer told the story this way:

Guillems de Cabestanh si fo us cavalliers de l'encontrada de Rossillon, que confina ab Cataloigna et ab Narbones. Mout fo avinens hom de la persona, e mout presatz d'armas e de cortesia e de servir.

Et avia en la soa encontrada una dompna que avia nom ma dona Soremonda, moiller d'En Raimon de Castel Rossillon, que era mout gentils e rics e mals e fers et orgoillos. En Guillems de Cabestaing si amava la dompna per amor e chantava de lieis e.n fazia sas chansos. E la dompna, qu'era joves e gentils e bella, si·l volia ben mais que a ren del mon. E fon dich so a·N Raimon de Castel Rossillon; et el, cum hom iratz e gelos, enqeric lo faich e saup que vers era, e fetz gardar la moiller

E quan venc un dia, Raimons de Castel Rossillon trobet paissan Guillem de Cabestaing ses gran compaignia et aucis lo; e fetz li traire lo cor del cors e fetz li taillar la testa; e·l cor fetz portar a son alberc e la testa atressi; e fetz lo cor raustir e far a pebrada, e fetz lo dar a manjar a la moiller. E qan la dompna l'ac manjat, Raimons de Castel Rossillon li dis: 'Sabetz vos so que vos avetz manjat?' Et ella dis: 'Non, si non que mout es estada bona vianda e saborida.' Et el li dis qu'el era lo cors d'En Guillem de Cabestaing so que ella avia manjat; et, a so qu'ell·l crezes mieils, si fetz aportar la testa denan lieis. E quan la dompna vic so et auzic, ella perdet lo vezer e l'auzir. E qand ella revenc, si dis: 'Seigner, ben m'avetz dat si bon manjar que ja mais non manjarai d'autre.' E quand el auzic so, el cors ab s'espaza e volc li dar sus en la testa; et ella cors ad un balcon e laisset se cazer jos, et enaissi moric.[55]

(Guillem de Cabestaing was a knight of the country of Rossillon, which borders on Catalonia and Narbonne. He was very handsome of his person and highly regarded in arms, service, and courtliness. An there was in his part of the country a lady called Madame Soremonda, wife of Sir Raimon of Rossillon castle, who was very nobly born and rich and formidable and brave and fierce and proud. And Guillem loved the lady truly and sang of her and wrote his songs about her. And the lady, who was young and nobly born and beautiful and pleasing, loved him more than anything in the world. And it was made known to Sir Raimon of Rossillon Castle; and he, like an irate and jealous man, inquired into the matter, and he learned that it was true, and he had his wife guarded. And a day came when Sir Raimon found Guillem passing by without great company and he killed him; and he had his heart taken from his body and had his head cut off; and he had the heart taken to his dwelling, and the head as well. And he had the heart roasted and made into a pepper stew and he fed it to his wife. And when she had eaten it, Sir Raimon said to her: 'Do you know what you have eaten?' And she said: No, except that it was good and tasty meat.' And he told her that it was the heart of Sir Guillem de Cabestaing that she had eaten; and in order that she might believe it better, he had the head brought before her. And when the lady saw and heard this, she lost her sight and

[55] Text from Boutière and Schutz, pp. 156-158.

hearing. And when she came to she said: 'My Lord, you have given me such good food to eat that I shall never eat anything else.' And when he heard her say this, he ran at her with his sword to strike her on the head: and she ran to a balcony and threw herself down, and thus she died.)

With this story as his base, and the poems of the Châtelain de Couci (a *trouvère* of the late twelfth century) as matter for specific amplification, Jakemon proceeded to construct an extended romance, one of the best made stories of the Middle Ages. It is obviously not the product of a professional *trouvère*; the versification is rather banal and prosy, but the structure is clear and logical. The combination need not surprise us, since the professional writers seem to have delighted in making their stories as long and as complex as the audience could bear, especially at this period.

Jakemon had one serious problem to overcome in fitting the Châtelain's poems into the structure of the *vida* of the southern poet: among the best poems of the *trouvère* there figured several crusade songs in which the poet lamented his separation from his beloved. Jakemon could, of course, have introduced a digression in which the hero went off on a crusade and wrote songs about the lady he left behind him, but he solved the problem more ingeniously by combining the crusade matter and the denouement. As Jakemon writes it, the hero is tricked by the husband into going on a crusade and there he meets death from a poisoned arrow. Before dying, however, he arranges to have his heart cut out and sent back to his lady. The husband intercepts the package, which also contains an informative letter, then has the heart roasted and fed to his wife, who, upon hearing what she has eaten, goes on a hunger strike and dies of starvation. The solution has obvious merits: the hero dies a more glorious death and a needless atrocity is removed from the story.

The question of the culinary merits of an organ that had gone through the mails in this manner probably did not trouble the medieval audience any more than it did the husband.

A good part of the story, as Jakemon writes it, is given over to the beginning, the drama of courtship, to which the *vida* gives no space at all. The lady quite properly says no for a long time, but Renaut, the châtelain, ultimately attains his goal.[56] After a tournament, elaborately described, in which the châtelain is wounded, he is taken to his lady's

[56] The historical Châtelain de Couci, the poet, was named Gui, not Renaut. The romancer would not have known this, since the manuscripts designate him only as the Châtelain de Couci.

castle. The standard development takes place: the lady's heart fills with pity, her resistance is broken, and she agrees to take him as her lover. They carefully plan their liaison: Renaut is to hire a boy, who is in turn to maintain contact with the lady's chambermaid, a trustworthy cousin. But the cousin is a cautious girl, and she persuades her mistress to test Renaut's love by making him stand outside the gate all night long in the rain. When on the following day, Renaut discovers that the husband had been absent all night from the castle, he concludes that the lady is making a fool of him. Overwhelmed with chagrin, he composes the following song:

> Quand li estés et la douce saisons
> Fait foelle et les prés reverdir
> Et li dous can menus des oisellons
> Fait li pluisours de joie souvenir,
> Las, cescuns cante, et je pleure et souspir;
> Et si n'est pas droiture ne raisons,
> Car c'est adïés tout m'ententïons,
> Dame, de vous honnourer et siervir.
>
> Qui aroit tout le sens k'ot Salemons,
> Si le feroit Amours pour fol tenir;
> Car trop est male et crueus sa prisons,
> Si le me fait assaiyer et sentir,
> Si ne me vuelt a son eus retenir
> Ni enseignier quelle est ma garisons,
> Car j'ai amé longhement em pardons,
> Et amerai tous jours sans repentir.
>
> Mierveilles ai dont vient ceste occoisons
> Qu'elle me fait a teil doulour languir:
> Chou est pour çou qu'elle croit les felons,
> Les maldisans, qu'elle devroit haïr,
> Qui moult sont pené de moi nuisir;
> Mais ne lor vaut lor mortels traïsons,
> Car en la fin iert grans li guerredons,
> Quant savera k'ainc ne li voch mentir.[57]

(When the summer and the sweet season makes leaves and meadows green and the sweet little songs of the little birds make many think of joy, alas! everyone sings and I cry and sigh, and yet it is not just or reasonable, for henceforth, Lady, I mean to honor and to serve you.

If one had all the wisdom of Solomon, yet Love would make him seem a fool, for his prison is very harsh and cruel, and he makes me feel and experience it and does not wish to keep me in his service, nor tell me how I shall be healed, for I have long loved in vain, and I shall always love without regret.

[57] *Le Roman du Castelain de Couci*, vv. 2591 ff.

I marvel whence might come the cause why she makes me languish in such pain; it is because she believes the felons, the scandal-mongers, whom she should hate, who have taken great pains to hurt me; but their deadly treason will avail them nothing, for in the end the reward will be great, when she knows that I never lied to her.)

It seems clear that the episode of the testing of the lover, essentially a delaying tactic, meant more to the writer as narrative background for the poem than as an event in the love story, which it in no way advances. The third stanza, platitudinous as it is, appears to have furnished the germ of the idea: the lover wonders why the lady makes him languish, and concludes that he has been slandered. Nothing is more common in the courtly lyric tradition, but here the romancer attaches it to a particular situation in which Renaut, after being subjected to a specific ordeal, finds it necessary to explain a specific contradiction between the lady's apparent willingness on the one hand, and on the other her decision to let him stand all night in the rain.

There follow a number of episodes in which Renaut and his lady have their troubles with the husband, but manage rather ingeniously to outwit him. But the husband finally hits upon a plan for ridding himself of Renaut. He announces to his wife his intention of going on a crusade and taking her with him. She falls into the trap and tells Renaut, who makes arrangements to go also. The prospect pleases him greatly: he sings a happy song:

> Au nouviel tans que mais et violette,
> Et lossignos me semont de canter,
> Et li dous coers me siert d'une amourette,
> Si douc present ne doit més refuser;
> Or me laist Deus a tel honnour monter
> Que celle k'aim entre mes bras nuette
> Tiegne une fois ains que voise outre mer.[58]

(In the new season when May and violet and nightingale summon me to sing, and the gentle heart presents me with a love, so sweet a gift must never be refused; now may God permit me to climb so high in honor as to hold naked in my arms the one I love before I cross the sea.)

The last three lines of the stanza are of course what determined the position of the song in the narrative, and, reciprocally, the course of the narrative as an introduction to the song. Its tone, in keeping with the usual pattern of the courtly lyric, is one of joy at the coming of spring. It would not have been entirely appropriate if at this time the

---

[58] *Ibid.*, vv. 7005-11.

châtelain had known that the husband's stated intention of joining the crusaders was only a trick to get rid of his rival. Thus when Renaut discovers that the husband, alleging ill health, has backed out of his crusade commitment, he is plunged into sorrow and sings another song, one of his most famous:

> A vous, amant, ains qu'a nul autre gent
> Est bien raisons que ma doulour complaigne,
> Car il estuet partir outreëment
> Et desevrer de ma douce compaigne;
> Mais quant la pierch, n'ain riens qui me remaigne;
> Et sace bien Amors seürement,
> S'ainc nus moru pour avoir coer dolent,
> Ja n'iert par moi mes meüs vers ne lais.
>
> Biaus sire Diex, qu'est-ce dont? Et comment
> Couvenra il qu'en la fin congé prenge?
> Oïl, par Dieu, ne puet estre autrement;
> Aler m'estuet sans li en terre estraigne;
> Si ne cuit nus que grans biens me souspraigne,
> Car je n'ai mais confort n'aliegement,
> Ne de nule autre avoir joie n'ateng,
> Si de li non—ne sai se c'iert jamais.[59]

(To you lovers, rather than to any others, it is right that I should painfully tell my suffering, for I must part from my lady and be completely separated from her, and when I lose her, nothing remains for me to love, and may Love know assuredly that if any man ever died of a grieving heart, never more will songs or lays be made by me. Beautiful Lord God, what then? How shall I take leave of her? Yes, by Heaven, it cannot be otherwise; I must go without her into foreign land; and may no man believe that good will come of it, for I shall have no more comfort or relief, nor do I expect joy from another, if not from her – I know not whether that will ever be.)

Jakemon used several different means of amplification to fill out his plot outline, the most noteworthy being the rhetorical amplifications in the form of considerable circumstantial detail and the general exploitation of the clichés of courtly love. But more to our immediate purpose, he amplified also by extending suggestions in the châtelain's poems into developed narrative sequences, incorporating the crusade songs into a new form of denouement. Throughout, however, we should note that Jakemon is respectful of the idea of verisimilitude. Whatever specific form his amplifications take, they rarely violate the principle that events should arise in accordance with necessity or probability. Evidently, Jakemon had a logical mind.

[59] *Ibid.*, vv. 7344-60.

Logic, however, has many forms. In fantasy, the sense of symmetry often dictates the logic of a sequence. Thus even in those stories that turn most completely away from everyday realities, logic in the form of symmetry may serve as an instrument of narrative invention.

For example, in the Arthurian vulgate there is a slight discrepancy between the initial and final episodes involving Arthur's sword Excalibur. Arthur first acquired the sword by drawing it from a magic anvil. He disposed of it, after the great battle on Salisbury plain, by having it thrown into a lake where it was taken by a hand reaching out of the water, which brandished it thrice, then vanished with it into the water. The two events are thousands of pages apart, but the discrepancy did not go unnoticed. The writer of a post-vulgate Grail cycle, known to us in a fragment called the *Huth Merlin* or the *Suite du Merlin*,[60] appears to have been concerned to explain why Arthur should get rid of his sword in so curious a way. He does this by means of an extended narrative sequence placed in the early part of Arthur's reign. News comes to Arthur's court that an unknown knight who lives in a nearby forest forces all passers-by to joust with him. Gifflet unsuccessfully tries to defeat him and Arthur is forced to fight him. After a long struggle, Arthur loses his horse and breaks his sword against that of his adversary. But Merlin's timely appearance saves him. Now a sword worthy of the young king has to be found. Merlin leads Arthur to a lake in the middle of which a hand holds up a sword:

Et voient une espée apparoir par desus l'iaue en un main et un brach qui apparoit tresque au keute, et estoit vestu li bras d'un samit blanc.[61]

(And they saw a sword appear above the water in a hand and an arm that appeared as far as the elbow, and the arm was draped in white samite.)

The scene is clearly calculated to prepare the reader for the concluding scene on Salisbury plain. Symmetry and consistency of design thus give a logical consistency to the narrative, for when the time comes for the magic circle to close, it seems only right that the magic sword should return to its point of origin.[62]

An explanatory impulse directed this narrative line. It is not very different in kind from the impulse we noted in the troubadour *razos* and in the story of Guillaume's nose. One rather peculiar form taken

---

[60]   *Merlin: Roman en prose du XIIIe siècle*, eds. G. Paris and J. Ulrich, 2 vols. (Paris, 1886).
[61]   *Ibid.*, I, 197.
[62]   See Vinaver's introduction to the *Roman de Balin*, ed. D. M. Legge (Manchester, 1942), pp. xi-xxii.

by this tendency to construct narrative through rationalization occurs in the amplification of stories through genealogy. Given the firm belief of feudal knighthood in what we now call hereditary or genetic determination, it seems hardly surprising that the story of one's parents should function as a rational explanation of one's own life and character. This is at least part of the reason why the cycle of Guillaume d'Orange grew along genealogical lines and proceeded in chronological reverse. If today at the end of a story we sometimes wonder what happened next, the contrary tendency seems to have prevailed in medieval times: the contemplation of the deeds of a hero inevitably raised the question of the nature of his ancestors. An extraordinary man must have had extraordinary antecedents.

We find in the story of *Tristan* an example of this sort of amplification. The original story, in all likelihood, did not contain the story of Tristan's mother and father.[63] Two things seem to have impelled some unknown *trouvère* to amplify the story genealogically: first, Tristan's name, originally the Pictish name Dryst, not known in French, but, by its similarity to the adjective *triste*, rich in poetic implications; second, the simple desire to enrich the hero's legend by recounting the exploits of the father, a procedure taken over from the epic tradition. Thus a story grew up about Rivalen, King of Leonois, who went to Mark's court and married the king's sister Blanchefleur. When Blanchefleur was delivered of a son and died in the pain of childbirth, the boy received the name Tristan, for he was born in sadness, and so too he lived and died.

We cannot say how extensively the matter was treated in Thomas's version, but if Gottfried von Strassburg's treatment is any indication, the story of the parents would not have exceeded 1500 verses, or something less than a tenth of the whole.[64] This question of proportion would be of relatively little interest if it were not for the fact that Chrétien de Troyes' *Cligés* appears to be a response to Thomas's *Tristan*. Perhaps somewhat piqued by the success of a rival poet, Chrétien presumably decided to write an *Anti-Tristan*, a story in which he took up the narrative data of the Tristan story and oriented them systematically toward a new meaning.[65] This transformation has been

---

[63] F. Ranke, *Tristan und Isolde*, pp. 3-6.
[64] Gottfried gives 1790 vv. to the story of the parents out of a total of 19548. His version is unfinished. Indications are that he amplified Thomas's version somewhat. Bédier estimates the length of Thomas's story as between 17000 and 20000 vv.
[65] *Cf.* J. Frappier, *Chrétien de Troyes*, pp. 107-108.

thoroughly examined on the conceptual level. Chrétien's preference for a form of love in which human choice and will prevail seems clear, and it is clear also that the idea of a fatal passion was repugnant to him. However, the matter has not yet been examined on a structural plane. My feeling is that in addition to its being a rebuttal to the latent conceptual content of Thomas's *Tristan*, *Cligés* was also intended to be viewed as an example of a more elegant poetic structure. And it is precisely with respect to the genealogical extension to the parents that the structural question seems most interesting.

In the *Tristan*, the story of Rivalen and Blanchefleur functions simply as a prologue of a roughly explanatory nature, without forming part of any structural pattern – so far as we are able to conjecture. Chrétien, however, chose to organize his version into a genealogical diptych, juxtaposing the extended romance of the parents to the romance of the son and his uncle's bride. The better to keep his two love stories separate, Chrétien arranges to have the parents die abruptly as soon as their love bears fruit in the person of their son Cligés, who is to be the hero of the second part of the story. The father falls ill and dies in the space of four verses (2556-2560); the mother dies of grief shortly afterward (2581-2584). There is some other transitional plot machinery in the middle relating to Cligés' uncle Alis, but Chrétien narrates it all with a minimum of amplification.

The story as a whole tends to have the general shape of a dumbbell: the first part – 2,383 verses – tells the story of the parents; the next two hundred verses are transitional; the story of Cligés and Fénice is the subject of the last 4,000 verses.

The first part is a simple story: Alexander, a young Greek prince, comes to Arthur's court, falls in love with the beautiful Soredamors, Gawain's sister, succeeds in winning her love, and they marry. The matter is considerably amplified by long psychological monologues. Alexander is timid in the presence of his beloved and does not confess his love to her, but he examines his own thoughts extensively. She, through modesty and decency, conceals her love for him, but she too spends a great deal of time analyzing her emotions. Guenevere finally intervenes, brings them openly to admit that they love one another, and sees that they get married. Fourteen months later their son is born.

In the transitional section, Alexander's father dies. As eldest son, Alexander should succeed him on the throne, but his brother Alis, upon hearing a rumor of his brother's death, usurps the throne. Alexander returns to Greece with his wife and son, and consents to leave his brother on the throne on condition that he promise not to marry, so that the crown will fall to Cligés. Alis accepts the condition; then Alexander dies, closely followed by his wife. The story of their orphaned son begins.

On the advice of bad counselors, Alis decides to break his promise and to marry Fénice, the daughter of the German Emperor. The marriage takes place at Cologne. But as soon as Cligés and Fénice see one another, they fall in love. Her marriage becomes a hateful burden. Her governess Thessala solves the main problem by providing a magic potion whose power is such that Alis will never possess her physically, except in his dreams, which he will take for reality. Alis drinks this potion at the marriage feast. On the way back from Cologne to Greece, the wedding party is attacked by an army, and Cligés performs great feats of prowess. He has not declared his love for Fénice, nor does he know of hers, and so in the grip of melancholy he decides to go to Arthur's court and try his hand at the chivalric life. He does very well at it, wins victory after victory, and accomplishes noble feats in England, Normandy, and France. But Fénice remains in his mind and her memory draws him ineluctably back to Greece, where Cligés finally confesses his love and begs Fénice to flee with him. But the maiden will do nothing of the sort. She would lose her reputation. Such behavior would be scandalous. The solution of Tristan and Iseut is not for her. She has a better idea: with Thessala's help she will counterfeit death. Cligés can then take her from her tomb and they will be able to live together happily – without scandal. And so it happens. The lovers live for fifteen months in an underground abode. One spring day, however, Fénice hears a nightingale and feels she must go out into the light. They exit through a secret door into a splendid walled garden, in the midst of which stands a magnificent tree whose branches shelter the lovers. But one day, unhappily, they are discovered by a hunter whose hawk alights on the tree. The hunter tells the emperor, and Cligés and Fénice are forced to flee to England. The emperor, however, conveniently dies of rage, and the pair return at last to Constantinople in glory; as Cligés is now emperor, he and Fénice are able to marry and live happily ever after.

By putting the stories of Soredamors and Fénice side by side, Chrétien evidently wishes to convey his ideas about love and marriage. The love of Alexander and Soredamors is ideally conducted and ended, and in the course of the story, Guenevere makes a little speech on the compatibility of love and marriage (vv. 2264-69). Fénice, however, has the misfortune of not marrying for love, and this enormously complicates her life. Had it not been for her faithful and resourceful governess, she might have been reduced to the scandalous behavior of Iseut, who allowed her body to be shared by her husband and her lover.

Chrétien obviously went to some pains to provide a clear and logical transition from one part of the story to the other. He quite as clearly invites the reader to seek out correspondences in detail. The bonds that unite the two parts are strong enough, and the author's design, to construct a narrative diptych, is perfectly clear. A writer, after all, would scarcely be led simply by a concern for logical development to write a story in this form. The story of Alexander and Soredamors is over when they marry. The story of Cligés and Fénice is entirely independent of it. The author's use of a logical nexus, we might say, served the purpose of justifying his real esthetic concern, the desire to write a bipartite story, one deliberately organized into two contrasting tableaux.

Thus, as I see it, the usual tendency to lengthen a story by providing preliminary matter of an explanatory nature has given way here to a structural purpose of considerable subtlety. Just as the device of repetition became a structural principle in *Erec*, here the principle of genealogical amplification is turned to account in what amounts to a well made narrative with a didactic undercurrent.

At this point, we begin to touch upon a problem of an entirely different sort, the question of unity. In the case of *Cligés*, we see for the first time a story which is deliberately organized into two parts in order to serve a higher principle which includes them both, and for which both parts are necessary. And that brings us to a new set of considerations.

III

THE QUESTION OF UNITY

A successful work of art, it is commonly assumed, must have some sort of unity. In narrative art, this usually means unity of action in terms of logical correlation and interdependence. More refined speculations as to metaphysical, tonal, or thematic unity in writers like Cervantes, Ariosto, and Chrétien are sometimes used to substitute for a less easily demonstrable type of unity.[1]

For example, we may say that the *Roman de Renart* derives unity from the nearly constant presence of a single figure, Renart himself, and to a lesser degree from the thematic value of the struggle between the fox and the wolf. The various episodes may be arbitrarily arranged and logically independent of each other; yet the impact of the whole has a certain oneness about it. Renart's world is unified by his presence and influence in it. Biographical romances may similarly be said to derive their unity from the presence of a central figure, such as Tristan or Lancelot, even though their various actions seem to have little to do with one another or with the main line of the story. In the many tales involving a quest there is an additional unity provided by our continual awareness of a terminal objective. The same may be said of the *chansons de geste*, where there is frequently a single battle to be won, and a single great military hero or family of heroes.

But we seldom stop to consider whether there might not be some advantage in relinquishing the idea of unity altogether and admitting at least hypothetically the validity of artistic duality, trinity, or some other form of multiplicity. As a principle of structure, the idea is repugnant to us, but I feel that it may have had some meaning for medieval writers. Their theoreticians laid no special stress on unity or simplicity, and seem rather to have been convinced that the secret of elegance lay

---

[1]   See for example Mario Casella, *Cervantes: Il Chisciotte* (Florence, 1938), I, 89.

not in the unification of the matter, but rather in the multiplication of its elements.[2]

Simple honesty compels us to grant that when a writer like Chrétien de Troyes, a man who so obviously knew what he was doing, wrote a story like *Cligés*, which so clearly divides into two parts, some artistic impulse toward narrative duality must have been a determining factor. It will not do simply to gloss over the matter by supposing that one or another part is later parasitic accretion, not originally intended as part of the story. On the other hand, the two parts of *Cligés* may be related conceptually. Even though they are quite independent as narratives, they are encapsulated by the idea which caused Chrétien to relate them within a single tale.

As a matter of fact, many of the important narratives of the twelfth century show this bipartite form. It appears to have been a standard structural device whose esthetic propriety was in some sense taken for granted. Before we begin to theorize about the unity of such works, we should first admit their duality. The problem of their unity can then better be considered in relation to the whole class of such stories on a more solid comparative ground. The obvious *étude à faire* is carefully to examine the way in which such stories are characteristically put together: the form of bipartition, the nature of the first part, the transition, and the second part.

Many critics have noted bipartition as a frequent medieval form.[3] Others have been inclined to see tripartite and quadripartite schemes, which should serve to remind us that analysis can be more or less refined, and that stories can be divided into parts in many ways to serve many different ends. Voretzsch, for example, argues that Chrétien's romances divide into five parts; Le Gentil sees a quadripartite division in the *Chanson de Roland*; Stefan Hofer, Jean Frappier, and Joseph Reason see, in different ways, a basically tripartite division in Chrétien's romances, particularly in *Erec* and *Yvain*. On the basis of the presumed conditions of oral presentation at court, Frances Titchener argues a division of Chrétien's works into twenty or so units averaging three hundred verses in length, each reasonably independent and suitable for a evening's entertainment. On the same principle, Wechssler

---

[2] See E. Vinaver, "A la recherche d'une poétique médiévale", *Cahiers de Civilisation Médiévale*, II (1959), 1-16.
[3] W. Kellermann, *Aufbaustill und Weltbild*, pp. 12-15; R. R. Bezzola, *Le Sens de l'aventure et de l'amour*, pp. 83-84; Werner Ziltener, *Chrétien und die Aeneis*, pp. 124-133; W. T. H. Jackson, *The Literature of the Middle Ages* (New York, 1960), pp. 56-57, 108-109.

proposes a tripartite division into units of about 2000 verses, and Witte two divisions of 3500 verses.[4]

All these schemes can be cogently argued, and it is not my purpose to contest their validity. It does seem, however, that there would be some advantage in reducing this diversity in such a way as to permit a broader basis for comparison. If I prefer in general to see a bipartite form in these narratives, it is because I feel that the primary structural peculiarity in this class of stories is that the writer normally carries his sequence of events to a perfectly satisfactory conclusion, then begins again and tells at considerable length matter neither implied nor necessitated within the framework of the first half of the story. The structure that results assumes, as I have suggested earlier, something of the shape of a dumbbell, two juxtaposed and reasonably developed narratives with a brief nexus between them. The nexus itself, in these cases, appears to serve no purpose beyond that of producing the bipartite form. Just what this means will become clearer as we look at particular examples.[5]

The *Chanson de Roland* is a typical case. Most modern readers would, I imagine, like to see the story end shortly after Roland's sublime death scene. Rychner undoubtedly speaks for many when he declares that the Baligant episode is an unwelcome intrusion in an otherwise great poem:

La *Chanson de Roland* me semble avoir été d'abord ... la chanson d'une

---

[4] Voretzsch, *Introduction to the Study of Old French Literature* (New York, 1931), p. 291; Le Gentil, *La Chanson de Roland*, p. 90; Hofer, "La Structure du Conte del Graal examinée à la lumière de l'œuvre de Chrétien de Troyes", *Les Romans du Graal*, p. 16; Frappier, *Chrétien de Troyes*, pp. 92, 227; Reason, *An Inquiry into the Structural Style and Originality of Chrétien's Yvain* (Washington, 1958), pp. 1-27; Titchener, "The Romances of Chrétien de Troyes", *Romanic Review*, XVI (1925), 165-173; Wechssler, *Die Saga vom heiligen Graal in ihrer Entwicklung bis auf Richard Wagners Parsifal* (Halle, 1898), pp. 159-161; Witte, "Hartmann von Aue und Chrestien von Troyes", *Beiträge zur Geschichte der deutschen Sprache und Literatur*, LIII (1929), 89.

[5] As to the possible influence of oral delivery on the structure of medieval narrative, assumptions vary considerably as to just how long the story-teller had for his performance. Titchener assumes twenty minutes, Witte five or six hours. It seems reasonable to assume that circumstances would have varied from time to time and from place to place. If so, the writer could hardly have been expected to predict what they might be. In any event, we simply do not know whether there was any uniformity such that writers could have taken the matter into consideration. Most such speculations are circular: the usual thing is to divide the story first into logically coherent units, then to estimate their average length, and then to assume that to have been the length of the performance. *Cf.* Ruth Crosby, "Oral Delivery in the Middle Ages", *Speculum*, XI (1936), 88-110; Kellermann, *Aufbaustil und Weltbild*, p. 5, n. 4; Rychner, *La Chanson de Roland*, pp. 9-25 and *passim*.

défaite douloureuse, se transformant finalement en victoire: c'est la souf-
france qui y domine et y rend le son le plus authenthique. Sans l'épisode de
Baligant, la composition du *Roland* est typiquement dramatique, avec sa
montée, son point culminant, et sa descente; aucune des parties ne se con-
çoit sans les autres: c'est une composition nécessaire.[6]

Undoubtedly, by our standards the *Roland* would be a more satisfactory piece of work without the Baligant episode. It is, for that
matter, entirely possible that in an earlier version, whether or not we
choose to designate that version as the 'original', it did not figure. But
for better or for worse, in the best version that we have, it is there, and
it is clearly intended to be there. We are therefore forced to admit the
possibility that a competent narrative artist saw the extension as desir-
able or even as formally necessary.

We may try to save the unity of the poem by arguing that the idea of
the holy war pulls the two halves together, that this idea is symbolized
in the person of Charlemagne, who as head of all Christendom must
find his opponent in Baligant, symbolic representative of paganism.[7]

Such considerations are no doubt entirely valid, but the fact remains
that they serve mainly to rationalize an unusual structure. The events
of the story lead inevitably to the disaster at Roncevaux: Roland dies
in triumph; Charlemagne returns to avenge his death. Then the writer
calls in Baligant, and the struggle resumes.

No doubt historical influences were working to determine the content
of this part of the story. At a time shortly before the First Crusade it
may have seemed necessary to Christian sensibility to complete the
poem with a symbolic defeat of Islam. But the way in which this is
done, producing a diptych with Marsile and Roland on the left, Charlemagne and Baligant on the right, the whole bound together by Ganelon's treason and punishment, seems clearly to reflect a concern for
elegance in form, a form based on a sharp medial division where the
story is once again set in motion.

An early, though less typical, example of bipartition may be noted
in the eleventh-century *Vie de Saint Alexis*. As we have already mentioned above, it was Curtius who first pointed out that the story divides
into two symmetrical halves, with Alexis' death occupying the center.
The death actually occurs somewhat beyond the center, in the 67th of
125 stanzas. Roland too dies somewhat beyond the center, in the 176th
of 292 *laisses*.

---

[6] *La Chanson de geste*, p. 40.
[7] *Cf.* Le Gentil, *La Chanson de Roland*, p. 62; A. Pauphilet, *Le Legs du Moyen
Age*, p. 94; E. Faral, *La Chanson de Roland: Etude et analyse*, pp. 241-246.

Anna Granville Hatcher, apparently disturbed by the mathematical discrepancy here, proceeded to propose a tidier structural analysis, which takes the following form:[8]

Stanza		No. of Stanzas	
1-2	Exordium	2	
3-10	Prelude to life	8	
11-15	Decision to leave home	5	
16-38	Flight and life abroad	23	
39-43	Decision to return	5	56
44-66	Life at father's home	23	
67	Death	1	
124-125	Conclusio	2	
68-77	Honored by Pope and Emperors	10	
78-100	Lamented by family	23	56
101-123	Honored as saint by world, at home in Paradise	23	

We may protest that, particularly in the subdivisions, Miss Hatcher is able to manage this admirably neat scheme only by a careful selection and grouping of certain sequences (flight AND life abroad; honored as saint in world, AND at home in Paradise), which under further analysis might have obscured the pervasive symmetry she sees in the poem. Still, it seems clear that the story does in fact separate into three parts in the ratio 8:56:56, or 1:7:7. I shall continue to refer to the eleventh-century *Alexis*, however, as a bipartite work, since I consider the primary peculiarity of the story to be the new narrative impulse that gives so lengthy a development to the final section of the story.[9]

It is of no small concern to see how the poet treated his source material in order to arrive at such an end product. So far, no one has examined the Latin and vernacular version to see what the structural relation is. The results are quite striking, I think, and throw considerable light on the question in general.

The Latin text furnished all but a very small part of the story material, but the proportions are quite different. Twenty-nine lines of

[8] A. G. Hatcher, "The Old-French Poem Saint Alexis: A Mathematical Demonstration", *Traditio*, VIII (1952), 156. Although even here I feel that certain reservations are in order, this is the most satisfactory application I have seen of the idea of numerical composition in a narrative work.
[9] It is worth noting that the rehandlers of the *Alexis* in the twelfth and later centuries must have been completely blind to the eleventh-century poet's concern with structure and proportion, a fact that should put us on guard against any assertions to the effect that medieval structural patterns were then known and recognized generally.

Latin prose describe Alexis' early life (the *prelude* in Miss Hatcher's analysis), one hundred fourteen his life as a saint, and seventy-two the events following his death.[10]

Thus what the eleventh-century writer did was to compress the prelude and extend the post-mortem sequence, so that what originally stood in a 1:3.8:2.4 ratio ultimately emerged as 1:7:7. How did he manage this? What was the basis of redistribution, especially of the compression? Medieval writers consistently tend to amplify; compression is rare.[11] It is therefore instructive to compare the two versions in this regard. The matter relating to Alexis' education shows us, I believe, what the writer was up to. The Latin text stresses the religious side of Alexis' education:

Puer autem ut ad aetatem disciplinae congruam pervenit, tradiderunt eum ecclesiasticorum, sacramentorum ac liberalium disciplinarium magistris, et Deo largiente edoctus est, ut in omnibus philosophiae et in maxime spiritua-libus floreret studiis.[12]

The vernacular version deviates significantly:

> Puis li bons pedre ad escole le mist.
> Tant aprist letres que bien en fut garniz.
> Puis vait li enfes l'emperedour servir.
> (vv. 33-35)

(Then the good father sent him to school. He studied his letters until he was quite proficient. Then the young man goes to serve the emperor.)

Much has been eliminated and an important detail has been added: the religious aspect of his education has been completely excised, and although nothing in the Latin text can be construed to indicate that Alexis was ever associated with the Emperor, the writer chose to invent that detail, an obvious corollary to the elimination of the religious matter.

The same tendency may be seen in the treatment of Alexis' father. The Latin text tells us that he gave generously to the poor, and three times a day set out tables of food for widows, orphans, pilgrims, and travelers; he himself dined with men of religion:

Hic namque erat justus et misericors, eleemosynas multas pauperibus ero-gans. Tres per singulos dies mensae parabantur in domo eius orphanis,

[10]   The line count is besed on the Latin text as it appears in J. M. Meunier's edition, *La Vie de Saint Alexis* (Paris, 1933), pp. 11-17.
[11]   The case of Chaucer's abbreviation of the beginning of Boccaccio's *Teseide* in the *Knight's Tale* is a well known example.
[12]   *Alexis*, ed. Meunier, p. 12.

viduis, peregrinis et iter agentibus. Ipse vero ad horam nonam comedebat cum viris religiosis.[13]

The vernacular text reads simply:

> Si fut uns sire de Rome la citet;
> Riches om fut, de grant nobilitet;
> Por çol vos di, d'un son fil veuil parler.
> Eufemiiens (si out a nom li pedre)
> Coms fut de Rome, dels mielz qui donc i eret;
> Sor toz ses pers, l'amat li emperedre.
>
> (vv. 13-18)

(He was a lord of the city of Rome; a rich man he was, of great nobility; I tell you this, since I wish to speak of his son. Euphemianus (so the father was named) was a count of Rome, one of the best that ever was there; above all his peers the emperor loved him.)

That completes the portrait of the father. Again there is the same tendency to secularize, again by the excision of all references to the father's piety. Twin purposes: compression and secularization. To what end? The general purpose of the prelude appears to be to locate Alexis at a high secular level. His family is rich and powerful; he himself is in the service of the emperor; and a highly advantageous marriage has been arranged for him. He marries the girl without any internal misgivings (*Danz Alexis l'esposat belement*, v. 48), and in short, at this point, the world is his. Very abruptly, however, we now discover that he does not want it. Two verses closing the prelude tell us that after the ceremony, Alexis realized that he wanted nothing further to do with the matter:

> Mais co'st tels plaiz dont ne volsist neient;
> De tot an tot a Deu at son talent.
>
> (vv. 49-50)

In the following scene, in the bedroom with his bride, his resolution crystallizes into action. He gives her a sermon on the beauty of chastity and stalks out into the night in search of sainthood.

We have here a sudden reversal of direction, a totally unprepared development, one obviously contrived to be so. The Latin text, with its heavy and insistent accent on the piety of his early life, makes Alexis' decision to renounce the joys of this world almost a psychological necessity. In the vernacular the effect is more striking. It smacks of the miraculous – which is, of course, entirely appropriate. This for-

---

[13] *Ibid.*

mal development, an unprepared peripety, frequently marks points of structural importance in medieval narrative.

Now that Alexis' life is rigidly oriented toward heaven, the vernacular writer follows the Latin text quite closely, up to the point of Alexis' death. But here again he diverges significantly. The Latin life tells us that Alexis knew he was going to die and requested that ink and parchment be brought to him so that he might write down the story of his life. The focus then switches to the voice that sounds in the sanctuary, instructing people to seek out the Man of God. The searchers finally discover Alexis, already dead, at his father's house. The vernacular text, on the other hand, goes to the trouble of marking the precise moment of death. It occurs during the search, at a particularly low point: while the pope and emperors sit in despair, wondering whether they will ever find the elusive saint:

> Li apostolies e li emperedour
> Siedent es bancs e pensif e plorous.
> Si les esguardent tuit li altre seignour:
> Deprient Deu que conseil lour en doinst
> D'icel saint ome par qui il gariront.
>
> En tant dementres come il iluec sont sis,
> Deseivret l'aneme del cors saint Alexis;
> Tot dreitement en vait en paradis,
> A son seignour qu'il aveit tant servit.
> E! reis celeste, tu nos i fai venir.
>
> (vv. 326-35)

(The pope and the emperors sit on the benches pensive and tearful. All the other lords look at them: they pray to God to give them counsel about the holy man by whom they will be protected. While they are seated there, the soul of Saint Alexis separates from his body, goes straight to Paradise, to his Lord whom he had served so long. Oh! celestial king, you make us come to you.)

The death interrupts and is superposed upon another narrative line. The writer wished to pinpoint that moment, the most important moment of his story. The death, coinciding with the despair of the rulers of this world, thus marks a second structural division.

What we should normally expect at this point would be discovery, lament, prayer, and a sense of awe at the saint's magnificent sacrifice. But the writer chooses instead to expand everything given in the text. He dilates the laments of the family to a length of twenty-three stanzas; he amplifies two incidents, the miraculous healing of the sick who touch the corpse, and the throwing of gold and silver by the emperor to disperse the crowd, who pay no attention to it; the poet adds of his own invention stanzas 119-121, which tell how Alexis' family continued to lament after his interment and finally attained salvation through him. The last two stanzas before the formal *conclusio*, also of the writer's own devising, show Alexis in Heaven with his bride in the presence of God himself:

> Saint Alexis est el ciel sanz dotance.
> Ensemble o Deu, en la compagnie as angeles,
> O la pulcele dont se fist si estranges;
> Or l'at o sei, ensemble sont lour anemes:
> Ne vos sai dire com lour ledece est grand.
>
> Com bon peine, e com bon servise
> Fist cil sainz om en ceste mortel vide!
> Quer or est s'aneme de glorie resplenide:
> Ço at ques vuelt, nen est neient a dire;
> Ensorquetot e si veit deu medisme.
>   (vv. 605-616)

(Saint Alexis is undoubtedly in Heaven, together with God, in the company of the angels, with the maiden he abandoned; now he has her with him. Their souls are together. I cannot tell you how great is their joy. What good pain and what good service this holy man did in this mortal life! For now his soul is resplendent with glory. He has what he wants, no question about it. Above all, he looks on God himself.)

In adapting the Latin text, the writer obviously did not approach his material uniformly. It was not simply a question of padding out a skeletal story. He condensed the beginning and amplified the end. Clearly there were other alternatives. Modern taste would dictate compression after Alexis' death, for the story line becomes diffuse at that point and develops into a hodge-podge of narrative motifs: Alexis is honored by pope and emperors, lamented by his family, and transported across the city; money is scattered in the streets; the lame and halt are healed by touching his corpse; his family lament further and are finally saved through his influence; and he finally appears in Heaven with his estranged wife. The eleventh-century writer chose instead to dilate this material and thus deliberately made his story assume the bipartite form.

Conversely, a modern writer would have been more concerned to expand the material relating to the early life, to indicate the stages of growth toward a full realization of the saint's vocation, the internal struggle that his impending marriage must have provoked, the conflict between the father's plans and God's will. But the medieval writer chose the opposite course. He chose not to prepare his audience for Alexis' renunciation of the flesh and the world. As we can see by comparing the vernacular and Latin texts, he demotivated the critical turn.

It seems clear that the writer knew what he was doing. He chose bipartition, and the form, it must be admitted, is particularly appropriate to his subject. But since the form is so generally in evidence in twelfth-century narrative, it seems likely that the bipartite form was not so much dictated by the subject matter as by prevailing modes of narrative organization. The author evidently wished to contrast the saint's earthly life with the events after his death; the bipartite form was available and popular, and so he deliberately cast his material in this mold.

The *Chanson de Guillaume* is a particularly interesting example of bipartition precisely because the writer did such a poor job of welding his two parts together. The suture is clear because he let a number of contradictions subsist between the two parts.[14]

It is generally agreed that the *Chanson de Guillaume* as we have it today results from the fusion of an original *chanson* with a *geste de Rainouart*. The first part, the *Chanson de Guillaume* proper, extends to line 1980; Guillaume's nephew Vivien is killed by the Saracens at verse 925, or about halfway through the first part. He has, however, sent for his Uncle William, who avenges his death, achieving a painful victory after which only he and his nephew Guiot are left alive. At line 1980 we read what appears to have been the last line of the original poem: *Or out vencu sa bataille Willame* (Now had Guillaume won his battle.) It is therefore with some surprise that we read in the lines immediately following:

> Li quons Willame chevalche par le champ.
> Tut est iriez e plein de maltalent.[15]

(Count Guillaume rides through the field. He is all wrathful and filled with anger.)

Even more surprising he now finds Vivien – still alive – which can hardly be made to accord with the account of his death a thousand lines earlier:

> Co fut damage quant si prodome chet.
> Sor li corent de plusurs parz paiens.
> Tut le detrenchent contreval al graver.

---

[14]   B. Valtorta, "La Chanson de Willelme", *Studj Medievali*, XXVIII (1939), 19-40.

[15]   *La Chanson de Guillaume*, ed. D. McMillan, I, vv. 1981-82. Further line references will be to this edition.

Od els l'emportent, ne l'en volent laisser;
Suz un arbre le poserent les un senter.
(vv. 923-927)

(It was a pity when so brave a man fell. Pagans ran upon him from all sides, cut him to pieces, down on the strand. They carried him away with them; they did not wish to leave him; they placed him under a tree beside a path.)

In this account, Vivien, it would appear, was cut to pieces by the pagans, then placed under a tree beside a path. When he is found by his uncle, which by internal indications would probably have been two weeks later, he is lying beside a pond and is still alive. His uncle then administers communion to him and decides to take his body back to Orange, which is again surprising, since he had come from Barcelona three days earlier. Now, from nowhere at all there appear fifteen pagan kings and hosts of Saracen warriors. Guillaume has to abandon Vivien's body; he returns to Orange, then goes to the Emperor Louis for help. He is coolly received. After describing the horrors of Archamps and detailing to the Emperor the pressing need for instant retaliation, he gains Louis' sympathy, but the Emperor refuses to lend his aid, rather petulantly remarking that Guillaume never visits him except to ask for favors (vv. 2209-2210). However, Guillaume has relatives at court who promise their aid and Louis himself finally gives him 20,000 men. Most important, as we have already had occasion to relate, the pagan giant Rainouart, who carries a tree trunk for a club, now offers his services to Guillaume. Rainouart's prodigies of strength carry the day; in a burst of heroic-comic violence he wipes out the pagan forces. And in the end he turns out to be Guiborc's brother.

Here, as in the *Chanson de Roland*, the center of the narrative is marked by two things: first, the death of the young hero, and second, the sudden appearance of a new pagan force. Vivien corresponds to Roland, Guillaume to Charlemagne. The writer who put the two parts of the story together transported Vivien's death from the middle of the original poem to the new middle, heedless of verisimilitude, in response to a definite narrative formula. The idea appears to be to concentrate misfortune at the center and then make the sequel a violent retaliation against those responsible for the misfortune. The death of the young hero in the *Roland* and in the *Guillaume*, while on the one hand constituting the end of one epic action, introduces a second movement, one of revenge.[16]

---

[16] The *Nibelungenlied* is similarly constructed: the first part leads up to Siegfried's murder; Kriemhilt marries Etzel in a brief transitional section; the second part leads to Kriemhilt's revenge.

Revenge is, of course, a familiar enough narrative theme, and by its very nature it is bipartite. However, the medieval writer does not begin *ex abrupto* with the act that provokes the revenge. He builds up his story slowly and carefully, so that the death will fall at a point quite advanced in the body of the story. It is this that gives the story its bipartite form and I believe that this is purposely done in the interest of providing a physical balance, a diptychal organization.

In the romances of Chrétien de Troyes, a new element is added. The center is no longer a real death, but a symbolic one, a descent into shame, from which the protagonist recovers by forcing himself through a series of rehabilitating adventures. This, at least, is the formula for *Erec* and *Yvain*. *Cligés*, as we have noted, is genealogically bipartite, a refinement of simple genealogical extension. *Lancelot* and *Perceval* show some of the standard structural devices, but not so clearly as *Erec* and *Yvain*.

Looking first at the *Erec*,[17] it is worth noting that Frappier proposes a three-part structure for it:

Structure en trois parties, à la fois souple et savante. C'est d'abord l'apparition d'un chevalier d'élite et une aventure d'amour au dénouement heureux; puis une crise psychologique donne un nouvel élan au récit; la troisième partie, de beaucoup la plus ample, fait s'évanouir d'épisode en épisode le drame intérieur, rétablit un bonheur menacé, s'enrichit d'une aventure prodigieuse entre toutes, qui accroît encore le prestige du héros dans sa quête de la perfection.[18]

The description is accurate and perceptive. For my part, however, I see here the same bipartite formula. The *crise psychologique* is merely transitional and exists only to provoke into existence the extended series of adventures that make up the second part. The main structural peculiarity is that the "aventure d'amour au dénouement heureux" should be followed by a psychological crisis providing a new burst of energy that sets the story off on a new narrative course. The postmortem sequence in the *Alexis*, the Baligant and Rainouart episodes in the *Roland* and the *Guillaume*, have the same effect: they give a new impulse to a story line that has already worked itself out.

The first part of the story consists of two rather tenuously intertwined motifs, the hunt for the white stag and the sparrow-hawk tournament. Arthur, in accordance with a long-standing tradition, announces that the knight who brings down the white stag will have the

17   *Erec et Enide*, ed. M. Roques (Paris, 1952).
18   *Chrétien de Troyes*, p. 92.

right to designate with a kiss the most beautiful lady at court. Gawain, ever alert to social complications, scolds Arthur for initiating a situation that can only end in quarreling and hurt feelings. But the King cannot unsay himself. Erec and Guenevere accompany the hunters at a distance. Since Erec is not participating in the hunt, he is unarmed, escorting the queen and her servant. They encounter a knight and his lady, accompanied by a dwarf with a whip. Guenevere sends her servant to ask them to ride over and introduce themselves. The servant is whipped across the face. Erec goes to them and gets the same treatment. He is furious but since he is unarmed there is nothing he can do but follow them until he finds an opportunity for revenge. He arrives finally at a fortified *burg*, where great crowds of people have assembled for the sparrow-hawk tournament, at which the knight encountered above, Yder son of Nut, will take on all comers, defending his lady as the most beautiful. Having neither arms nor a lady in whose name to fight, Erec is particularly fortunate in spending the night with a poor but genteel vavasour who provides him with horse, armor, and his daughter Enide, whose ragged clothes cannot conceal her extraordinary beauty. Erec wins the joust and the sparrow-hawk, sends Yder to Arthur's court as prisoner, and returns with the beautiful Enide on his arm. Arthur, who happened to bring down the white stag, confers on Enide the kiss of the most fair. There is no dispute. Everyone agrees that she is ravishing. And now Chrétien tells us that the first part of the story is over: *Ci fin li premerains vers* (v. 1844). Indeed, the story is done. The two motifs have been gracefully drawn together; nothing remains to be added. "Le récit", writes Frappier, "est si bien ajusté qu'à lui seul le 'premier vers' mérite d'être loué comme une belle conjointure."[19]

But the action rebounds. Erec and Enide marry. The celebration culminates in a tournament at Tenebroc from which Erec emerges as grand champion. Then, suddenly, he becomes so engrossed in his bride that he loses interest in arms and chivalry, as we have already noted. His loss of reputation now provokes into existence the extended series of graduated and symmetrically arranged adventures we have examined above (pp. 89-91).

The story formula seems clear: there are two series of adventures separated by a psychological crisis. In the first, Erec moves out of Arthur's court unprepared for adventure, is passively absorbed into a

---

[19]   *Chrétien de Troyes*, p. 85.

sequence of events that culminate in his winning chivalric glory and a
lovely bride. Success is his, but by neglecting to maintain his involvement in chivalry, he loses his *prix*. Hearing Enide's lament, his pride
in his military and amatory prowess shatters. He realizes that he is no
longer worthy of chivalric society. He therefore excommunicates himself and with laudable determination puts himself through a series of
graded trials of strength and courage, culminating in a second and this
time definitive attainment of both chivalric glory and wedded bliss.
Enide passes with him through the series of ordeals, for she too is
being tested. Doubt of her husband's prowess had insinuated itself
into her mind and that doubt had to be purged.

At the center of the story we find a peripety, a fall from glory into
shame. The peculiar thing about this reversal is that it is produced, so to
say, *ab nihilo*. Up to verse 2434, there is no indication that Erec is likely
to fall prey to the evils of uxoriousness. After all, Enide originally
functioned in a purely ancillary way. Erec needed a lady whose beauty
he could defend against Yder. Not for love of her, but rather to avenge
the insult against his queen does Erec participate in the sparrow-hawk
tournament. The bellicose aspect of his temperament is further under-
scored by his success in the tournament at Tenebroc. Chrétien, it
would appear, went to some lengths to emphasize Erec's strongly
military inclinations, even to the point of showing him to be relatively
insensitive to the charms of amorous dalliance. Here, one feels, is a
man of steel. My guess is that Chrétien deliberately exaggerated Erec's
military disposition, in the same way that the writer of the *Alexis*
chose to emphasize his hero's secular status, in order that the reversal
of fortune, when it came, should be the more astonishing. The development of the crisis is, accordingly, extremely brief. It crops up suddenly and in Chrétien's first mention of it, the situation is already
completely clear:

> Mes tant l'ama Erec d'amors
> Que d'armes mes ne li chaloit,
> Ne a tournoiemant n'aloit,
> N'avoit mes soing de tornoiier;
> A sa fame aloit donoiier.
> De li fist s'amie e sa drue:
> Tot mist son cuer et s'antandue
> An li acoler et besier.
>
> (vv. 2434-42)

(But Erec loved her so tenderly that he no longer cared about arms, nor
went to tournaments, nor cared to participate in them. He spent his days

wooing his wife, and he made her his beloved and his mistress. He put all his heart and purpose in embracing and in kissing her.)

If Chrétien's primary interest in the story was, as seems likely, to pose the problem of the reconciliation of *amor* and *militia*, to define their proper relation and maximum resonance, one may legitimately wonder why he chose to postpone the matter to so advanced a point in the narrative. Since what Chrétien calls the 'premerains vers' contributes in no important way to the social and psychological problem of his story, he might have summarized its content, telling us in a few dozen verses that Erec was a mighty warrior who vanquished Yder, son of Nut, and married the beautiful Enide. Then he could have got right into the core of the matter. He chose instead to bring all that preliminary matter into the foreground and even to give it the specious look of a story whose ending could not be other than happy. We are reminded of the *Roland* and the *Guillaume*, in which the writers brought their stories to a perfectly satisfactory close in painful victory, then introduced new elements requiring that this victory be reobtained and re-emphasized through a repetition of battle. Furthermore, Erec's descent into shame and his self-excommunication from courtly society is a symbolic death from which he resurrects himself in a series of penitential trials. Chrétien is giving a spiritual regeneration formula. In any event, the correspondence with the actual deaths of Roland and Vivien is suggestive and not likely to be entirely fortuitous. Just as the young and impetuous hero (Roland, Vivien) is replaced by the older and wiser one (Charlemagne, Guillaume), so from the penitential ashes of the young knight there arises a second and greater Erec.

It is worth noting that there is a distinct change in the sequential pattern from the first part to the second. The first part is reasonably well concatenated, having a beginning, middle, and end. The second half is a *roman à tiroirs*. It looks as though Chrétien amplified a simple short narrative *lai*, by carrying it beyond its natural endpoint – the end of the 'premerains vers' – introducing a peripety based on a point of courtly ethic (the *sen* of the story) and resolved in a rehabilitation sequence.

It seems not unlikely that Chrétien's designation of the first part of the story as the first *vers* may throw additional light on the formula he was using, for the word *vers*, which seems strangely inappropriate in this context, can and often does mean *stanza* in Old French. Since in the first stanzas of the courtly love lyric the poets generally put a summary description of springtime, a *départ printanier*, Chrétien may have been pointing up an analogy between the construction of narrative and lyric art.[20] The *Erec* begins on Easter Day; the tone of the first part of the story is fresh, youthful, and enthusiastic; morbidity and guilt are generally absent; the hero sails easily and gracefully through all obstacles. *La Vie de Saint Alexis* also begins, we remember, by recounting the pleasant unopposed rise of Alexis to high secular status; Roland and Vivien lend to the first parts of the poems in which they figure an appropriate tone of youthful impetuosity; of Chrétien's other poems, *Yvain* begins at Pentecost, *Lancelot* on Ascension Day, and *Perceval*, somewhat less precisely, "au tans qu'arbre florissent", *i.e.*, in spring (v. 69). Many minor romances – *Galeran de Bretagne, Escoufle, Guillaume de Dole* – also exhibit this sort of *départ printanier*, which appears to have been part of a standard narrative pattern.

Chrétien tells us that in writing the *Erec* he was adapting a *conte d'avanture:*

> Por ce dit Chrestïens de Troyes
> Que reisons est que totesvoies
> Doit chascuns panser et antandre
> A bien dire et a bien aprandre,
> Et tret d'un conte d'avanture
> Une mote bele conjointure.
>
> (vv. 10-14)

(And that is why Chrétien de Troyes says that each of us must think and try to speak well and teach aright, and he draws from a tale of adventure a beautiful *conjointure.*)

It may well be that the *conte d'aventure* to which he refers was, in its general outline, the 'premerains vers', a simple story that he chose to amplify into a 'bele conjointure' by tacking onto it a narrative peripety with a didactic purpose, one intended to illustrate how the ideal of *mesure* applies in the adjustment of marriage and chivalry. Thus to the simple *matière* of the *conte* he added a courtly *sen*.[21]

In corroboration of this view we may note that the *Roland* appears to have been amplified in much the same way; the case of the *Chanson de Guillaume* is quite clear, precisely because it is so badly conjoined. We may note also that the Breton stories Marie de France chose to versify are not bipartite in form; they are simple stories with a be-

---

[20]   E. Hoepffner, "Matière et sens dans le Roman d'Erec et Enide", *Archivum Romanicum*, XVIII (1934), pp. 447 ff.

[21]   The terms, *matière* and *sen*, roughly translatable as 'matter' and 'meaning', occur in Chrétien's prologue to the *Lancelot*, in which he casually remarks that the Countess of Champagne provided him with both "matière et san" (v. 26).

ginning, middle, and end, without peripety, without the strenuous up-
ward march from shame to moral perfection. Frappier takes oblique
note of this fact when he writes, apropos of the "premerains vers":

Ce prélude possède son unité. Chrétien aurait pu s'en tenir là s'il n'avait
songé qu'à écrire un lai sur un sujet légendaire et courtois.[22]

From our point of view it does not particularly matter whether it was
Chrétien or a predecessor who originally amplified the story to make
it bipartite in form. What is significant is that from a purely compositional point of view the two halves are discontinuous enough to postulate an earlier version of the story in which the 'premerains vers' was
all there was. A simple form no doubt preceded the compound form,
just as the *Roland* and the *Guillaume* were at one stage of their development almost certainly independent of the Baligant and Rainouart
episodes. What is important for our purposes is not whether the earlier
forms were artistically superior, but that very able writers like Chrétien
de Troyes and the writer of the Oxford *Roland* chose the bipartite
form for their tales. We can only assume they did so because they
found the form esthetically superior.[23]

Yvain offers very much the same structural formula as the *Erec*.
The hero triumphs militarily in his defeat of the Knight of the Fountain, Esclados le Roux, and amatorily in his marriage with the knight's
beautiful widow. Like Erec, he annihilates both triumphs through
démesure, but the nature of his fault is the exact opposite of Erec's.
While Erec had become uxorious, Yvain leaves his wife to dabble in
chivalric games. When he forgets to return to her on the appointed day,
he is shamed at court by the tongue-lashing he receives from her messenger. After a period of insanity and grief, he accomplishes prodigious
feats of bravery and strength in the service of various distressed females,
and finally wins back his wife.

Parallels with the Erec are evident and striking, as several scholars
have already pointed out.[24] Both stories tell how a knight won, then

---

[22] *Chrétien de Troyes*, p. 85.
[23] The presence of the bipartite form in the Welsh Mabinogion versions of *Erec*
and *Yvain* probably derives from Chrétien. As J. Vendryès remarked at the
Strasbourg colloquium: "En ce qui concerne les romans arthuriens qui sont rangés
traditionnellement dans les mss gallois, il est depuis longtemps établi qu'ils dépen-
dent étroitement de Chrétien et qu'ils ne sont que des arrangements, assez malad-
roits souvent, des poèmes correspondants du romancier français." *Les Romans du
Graal*, p. 26.
[24] See, for example, Foerster, *Yvain*, kleine Ausgabe, p. xxii; Frappier, *Chrétien
de Troyes*, p. 150.

lost, then won again a bride and a reputation for chivalric prowess. The center of both narratives is marked by a revelation of courtly guilt and a subsequent auto-excommunication from Arthurian society. Beyond the center, the story line in both romances tends to become diffuse,[25] to take the form of a *roman à tiroirs* whose principle of sequence is varied repetition supported by gradation, a progress of the knightly soul toward perfection. Otherwise the sequences are discontinuous, the various episodes being related to one another neither logically nor in terms of their leading consistently toward a narrative goal.[26]

The beginning, on the other hand, has a fairly concerted narrative movement. Events mysteriously draw Yvain deeper and deeper into an unknown world in which the main adventure, the combat with Esclados le Roux, leads directly to an amorous involvement with the widow Laudine, which turns out brilliantly for him. The twin victory is celebrated upon the arrival of Arthur's court. The story, neither particularly overwhelming, nor entirely coherent in its details, has none the less a clear beginning, middle, and end. It is only in the second half that the story line begins to wander aimlessly.

The catastrophe in *Yvain* is treated with customary brevity: a short but neatly turned speech by Gawain on the dangers of inactivity resulting from marriage suffices to persuade the hero to leave his new bride, although he does so much against his will (*mout a anviz*). Their parting is so touching as to lead the reader to suppose that wild horses could not prevent Yvain's returning to his beloved on the appointed day. Yet Gawain, somehow,

> ... le fist tant demorer
> Que trestoz li anz fu passez
> Et de l'autre an aprés assez
> Tant que a la miaost vint.
>
>   (vv. 2676-79)

(... made him delay so long that the whole first year passed by and most of the next, until mid-August came.)

Less than one hundred lines cover the two-year period between his

---

[25] See Frappier, *Chrétien de Troyes*, p. 155: "Si la première partie formait un tout pourvu de son unité, Chrétien courait ensuite un risque de dispersion." See also Andrée Bruel, *Romans français du moyen âge* (Paris, 1934), p. 132; and Roetteken, *Behandlung des einzelnen Stoffelemente in der Epen Veldekes une Hartmann von Aue* (Halle, 1887), p. 2.

[26] Herbert Drube sees a thematic progression in the sequence, but he does not try to argue a concatenation. *Hartmann und Chrétien* (*Forschungen zur deutschen Sprache und Literatur*, Heft II, Munster, 1931), p. 116.

departure and his denunciation. Chrétien takes no pains whatever to uncover the psychological causes for Yvain's failure to return, although he spent nearly a quarter of the first part of the story developing the delicate psychological movement of Laudine's passage from bereaved widow to eager bride of her husband's murderer, a three-day affair. It was, we may assume, something of a law of the genre to concentrate improbable misfortunes at the center. It is, in a way, a form of *diabolus ex machina* device, used to precipitate a catastrophe.

In *Yvain*, as in the *Erec*, I am inclined to see the first part, up to the celebration of the marriage, as the subject of a *conte d'aventure* that Chrétien used as his source. The moral peripety and the diffuse adventures that follow upon it appear to me to be Chrétien's own invention. Their content and movement, stemming from free association of odd narrative bits and worked into a general graded pattern, imply a purely artificial grouping hardly likely ever to have constituted an independent story. Again we have a *conte d'aventure* with a happy ending, a suddenly introduced peripety containing a point of courtly ethic, and a series of ordeals through which the hero redeems his faults.

The *Lancelot* tends, I think, to confirm this intuition, for while scholars have not been able to locate narrative sources for the first part of the *Erec* or the *Yvain*, the narrative pattern of the *Lancelot* has been clearly identified. Not only does the story of Guenevere's abduction figure in the *Vita Gildae* by the Welshman Caradoc of Lancarwan, there are also several variants on the same narrative theme in Welsh and Irish literature.[27] They reduce in general to the following narrative outline: A mysterious stranger claims another man's wife. He obtains her by force or by ruse (frequently by the *don contraignant*) and takes her to his otherworld kingdom. The husband pursues and, after surmounting formidable obstacles, he penetrates into the presumably inaccessible realm and delivers the captive. That this story has parallels in classical mythology – Orpheus and Eurydice, Theseus and Persephone, Hercules and Alcestis – has been frequently pointed out.

Let us assume that Chrétien began with just such a story: this was his *matière*. But his patroness, Marie de Champagne, wanted that sort of story to be given a new courtly twist. Chrétien was to tell it in such a way that it might have contemporary appeal, thanks to the injection of the new spirit of courtly love, as it appeared in the poems of the troubadours: a spirit of utter servitude to the lady.

---

[27] See R. S. Loomis, *Arthurian Tradition and Chrétien de Troyes* (New York, 1949), pp. 202-204, 335; Frappier, *Chrétien de Troyes*, p. 136.

After going through a host of nightmarish adventures, Lancelot, who has replaced the husband of the original plot as rescuer, crosses the sword bridge into the land of Gorre, defeats Meleagant and thus rescues the queen. But the story is far from over. At this point Chrétien introduces his astonishing peripety, Guenevere's rejection of her rescuer for his hesitation in getting into the cart. Lancelot, at this point unaware of the queen's reasons, even supposing it was because he HAD entered the cart that the queen was displeased, wanders off in despair and into captivity. He makes an abortive attempt at suicide that sends a false rumor of his death to Guenevere. She repents her harshness and when the pair meet again a little later, she accords him the supreme recompense, a night of ineffable love. All that remains now is for them to return in glory to Arthur's court. But the law of the genre prevails: an unmotivated catastrophe starts the story rolling again. Lancelot falls inexplicably into captivity. Guenevere returns to Arthur's court with Gawain. A year later, Lancelot must again defend her from the same abductor's pretentions. In between, the better to flesh out an otherwise barren second half, there is a lengthy description of the tournament of Noauz, in which Lancelot participates by temporarily and honorably breaking jail. At this tournament, he unhesitatingly consents to play the coward for two days at his queen's behest. Then, when she finally reverses her command, he shows what a splendid fighter he really is. This is evidently his rehabilitation.

Chrétien did not finish the *Lancelot*. Midway through the second half, he gave it over to Godefroi de Lagny, who carried the story to its conclusion. It is not entirely clear why he did this. If, as has been suggested, he simply tired of the story, one would be hard put to it to explain why he did not simply end with the reconciliation of Lancelot and Guenevere, which makes a satisfactory end. It would appear that to Chrétien the bipartite form was in some obscure sense obligatory. Elegant form required that the story be stretched out by introducing a reversal of fortune after success. I imagine that Chrétien must have realized that after producing such a masterstroke in making the story reverberate with courtly *sen* in Lancelot's startlingly unforeseen rejection, the ending could only be a banal anticlimax. For that, the talents of Godefroi de Lagny would suffice.

Here, at any rate, is a clear case of a story originally Celtic and unipartite, whose matter in Chrétien's hands has been enriched by a reversal of fortune turning on a point of courtly ethic. It seems reasonable to assume that *Erec* and *Yvain* underwent a parallel transformation.

The bipartite form was very widespread in the twelfth century.[28] The Middle High German Spielmannsepos *König Rother* shows the same form without courtly overtones. There may have been some classical influence working here. The *Aeneid* is split at the center by a descent into hell, after which the narrative changes direction because of the spiritual regeneration of Aeneas. The famous story of Cupid and Psyche in Apuleius' *Metamorphoses* concludes with a series of penitential trials following upon the violation of a taboo. But while this seems clear enough, the basic impulse in the medieval stories seems to be simple amplification, a desire to spin out the story. But the extension is counterbalanced by a concern for symmetric form, and in the case of Chrétien by a modest didactic penchant.

The pervasive presence of such a form argues for the authenticity of intention as far as the Baligant episode of the *Roland* is concerned. We ought, moreover, to be on our guard against explanations of bipartition that fail to take into account how widespread a formula it is. Bezzola, for example, rationalizes the bipartition of the *Erec* in terms of the historical development of feudal society. At the beginning of the twelfth century, he tells us,

la société féodale, où tout convergeait encore vers le suzerain . . . se transformait en une société courtoise, où tout convergeait vers l'idéal du chevalier que chacun réalise dans sa propre vie.

Chrétien accordingly depicts the knight as engaged on a double quest. He is

à la fois à la recherche de lui-même comme individu et comme membre d'un organisme fondé, non sur le pouvoir suprême, mais sur l'idée universelle destinée à s'accomplir dans la vie de chacun. Ce dualisme explique tout naturellement . . . la bipartition des romans.[29]

The sort of dualism Bezzola refers to, even if it could be fully demonstrated with reference to the courtly romance, could hardly be made to apply to the *chansons de geste* or the saint's lives, much less to stories like *König Rother*, in which the king simply goes through a series of adventures and wins the hand of an Eastern princess, then has her stolen from him and goes through another series of adventures to win her again. It seems more simple to assume that Chrétien inherited the bipartite form and through it managed, as artists will, to express his own artistic mind.

[28] W. T. H. Jackson calls it a "nearly universal type", *The Literature of the Middle Ages*, pp. 56-57.
[29] Bezzola, *Le Sens de l'aventure et de l'amour*, pp. 83-84.

We ought also to be on guard against theories of structure that would confer a specious unity on stories that clearly divide in half. Hofer, for example, sees the following three-part structure in Chrétien's romances:

Une *exposition* introduit le héros et pose le problème, une *partie principale* en donne le développement, la *solution* termine le roman. L'exposition comprend en génèral plus de 2000 vers et raconte les données qui seront développées plus tard.[30]

It seems clear that Hofer is describing well-made narrative. But if we examine the stories closely, we see that in the *Erec*, for example, what Hofer calls the *exposition* is in fact a reasonably complete story, almost entirely unrelated to the *partie principale*. Nothing in this exposition in any way announces Erec's *recreance*. The actual exposition of that problem begins at verse 2434 precisely. Erec's disposition to love and idleness emerges suddenly at that point, not to develop the preceding matter, to which it is not at all related, but to introduce a fresh narrative impulse. The story line from that point forward does indeed revolve around Erec's rehabilitation up to the *Joie de la Cour* episode, which brings the story to a conclusion. But that episode is anything but a solution. It is rather an entirely gratuitous extension. Erec and Enide are perfectly reconciled: no serious doubt remains of Erec's hardihood. The episode is a conclusion only insofar as it stands as the symbolic recapitulation of the themes of the story. Of Chrétien's other romances, only *Yvain* comes close to fitting the pattern Hofer describes, and there again, it is only by profoundly modifying our understanding of the meaning of *exposition* as a literary term that we can see the first part of the story as having any bearing on the *partie principale*.

There is, of course, a good bit of medieval narrative, even in the twelfth century, that is not bipartite. The importance of the form derives from the fact that the really first-class narratives of the period – the Oxford *Roland*, Chrétien's romances, the *Nibelungenlied*, and, earlier, *Beowulf* – make use of this pattern. Conversely, the absence of such a form in the *fabliaux* and in other examples of popular narrative indicates that the bipartite form was essentially an artificial refinement.

It is difficult to justify this sort of procedure if we persist in believing that unity is a necessary condition of artistic success. What we should see is that the writer of the Oxford *Roland* used the form to advantage,

---

[30] S. Hofer, "La Structure du Conte del Graal examinée à la lumière de l'œuvre de Chrétien de Troyes", *Les Romans du Graal*, p. 15.

and that Chrétien was able to communicate some rather subtle points of courtly ethic by working them into the central peripety. The form itself, once established, can be very subtly used. The *Conte du Graal*, for example, would lose much of its point if the bipartite form were not part of the background of the tale; for Perceval behaves as though he had read *Erec* and *Yvain*. He follows the formula but misses its meaning. At the center of the narrative, when Perceval sits in glory among the Arthurian company, the Loathly Damsel bursts in upon the court and, singling him out from the others, roundly berates him for having failed in the one great test of his life, the question test at the Grail Castle. By neglecting to ask the right questions, he failed to bring about the healing of the Maimed King and the refertilization of the land. Indeed, there is worse: ladies will be widowed, knights will die, children will be orphaned, and all because of him. But Perceval is undismayed: he knows what to do. He goes out in search of adventure and further glory. For five years he rides, sending back to Arthur's court no fewer than fifty *chevaliers de prix* in witness of his prowess. All in vain. He has failed to understand the religious nature of his quest. He has forgotten God. He has not repented in his heart. Not until he meets the pilgrims on Good Friday does he realize how hopeless his search has been.

Chrétien has here returned to orthodoxy, but even in his mundane romances, the idea of penance does not seem to have been far from his mind. It appears as a modified form of the Phoenix myth. His heroes fall but rise again in greater strength. The heroine of *Cligés* is named Fénice: she undergoes a seeming death. To the medieval mind, with its absorbing interest in the story of Lazarus – a story commonly told to illustrate the miraculous nature of penance and the equivalence of sin and death[31] – such stories may well have provided a sense of unity rather than of duality. For this is the pattern of life itself: youth and innocence followed by sin and despair, then health restored by penitential trial. Thus the form of narrative, viewed as an analogous development, may have seemed to present a necessary cycle. And of course Aeneas' descent into Hell and subsequent rededication to his destiny must have seemed a perfectly obvious parallel to the story of Lazarus, and thus functioned as a powerful literary model.

The *Roman de la Rose*, although an allegory and therefore subject to different kinds of structural principles from those we find in non-

---

[31] Beryl Smalley, *The Study of the Bible in the Middle Ages* (Oxford, 1952), p. 25.

allegorical narrative, quite clearly follows this same pattern of initial success, unexpected failure and despair, then rehabilitation and definitive success. In the familiar springtime atmosphere of the opening the lover manages, without inordinate strain, to get into the garden, to fall in love, to learn a few things about love – its pains and pleasures – and ultimately to kiss his rose. For although Dangier and Raison work against him, he has the powerful aid of Bel Accueil, Franchise, and Pitié. Thus after about 3500 verses of moderate effort Amant achieves his preliminary goal. So ends, as it were, the *premerains vers*. Suddenly Male Bouche – not previously mentioned – opens his ugly mouth, blabs to Jalosie and in a trice Bel Accueil and the Rose are immured in a tower, plunging Amant into the depths of despair. And of course the rest of the poem is devoted to the lover's rehabilitation. While we can scarcely say that he endures a series of penitential trials he is nevertheless made to absorb a staggering amount of instruction, not all of it directly relevant to his purpose. Yet somehow this all helps to prepare him for his final victory. What the lover learns, I believe, is self-control.[32]

Dante's *Commedia*, we may note, begins in the middle of his journey through life, lost in a dark and savage wood. Under Virgil's tutelage, Dante has properly begun *in medias res*, that is, at the catastrophe, rather than in the springtime of the new life. The graduated descent through the several circles of Hell, then up through Purgatory and Paradise, corresponds in some sense to the progress of Chrétien's heroes. The apparent tripartite structure of the *Commedia* should not blind us to its real structure. The whole of the *Commedia* is in fact a unified progression which balances the unwritten fall of the hero, which is alluded to by Beatrice (*Purg.* xxx, xxxi). At any rate, however we choose to rationalize the bipartite form – it was susceptible of various applications – the fact of its existence is the main thing. The medieval writer steadfastly declined to subordinate one story to the other, as he might have done by beginning *in medias res*. He began *ab ovo* and made his stories stand sharply side by side, their independence guaranteed by a medial discontinuity. As we have seen, genre seems not to have been a controlling factor: saints' lives, *chansons de geste*, and

[32] As allegorically represented by Faux Semblant, who as the slayer of Male Bouche is the true hero of the *Roman de la Rose*. For Faux Semblant is not simply hypocrisy – Jean de Meung apparently misunderstood his allegorical blueprint – but the lover's capacity to deceive scandal-mongers by controlling his facial expressions and thus keeping the secret.

courtly romance all show this tendency, however much they may differ in other ways.

THE TRANSITION TO INTERLACED STORY. If during the twelfth century the prevailing notion of elegant narrative seems generally to have found expression in bipartite form, the thirteenth-century writers appear to have dropped it altogether and substituted for it the technique of narrative interlacing. The story of that evolution can be read in the developing compositional techniques of Chrétien de Troyes, who not only brought the bipartite structure to its apogee, but also inaugurated a new movement in narrative form that was to dominate most of the thirteenth-century story-tellers and be carried on by Boiardo and Ariosto in the fifteenth and sixteenth centuries. It was also to provoke Tasso to perform a great critical synthesis by announcing the principle that multiplicity and unity are compatible through the agency of logical interdependence.

The first indications of this development occur in Chrétien's *Yvain*. Not content, as in the *Erec*, to conclude his story with a rehabilitation sequence consisting of a series of graduated episodes, one following the other like beads on a string, he takes the trouble to suspend two episodes by introducing another, whose content is quite extraneous, before returning to the conclusion of the first. That is, instead of telling two episodes one after another, he inserts the second between the beginning and the end of the first.

He begins to do this at the point where Yvain and his lion come upon Lunete, who is to be burned at the stake on the following day. At this point, Chrétien could simply have written: "The next day, Yvain was there, and so on", but he chose not to. He draws Yvain off into quite another adventure at a castle where he learns that on the following day the daughter of the lord of the castle – and, incidentally, Gawain's cousin – is to be handed over to an evil giant, Harpin de la Montagne. Yvain would gladly help but for his previous commitment to help Laudine. On the following day, he waits until the last minute before leaving; the giant arrives in time for Yvain to defeat him, then return to Lunete and defeat her accusers. The first episode is begun, then suspended while the second is told, then ended.

This procedure is no accident. The two episodes are logically independent and could have been related in sequence, but Chrétien chooses to thread the one into the other and to exploit the possibilities of suspense the technique offers.

He repeats the procedure in the following two episodes, in which Yvain liberates three hundred captive maidens from the *Château de Pesme Aventure*, and combats Gawain to settle an inheritance dispute. The matter relating to the captive maidens is inserted between the beginning and end of the inheritance question. Chrétien introduces these developments by telling us that while Yvain and his lion were convalescing, after their struggle with the giant and with Lunete's accusers, a certain lord of the Black Thorn has died, leaving two daughters to share his inheritance. The elder decides to keep everything for herself. The younger threatens to request the aid of Gawain, but her sister shrewdly hurries to court and engages Gawain to uphold her side in the quarrel. The younger sister hears of the Chevalier au lion and sends a servant in search of him. The servant finds him, but on their way to Arthur's court they spend the night at the *Château de Pesme Aventure*. Here another story begins: captive maidens at the chateau are forced to weave cloth at shockingly low wages in a sweatshop operated by two devils (*maufés*), over whom Yvain triumphs. He sets the maidens free and returns to the matter of the disputed heritage. That dispute, we realize, was carefully engineered by the author in order to bring Yvain and Gawain into opposition. Their struggle is inconclusive, and when they finally recognize one another, each courteously insists on conceding victory to his friend. Arthur has to step in and settle the question with a Solomonic judgment. Now, however, having reached the pinnacle of knightly perfection – not to be bested by Gawain, whether in arms or in courtesy – Yvain returns to his wife and manages to win her back, profiting again from the good offices of Lunette. And so the story ends.

Apparently Chrétien was well pleased with this refinement of episodic sequence, for he took it up again in the *Conte du Graal*. It looks as if he constructed the first part of this romance in such a way that the events at the Grail Castle should occupy the structural center. A number of matters are begun before that episode and allowed to hang suspended, not to be resolved until after Perceval's exit from the Grail Castle.

For example, Perceval leaves his mother to go in search of the chivalric life and Arthur's court. She falls to the ground, but neither Perceval nor the reader knows that she has died until after he leaves the Grail Castle, when his cousin accuses him of causing his mother's death. Again, after leaving home, he breaks in on a girl in a tent, eats her cakes, takes her ring, kisses her, and then rides off. Later, after talking to his cousin and learning of his mother's death, he meets this same maiden being brutally treated by her jealous lover, L'Orguelleus de la Lande. Perceval defeats him in combat, and sends him to Arthur's court to bear witness to Perceval's prowess. Two other matters are begun before Perceval's arrival at the Grail Castle: he becomes involved with Blanchefleur, defends her against Clamadeu des Iles, and spends a night in her arms; secondly, he arrives at Arthur's court and then leaves to win the armor of the Red Knight. These matters too are resolved after the visit to the Grail Castle. After defeating L'Orguelleus de la Lande, he comes upon three drops of blood in the snow and he begins to see the meaning of his experience with Blanchefleur. He goes into a state of trance, provoked by the three drops of blood, which remind him of the rosy lips and cheeks of his now distant *amie*. His revery, however, is interrupted by the arrival of Arthur's court. He is now at last received as a full-fledged member of this company, and the first cycle of adventures ends.

It seems tolerably clear that this sequence is structurally a complex extension of the technique used in the *Yvain*. Instead of interrupting one adventure with another, Chrétien arranges a series of episodes so that four matters are left in suspense, each an interruption of the preceding one, then all four are resolved in turn, the whole culminating in Perceval's admission to Arthurian society. At the center there stands the Grail episode, the major unfinished business of the romance as a whole.

Chrétien now begins something new, but not structurally unrelated. He interrupts the story of Perceval and begins the story of Gawain. The point of departure for the Gawain sequence is the arrival in court of the Loathly Damsel. Perceval, at the height of his glory, now finds himself called a complete failure. He determines, as we have already mentioned, to repair his reputation by setting out in quest of the Holy Grail. At this point, however, Chrétien introduces a certain Guingambresil, who accuses Gawain of having murdered his lord and challenges him to combat. This is fixed, in accordance with custom, for forty days later. Chrétien then follows Gawain through other adventures and for nearly 1500 lines (4708-6180) Perceval is totally absent from the scene. Chrétien then abandons Gawain and gets back to Perceval. The formula of transition is the one we find in later examples of interlaced narrative:

> De mon seignor Gauvain se test
> Li contes ici a estal.

> Si parlerons de Perceval.
> Perceval, ce conte l'estoire,
> A si perdue la memoire
> Que de Deu ne li sovient mais.[33]

(The story here ceases to speak of my lord Gawain, so we shall speak of Perceval. Perceval, the story tells, so lost his memory, that he no longer remembered God.)

Now comes a critical period in the story of Perceval. After five years of fruitless wandering,[34] an encounter with a group of pilgrims – an encounter that evidently parallels the earlier encounter with a group of Arthur's knights – causes him to realize that he has forgotten God. He is directed to a nearby hermit – his uncle as it happens – from whom he learns the importance of penance and embarks on a program of purification of his soul. He is now ready, we imagine, to complete his quest. But Chrétien turns the tale back to Gawain, again in the standard way:

> De Percevax plus languemant
> Ne parle plus li contes ci.
> Einçois avroiz asez oï
> De mon seignor Gauvain parler
> Que plus m'oiez de lui conter.
> (vv. 6476-6480)

(Of Perceval at greater length the story at this point says no more. Instead, you will have to hear much about Gawain, before you hear me speak of him again.)

Chrétien, unfortunately, died before he was able to get back to Perceval, so we do not know how he would ultimately have brought his story to an end. No doubt Perceval would have completed his quest, but just how this denouement could be tied in with Gawain's adventures it is hard to imagine.

Here, at any rate, seems to be the beginning of narrative interlacing.[35] A further development along the same line occurs in a romance of disputed authorship, *Guillaume d'Angleterre*, which many critics have attributed to Chrétien.[36] If Chrétien did write it, it may be that he did

---

[33]   *Chrétien de Troyes: Li Contes del Graal*, ed. G. Baist (Freiburg, 1909), vv. 6176-6181.
[34]   Note the chronological discrepancy: Gawain's forty days are not yet up. Later romancers were more careful.
[35]   There are earlier examples of its use – for example, in *La Vie de Saint Alexis* and the *Roman de Troie* – but I feel that this is the first systematic exploitation of it as a structural pattern.
[36]   *Cf*. Frappier, *Chrétien de Troyes*, pp. 75-84.

so as a structural exercise, since it is quite different from his usual structural pattern, but it carries the development of interlaced narrative one step further, the addition of a third party.

As the story begins, King William and his wife Gratienne are about to have a long-awaited child. There is no indication that they are anything but pious, charitable Christians. But catastrophe strikes. William is admonished in a dream to go into exile in the name of the Father and of the Son. He tries to avoid the issue by giving away his property and riches, but when the voice admonishes him a third time, he feels he must leave. Gratienne, heavy with twins, goes with him. She gives birth beside the sea. William goes off in search of food, meets a group of merchants, and leads them to his wife. They find her very pretty and take her away with them. While William protests this injustice, a wolf carries off one of his children. While he chases the wolf, a group of merchants carry off the other child. The same group of merchants takes the other child from the jaws of the wolf. The boys, Louvel and Marin, are adopted by merchants and become friends later on.

Now that the family has been separated, the author begins to interlace his narrative. He leaves the two sons and their newly acquired fathers, saying:

> Mais d'aus vos lais ci la parole.
> Del roi cui deus et ire afole
> Tant qu'il ne se set consillier,
> Oiés qu'il fist au reveiller.[37]

(But I cease to speak of them here. Of the king, whom dole and anger drive mad, so that he knows not what to do, hear what he did when he woke up.)

We follow the fortunes of the exiled king, who enters the service of a good merchant and shows an extraordinary aptitude for commerce. Then the author turns to the queen:

> Mais or me voel del roi taisir,
> Car drois est que jou vos redie
> De la roïne et de sa vie.
> (vv. 1034-36)

(But I wish to be silent about the king. For it is right that I tell you of the queen and of her life.)

The merchants return to their country and squabble over her. The dispute is settled by the lord of the country, an aged knight named

[37] *Chrétien de Troyes: Guillaume d'Angleterre*, ed. M. Wilmotte (Paris, 1927), vv. 839-942.

Gleolais, who protects her. His wife, however, dies soon afterward, and he asks Gratienne to marry him. She agrees, but only on condition that there be no sexual intercourse for a year. She invents a story about having led a life of whoredom that it will take her a year to expiate. She thus becomes first lady of the country, and is soon loved by all. Then the author returns to the sons:

> Mais or ne vuel plus demorer
> En ces paroles u jou sui.
> Conté vos ai tant con je dui
> De la roïne a ceste fois.
> Des deus enfans est ore drois
> Que vos saciés que il devinrent.
>
> (vv. 1324-29)

(But I wish no longer to remain in these words where I am. I have told you as much as I should about the queen this time. It is now right that you know what became of the two children.)

Because of their violent distaste for commerce, both boys leave their adoptive fathers and go to a neighboring country where they kill a doe on the king's game preserve. Brought before the king, they impress him with their aristocratic bearing and are therefore employed as squires. But now it is time to return to William:

> Des enfans au roi m'en revois,
> Que ciés le borgeois vos laissai;
> Des enfants tant conté vos ai
> Que plus dire ne vos en doi.
> Si recommencerons del roi.
>
> (vv. 1945-50)

(From the children I go back to the king, whom I left with the merchant. I have told you so much about the children that I must not tell you more. So we shall begin again with the king.)

William goes as a merchant to his wife's country. Since now twenty-four years have passed, they recognize one another with difficulty. They sit down to dinner, but when hunting dogs enter the hall, William is reminded of his sporting days of long ago. He goes off to hunt, warned by his wife not to cross the river separating her country from that of a hostile neighbor. In the enthusiasm of the hunt, he crosses it. There two young knights prepare to take him prisoner. When he tells them who he is, King William of England, and how he lost his wife and two sons, they realize this must be their father. They return with him and are reunited with their mother. So all ends well. William goes back to England and resumes his duties as king.

The story breaks into three major movements – an introduction leading up to the separation (1-836), then the three parallel biographies (839-2395), and finally the reunion of the disunited members (2395-3310). The center section is itself divided in three parts: that relating to the king (839-1033), to the queen (1034-1323), and to the sons (1324-1944).

If Chrétien actually wrote this rather foolish story, it must have been after he wrote *Cligés*, which Chrétien begins by giving a list of his previous works, among which the *Guillaume* does not figure. It has in fact been held that the pious flavor of the story would place it around the period of the *Perceval*. Structurally speaking, this would accord with the general tendency in his works toward the form of narrative interlacing.

At any rate, scholars generally agree that the finest example of this technique occurs in the early thirteenth-century prose cycle, the *Lancelot-Graal*. Not long afterward, about the middle of the thirteenth century, the technique entered a decadent phase in the prose *Tristan*.

The technique as we have seen it used so far seems simple enough, and it remains so as long as the writer works on a small scale. But when the scale is expanded to involve almost all the knights of the Arthurian circle in a romance running to over a thousand pages, as in the prose *Lancelot*, the matter becomes extremely complex. In the first place, there are so many threads carried forward simultaneously that there is a considerable danger of forgetting some minor knight in the midst of an uncompleted quest. But the writer of the prose *Lancelot* scarcely ever drops a stitch in his tapestry. Every series of actions, no matter how often it is interrupted, is taken up exactly where it was left off; no thread is abandoned once it is begun.

In the second place, since all these actions are presumed to be going on simultaneously, and since from time to time paths cross, it should be possible to construct a calendar around the central events of the story, the feasts and the tournaments, and to see whether the various events of the several stories can be fitted into it. In the prose *Lancelot*, the chronology is carefully worked out. The writer apparently had devised a meticulous time-scheme of days and hours, so that at any given time he knew precisely where the several knights stood in relation to one another.[38]

---

[38] F. Lot, *Etude sur le Lancelot en prose*, pp. 17-64. Chronology is most carefully handled in the *Lancelot* proper. It is somewhat less precise in the *Mort Artu*, hardly present at all in the *Queste*.

Clearly this is a technique that requires considerable vigilance, hindsight, and foresight. Indeed, it seems reasonable to assume that the story was diagrammed before it was written. The sequence of the various biographical sections and the time relations between them were probably planned in advance.[39]

The extravagant length of the prose romances in this form had its effect on structure. For while Chrétien seems arbitrarily to have fixed the length of his romances at approximately 7,000 lines the better to plan his repetitions and climaxes, the writers of interlaced romances abandoned the ideas of both fixed length and of graded sequence. After all, one cannot reasonably be expected to make every adventure more difficult than the previous one when their number runs to several thousand. The principle of gradation was thus replaced by the principle of textural variety. In accordance with this principle, each knight's character assumes a differentiating function: each biographical line has some distinctive coloring.

The principle is best illustrated in one of the shorter romances of the *Lancelot-Graal*, the *Queste del Saint Graal*. Since it also serves to indicate how interlacing works in its detail, I shall take the liberty of including here a brief but complete summary of the narrative here, leaving out, except for a few examples, the allegorical commentary which the writer chose to incorporate into the body of his story. This romance has the advantage of presenting a structure sharply analogous to that of the *Guillaume d'Angleterre*: there is a beginning section in which everyone starts out together, then a central section in which the various biographical lines are interwoven, and an end in which the tapestry is finished off and everyone finds his final resting place.[40]

The story begins the day before Pentecost. A messenger arrives who takes Lancelot to a nearby nunnery where on the following morning he knights his son Galaad. Lancelot returns to court to find the Perilous Seat miraculously inscribed to the effect that it is about to find its rightful occupant. A stone with a sword fixed in it floats to shore nearby; an inscription notes that only the best knight in the world will be able to draw the sword from the stone. Lancelot refuses to try.

[39] J. Frappier, *Etude sur la Mort le Roi Artu*, pp. 122-146.
[40] The *Queste* is one of the few romances of this sort in which the writer's concern is fundamentally didactic. At various points through the story white-robed Dominican friars appear, provide a symbolic interpretation of the events of the story, then vanish. The writer, it will be noted, admirably adapts the interlaced form to suit his didactic purpose. Page references in the text are to *La Queste del Saint Graal*, ed. A. Pauphilet (Paris, 1923).

Gawain and Perceval try in vain. Then Galaad arrives, passes the test of the Perilous Seat, and draws the sword from the stone. A thunderclap announces the appearance of the Holy Grail, which floats into the hall bathed in light. It circulates through the room providing each knight with what he most desires, then mysteriously vanishes. All the knights of the Round Table, one hundred fifty strong, swear to go in quest of it (pp. 1-25).

It is at this point that the writer begins systematically to interlace his narrative. The knights start out together, but their paths diverge, and their adventures are recounted severally. The author concentrates on five major figures: Galaad, Bohort, Perceval, Lancelot and Gawain. Several others, including Baudemagu, Lionel, Hector, and Yvain, figure peripherally in the development of the story.

The writer first follows Galaad to a white abbey where he meets Baudemagu and Yvain. The former boldly but unwisely rides off with a white shield bearing a red cross, which has been conserved at the abbey, fabled to bring misfortune to all but its destined bearer. A knight in white armor roughly unhorses him and thus punishes his temerity. He returns to the abbey and learns that the shield was predestined for Galaad, who now takes it up and rides out to meet the knight in white armor, who tells him of the shield's illustrious owners from the time of Christ. The knight in white armor, having served his purpose, now vanishes into thin air. Galaad returns to the abbey, where he lifts a tombstone covering a knight in full armor. A white-robed friar explains the symbolic significance: the tombstone is the hardness of sin, the knight is humanity dead and blind under sin's crushing weight, Galaad is the predestined deliverer of humanity, and so on. He now knights a young squire, Melian. The two ride until they come to a fork in the road. Their paths diverge and the writer turns from Galaad to Melian (26-41).

Melian comes upon a crown on a chair in the middle of the road. He puts the crown on his head and rides off, then meets a knight who unhorses him, wounding him severely, and who tells him that the crown is not for him – the motif plainly parallels Baudemagu's adventure. Galaad now happens along, triumphs over the knight who had struck down Melian, and takes the latter to a nearby abbey to be cared for. One of the friars explains the symbolic meaning of the adventure. Galaad now rides to the Château des Pucelles, where he fights with seven evil brothers, who take flight at midday. Then he enters the castle and delivers a crowd of captive maidens. News arrives that the seven brothers have been killed by Gawain, Gaheriet, and Yvain. Galaad rides off and the story turns to Gawain (44-51).

It is no accident that Gawain should have been mentioned at the end of the preceding sequence. This mention brings Gawain into the picture peripherally and makes the transition more graceful. We do not, however, take up the story of Gawain from this point on. There is a chronological retrogression to the point of departure. Gawain follows Galaad from the beginning, so that his appearance at the *Château des Pucelles* does not seem entirely accidental. After several days of questing uneventfully, Gawain comes to the abbey where Galaad won his white shield. He sets off in search of Galaad and comes to the abbey where Melian is convalescing. From him he gets further news of Galaad. Gaheriet and Yvain arrive just before Gawain sets out to continue his search for Galaad. The three of them start together for the *Château des Pucelles*, meet the seven knights fleeing from Galaad, and kill them. We are now at the point where the Gawain sequence began. It closes with Gawain's going to a nearby hermitage where he confesses to a recluse, who sharply rebukes him for killing the seven knights before they had a chance to make their peace with God. The recluse goes on to explain that the seven knights were the seven deadly sins, but one must not confuse levels of interpretation by wondering just how abstractions are supposed to have human souls. At any rate, the story now turns to Galaad (51-55).

Galaad is still fresh in our memory, but this next section is not really about Galaad at all. Its hero is Lancelot. The way in which the writer shifts the emphasis is quite interesting. After leaving the *Château des Pucelles*, Galaad rides off and meets Perceval and Lancelot. They do not recognize him. He strikes both to the ground, then gallops off. The writer then turns his attention to Lancelot, conveniently disposing of Perceval by sending him to a nearby recluse. The writer does not in this case return to the point of departure: Lancelot's adventures begin here. Perceval's momentary presence at this point makes it possible for the writer to return to him when he has finished the section on Lancelot. All the major figures, with the exception of Bohort, have now been introduced.

Lancelot sees a sick knight healed by a sudden appearance of the Grail. Then a mysterious voice curses him as a hardened sinner. A white-robed friar gives him a detailed interpretation of the curse. Lancelot confesses to him and renounces his guilty passion for Guenevere, and the writer now turns to Perceval (55-71).

Galaad is clearly the hero of the story. Gawain's prospects are decidedly negative; this is not his sort of quest. Lancelot occupies a middle ground as a repentant sinner. The writer's job was to fit in Perceval and Bohort.

As to Perceval, there was already in existence a considerable amount of material in the Grail tradition: in two of the continuations of Chrétien's *Conte du Graal* he had accomplished the quest, and some place had to be made for him in the rehandling of the story. So at this point we learn something of the writer's intention as to the outcome of all these adventures.

Perceval, after the encounter with Galaad, goes to a nearby recluse to find out who the knight is who has just triumphed over him. The recluse is his aunt, former queen of the Blighted Land. She brings in many details of the story from Chrétien's version. She exhorts him above all to conserve his virginity. She assures him that Galaad is a far better knight than he, but that both he and Bohort will be with Galaad when the quest is finally accomplished. On his aunt's advice he begins to search for the castle of Corbénic. Somewhat later, Perceval is assailed by twenty knights and would succumb but for the timely intervention of Galaad, who aids him without being recognized. After several strange adventures and visions, explained by a mysterious personage in a strange boat draped in white samite, Perceval's chastity is tested by a beautiful maiden. At the last moment he catches sight of a cross engraved on the pommel of his sword. The maiden disappears. The man in the white boat returns and explains the adventure to Perceval, who repents his weakness, then gets into the boat. Now the story moves back to Lancelot (71-115).

The next thirty pages of the tale (115-146) contain diverse adventures of Lancelot, beginning at the chapel where he entered upon his program of repentance. He is now wearing a hair shirt that will protect him from sin as long as he wears it. He enters a tournament and tries vainly to turn the tide of combat in favor of the knights in black armor. He discovers that the reason he could not prevail is that the tournament was a symbolic representation of the quest itself, which can only be won by the pure, the knights in white armor. The symbolic situation here is quite complex: the quest symbolizes the spiritual quest which the tournament also symbolizes. Lancelot, at any rate, goes on until he halts before a marsh he cannot cross. Out of its dark waters there appears a black knight who kills Lancelot's horse. Lancelot despairs and kneels to pray. But now the story turns to Gawain.

Gawain's situation is clear: this sort of quest is not for him. Neither he nor Hector, whom he now meets, has come upon any worthwhile adventure. Nor have some twenty others whom Hector has met in his wanderings. Gawain jousts with a knight, kills him, and discovers to his sorrow that it is his friend Yvain. A hermit explains why they have been so unsuccessful. The quest for the Holy Grail is a spiritual adventure in which knights like them, weighted down with unrepented sins, cannot fruitfully participate. They therefore decide to return to Camelot. (142-62).

Now a curious thing happens. The writer tells us that the story ceases to speak of them and returns to Bohort. Of course, Bohort has not yet figured in any of the adventures; he has simply been mentioned by Perceval's aunt. I do not think that the writer was quite sure of what he intended to do with Bohort, so he put off the problem as long as he reasonably could. He probably decided to include Bohort among the elect only in order that there might be three knights, a trinity, at the final Grail service. At any rate, undisturbed by the fact that he has not yet managed to work Bohort into the story, the writer simply says: "Or dit li contes que quant Bohorz se fu partiz de Lancelot, si come li contes a devisé, qu'il chevaucha . . ." (162).[41]

Bohort rides until noon and then meets a holy man, who talks to him at length about the quest, telling him that he will be among the elect. Bohort goes on and sees a bird circling over a dead tree. Its little ones having died of hunger, the parent punctures its breast with its beak, revives its young with its own blood, then dies. Bohort feels that there must be some religious significance to this, but before he gets to the bottom of it he comes across a disinherited lady, whom he champions against her sister's knight (possibly a reminiscence of *Yvain*). After an adventure in which he quarrels with his brother Lionel, Bohort joins Perceval in the boat draped in white (162-195).

The tale returns to Galaad. After helping Perceval in his fight against the twenty knights, he enters a tournament in the course of which he delivers a terrible blow to Gawain.[42] Clearly the writer has taken us back to a point before Gawain's withdrawal from the quest.

[41]   Malory's adaptation takes this transition all the way back to the beginning: "Whan that Sir Bors was departed from Camelot, he mette with a holy man . . .". *The Works of Sir Thomas Malory*, ed. E. Vinaver (Oxford, 1947), II, 1955.
[42]   The blow is important, illustrating a procedure typical of intercomplication in the Vulgate cycle. When Gawain at the beginning of the story tried to pull the sword from the stone, Lancelot commented that "ceste espée vos tochera de si prés que vos ne la voldriez avoir baillée por un chastel" (6).

The technique obviously obliges the writer to reverse his chronology for at least some of the sections, but it is a little unsettling for the reader, who feels that Gawain is now definitely out of the quest and resting comfortably at Camelot.

A maiden leads Galaad to the shore, where he sees the boat in which Bohort and Perceval are traveling. He enters with the maiden, who turns out to be Perceval's sister. Later, the sister gives her blood to heal a leprous woman and she dies. Her body is placed in the ship – the three knights have found another one, built by Solomon to carry a message to Galaad, the last of his line – and committed to the waves. The boat carries both her and us to Lancelot, of whom we have not heard for some time: "grant piece s'en est teuz" (195-246).

After wondering at some length how he will cross the marsh, Lancelot sees the boat carrying the body of Perceval's sister. He gets aboard and finally arrives at the castle of Corbénic, where he is permitted to witness from a distance the celebration of the mystery of the Holy Grail. He falls into a swoon for fourteen days, equal to the number of years of his service to Guenevere, then returns to Arthur's court (246-62).

In the next section we get a closer view of that mysterious service, for the story returns to Galaad and his two companions. The three are welcomed at Corbénic, and in a scene of great solemnity, described in considerable detail, the Grail service is performed in the presence of the Maimed King. Higher revelations await the heroes at Sarras. There Galaad dies in ecstasy after seeing openly the mystery within the Grail itself. A hand then reaches from Heaven and removes the Grail from the Earth. Perceval dies a year later. Bohort returns to court to tell the story, and thus ends the high history of the Holy Grail (263-280).

It seems clear that the writer chose to use the cadre of interlaced romance to symbolize what seemed for him to be the great collective adventure of humanity, the search for God. Summing up humanity in a few typical personality types, he interwove their biographies, presenting each separately, but for purposes of instructive comparison each one is interrupted by another, and none is permitted to be lost from view for too long. But since there are only two possibilities, salvation or damnation, God finally gathers together those whose merits place them on one side or the other. Gawain and his friends realize the hopelessness of their efforts and return to Camelot. The elect, separated through the early stages of their questing, join together in the supreme experience. The narrative web is woven of biographies, like threads of different color, which form by turns the central design, then disappear, reappear, and cross; the most brilliant of them come together at the end to form a last magnificent motif.[43]

Here the fusion of form and doctrine, of *matière* and *sens*, has been managed admirably. We could hardly get the same effect by separating out the story of Galaad. Somehow the full meaning of his experiences depends on their juxtaposition with those of the others. The unity that we perceive in the work is therefore in part the unity of form and substance.

Even without the help of metaphysics we may see a certain structural unity here, one that has been very well described by Bishop Hurd in connection with Spenser's *Faerie Queene*. His observation fits the *Queste* so much better than it does Spenser's unfinished romance that it deserves to be cited:

If you ask then, what it this *Unity* of Spenser's poem? I say, it consists in the relation of its several adventures to one common *original*, the appointment of the *Faerie Queene*, and to one common *end*, the completion of the Fairy Queen's injunctions. The knights issued forth on their adventures on the breaking up of this annual feast; and the next annual feast, we are to suppose, is to bring them together again from the achievement of their several charges.

This, it is true, is not the classical Unity which consists in the representation of one entire action; but it is an Unity of another sort, an unity resulting from the respect which a number of related actions have to one common purpose. In other words, it is an unity of *design*, and not of action.

This Gothic method of design in poetry may be, in some sort, illustrated by what is called the Gothic method of design in gardening. A wood or grove cut out into many separate avenues or glades was among the most favourite of the works of art which our fathers attempted in this species of cultivation. These walks were distinct from one another, had each their several destinations, and terminated on their own proper objects. Yet the whole was brought together and considered under one view, by the relation which these various openings had, not to each other, but to their common and concurrent center.[44]

The notion that unity of a sort results from having a common origin and a common end seems to have been entirely present to the writer of the *Lancelot* proper, for at one point when Gawain and twenty other knights go off in search of a knight in vermilion arms, the writer tells us that "chascuns de ces .xx. chevaliers a son conte tout entier, qui

[43]   Pauphilet, *Etudes sur la Queste del Saint Graal* (Paris, 1921), p. 163.
[44]   *Letters on Chivalry and Romance*, Letter VIII, in *The Works of Richard Hurd* (London, 1811), IV, 300-301.

sont branques de monseignor Gauvain, car chou est li chiés, et a cestui en la fin convient tous ahurter pour che que il issent tuit de cestui".[45] At yet another point, the writer points out that "li contes Lancelot fu branche del Graal".[46]

It seems therefore that we may at least provisionally speak of a unity of design in such works as these, as long as the writer manages to relate the multiple adventures to some common point of origin and lead them to some common end. Unfortunately, this is by no means always the case among the imitators of the technique, who seem to have been conspicuously unaware of the technical proficiency required in the 'proper' use of such a narrative procedure. That this should have happened is no surprise. It takes attentive study to find out that the structure of the prose *Lancelot* is firm. Before Lot's careful study appeared, most scholars were of the opinion that the story was one of the most rambling productions of medieval literature.

The prose *Tristan*, a vast prose romance on the order of the Arthurian Vulgate, shows what happens when the manner is taken up by a less talented writer. The fabric disintegrates, loose threads are scattered, quests are undertaken and then abandoned, long narrative developments occur that have no bearing on earlier or later developments; the work as a whole takes on the look of a vast *roman à tiroirs*.

One example should suffice to indicate the quality of the narrative structure of the *Tristan*. It may be taken to represent the ultimate poetic development of the motif of the unknown knight. In this case, Tristan and Palamedes simply come across such a one sleeping beside a fountain. They decide to wake him up and talk to him. But the knight immediately attacks Tristan, bowls over both him and his horse, then unhorses Palamedes and calmly rides off. Amazed by this display of virtuosity, Tristan and Palamedes follow him, determined to find out his name. They meet a maiden whose knight has just been killed by their man. Next we see the unknown knight in a dispute with Gawain and Blioberis. Gawain challenges him, but the knight does not feel like jousting. Instead he expresses himself at some length on the worth of certain knights who are supposed to be among the best

---

[45] "Each of these twenty knights has his own full story, which are branches of Monseigneur Gawain, for he is the leader, and toward him it is fitting that in the end all should converge, for they all proceed from him." *The Vulgate Versions of Arthurian Romances*, ed. Sommer, III, 276.
[46] "The story of Lancelot was a branch of the story of the Grail." *Ibid.*, p. 429.

in the world, but whom he considers to be worthless. Blioberis, after vainly asking the stranger to identify himself, finally presents an ultimatum: name yourself or joust. He is struck from his horse and wounded. Gawain meets the same fate. Once the stranger leaves, Tristan arrives. The squires of Blioberis and Gawain tell him what he just happened. Tristan follows after him, more determined than ever to find out who he might be. His adversary takes lodging that night with a widow, and Sir Kay and Sir Dinadan arrive a little later. They have a long conversation in which the stranger expresses his violent hatred for Guenevere. Kay passes a sleepless night, determines to joust with the stranger the next day, but the following morning the stranger leaves without saying goodbye. Kay catches up with him and invites him to a joust. Kay is knocked senseless and remains in a swoon until noon that day. Tristan arrives and learns from Dinadan what has happened, then continues his pursuit. But he loses the trail, goes to the right when he should have gone to the left, and after five days he abandons the search. Neither he nor we ever find out who that unknown knight was. Nor is it likely now that we shall ever know.[47]

This sort of sequence is by no means atypical. It takes up a dozen or so leaves of many hundreds in the manuscript. Others of the same general nature occur throughout the story. This sequence really begins nowhere, ends nowhere, feeds on its own substance, and finally vanishes. A story constructed in this way cannot be said to be interlaced, since the term implies a regular procedure of continuing matters begun earlier. A development such as this constitutes nothing more than a *roman à tiroirs*, for it is quite evident that this sequence could be put anywhere in the story, or left out entirely, without having any effect on the total economy of the work. However, I do not doubt that the writer felt he was doing much the same thing as the writer of the prose *Lancelot*.

FROM DECADENCE TO ANALYSIS. The next development in the history of narrative structure seems to be decisive in the passage from medieval to modern narrative style, from multiplicity to unity. The period and the development have scarcely been studied at all, except by Vinaver, whose studies bear particularly on the relation of Malory to his French sources.

---

[47] The events summarized above appear in a fuller narrative summary in E. Löseth, *Le Roman en prose de Tristan* (Paris, 1891), pp. 143-146. Löseth's extensive summary of the many mss is so far all we have.

While the style of the prose *Tristan* continued to reign in France as the dominant form of narrative through the fourteenth, fifteenth, and most of the sixteenth centuries in works like *Meliador, Perceforest, Amadis de Gaule,* and the successive prosifications of the *Quatre Fils Aymon,* important things were happening in the derivative literatures abroad, particularly in the works of such writers as Boccaccio and Chaucer in the fourteenth century, Sir Thomas Malory in the fifteenth. The three of them may fairly be said to have anticipated the new narrative style, the Renaissance movement toward classical standards of unity. On the whole, their work appears to be a reaction against the extravagances of the French romances, and notably against their undue length and complexity. A process of analysis and reduction was in order.

The first well-made story of any considerable length in Western literature is Boccaccio's *Filostrato.* The story of its development from Benoît de Sainte-Maure's *Roman de Troie* has often been told,[48] but in order properly to appreciate the full meaning of that transformation, it has to be viewed against the background of interlaced story. What Boccaccio did was to disengage one narrative thread from the *Roman de Troie,* amplify its beginning, and thus make one story from a part of a lengthy romance.

Benoît seems to have introduced the love story solely for the purpose of creating a diversion from the long and monotonous series of battles and single combats between the Greeks and Trojans. But in order not to interrupt the progress of his war narrative, he grafts the love story piecemeal to the trunk of the main narrative. He opens the love story, then drops it to return to the war story. He repeats this operation nine times, so that the love story is broken into nine sections of varying lengths, inserted at varying intervals into the main narrative. This, we recognize, is a form of interlaced narrative. Its use in the *Roman de Troie* is not at all systematic; it appears to result from the desire to relieve the monotony of the main narrative line. Elsewhere in Benoît's romance the narrative technique is simply a straightforward episodic sequence.

At any rate, Boccaccio discards all the intervening matter of the Trojan War and concentrates his narrative on the love of Troilus and

---

[48] *Cf.* particularly Karl Young, *The Origin and Development of the Story of Troilus and Criseyde* (Oxford, 1908); see also N. E. Griffin's introduction to the *Filostrato of Giovanni Boccaccio* (Philadelphia, 1929).

Griseide, pulling the nine narrative patches together into one continuous story. But he also amplifies his original by a little more than
four times. His primary contribution to the story is a fully developed
expository beginning. Benoît had begun the story when Troilus and
Griseida were already in love and the exchange of prisoners was about
to take place to separate the two. Boccaccio chose to tell at length how
the two came to be lovers, and for this purpose he invents Pandaro,
Griseida's brother and Troilus' friend, who serves as go-between for
them. It must have seemed to Boccaccio that the story gained considerably in depth when the treachery of Griseida was understood against
the background of her enamourment. Thus the story emerged with a
legitimate beginning – the courtship and conquest of the girl – pro-
gressed to a crisis – her betrayal of her lover – and finally to the end –
the death of Troilus.

When Chaucer took over the story, he amplified the beginning still
more, developing and shading the main characters, especially Pan-
darus. The result was that this story, which originally began as a narrative *hors-d'oeuvre* woven loosely into the fabric of the *Roman de
Troie*, and which originally was no more than 1300 lines in length, was
amplified to 5470 lines by Boccaccio and to 8239 by Chaucer. This
development is symptomatic of a shift toward unity through the reduction of interlaced narrative. It is the product of analysis, of pullling
out one strand from an elaborately diversified fabric and working it
into a full and complete narrative by expanding it backwards, by
developing the initial situation from which the rest arises.

The same tendency toward analysis can be seen elsewhere in Italian
literature. One of the earliest collections of short stories in Italian, the
Conti di antichi cavalieri, contains a "Conto di Brunor e di Galeotto
suo figlio", a story of the youth and early career of Galhaut, and how
he came to be associated with Lancelot and Tristan. The story was
apparently unravelled from the more complex narrative materials of
the Vulgate Cycle and the prose *Tristan*.[49]

Other Arthurian *novelle*, separated out from the complex tissue of
interlaced narrative occur in the *Cento novelle antichi*, a late thirteenth-
century collection of stories. The story of King Meliadus and the
Knight without Fear, the moonlight meeting of Tristan and Iseut in
which Mark spies on the lovers and is deceived by what he overhears,
and several stories about Lancelot are all of this same general char-

---

[49] See Edmund Gardner, *The Arthurian Legend in Italian Literature* (New York,
1930), pp. 85-88.

acter. The best example of the technique, however, is the story, retold from the *Mort Artu*, the last romance in the Vulgate cycle, of the death of the fair maid of Astolat: "Come la damigella di Scalot morí per amore di Lancelotto del Lac".[50]

The story, in the French source, is broken up into five sections, and is intimately bound up with Lancelot's relation with Guenevere and Arthur. Lancelot goes incognito to a tournament and stops at the castle of Escalot, where he rather foolishly promises to wear at the tournament a red sleeve belonging to Escalot's daughter, who has fallen in love with him. Arthur penetrates his disguise at the tournament, which allays his suspicions that Lancelot might have stayed behind at Camelot to be with the Queen. But when Guenevere hears Gawain and Arthur talking of the red sleeve, she immediately assumes that Lancelot has betrayed her, and she sends him away from her. Not long afterward, she is accused of murder and Lancelot is not there to defend her. At this point the body of the maid of Escalot floats to court with a letter explaining that her death was due to Lancelot's refusing to grant her his love. Guenevere now realizes that Lancelot had been true to her all along. The story of the maid of Escalot thus functions essentially to provide complications. But in the *Cento novelle antichi*, as well as in Malory, the story is disentangled from that complex web and told as a story in itself. The Italian version is very short; it has been called by W. P. Ker "one of the beautiful small things in medieval art":[51]

A daughter of a great baron loved Lancelot of the Lake beyond measure. But he would not give her his love, because he had given it to Queen Guenevere. So much did she love Lancelot that she came to death therefrom. And she bade that when her soul should be parted from her body, a rich barget should be arrayed, covered with red samite, with a rich bed therein, with rich and noble coverings of silk, adorned with rich precious stones, and that her body should be put in that bed, clad in her noblest clothes, and with a fair crown upon her head, rich with much gold and with many precious stones, and with a girdle and purse. In that purse was a letter, of which the intent is written below. The damsel died of the sickness of love, and it was done with her as she had said. The barget, without sails or oars, was set upon the sea with the lady. The sea guided it down to Camelot, and it stayed at the shore. The tidings went through the court. Knights and barons went down from the palaces. And the noble King Arthur came thither, and wondered much that it had come there without any guide. The King entered; he saw the damsel and the array. He had the purse opened. They found the

---

[50] On the stories mentioned above, see Gardner, *Arthurian Legend*, pp. 88-93.
[51] Text from Gardner, pp. 93-94.

letter. He had it read, and it said thus: "To all the knights of the Round
Table, the maiden of Astolat sends greetings as to the best folk of the world.
And if you would know for what I come to my end, it is for the best
knight of the world and for the most churlish (*villano*); to wit, my lord Sir
Lancelot of the Lake, whom in sooth I knew not how to beg for love so that
he might have pity on me. And so, woe's me, I have died through loving
well, as ye can see."

Sir Thomas Malory tells the story in considerably more detail,[52] but
the principle of analysis is the same. The story is disentangled from the
total frame of the French romance in such a way as to constitute in
itself a complete and autonomous narrative.

Malory, in fact, provides the clearest example of this literary phenomenon, the movement from diversity back to unity. His main sources,
the *Suite du Merlin*, the prose *Tristan*, and the Vulgate cycle, were
all apparently too complicated and verbose for his taste. He systematically disentangled his various romances, collecting the various stretches
of any given thread so as to reduce interlacing to a minimum. He
realized that to perform such an operation on the *Quest of the Holy
Grail* would be foolish. To remove the story of Galahad and tell it as
a single romance would have destroyed its meaning. And so he left it
structurally the same as he found it, contenting himself with a brutal
reduction of the symbolic and allegorical commentary that made the
Old French text more a didactic than a narrative work. But in general
he adhered with great consistency to the principle of 'singleness'.

For example, his *Noble Tale of Sir Launcelot* consists of three
carefully chosen short episodes which in the French prose Lancelot are
hundreds of pages apart. Discarding all the intervening matter, Malory
makes these episodes into one tale. His handling, however, of the story
of Balin, the Knight with Two Swords, is even more significant. The
French version, which appears in the *Huth Merlin*, or *Suite du Merlin*,
a fragment of a post-Vulgate Grail romance, is essentially an explanatory amplification inserted into the story of Arthur's early reign in
order to prepare the theme of the Maimed King and the Blighted Land,
mysterious elements of the story originating in Chrétien's *Perceval* and
carried into the Vulgate cycle without much in the way of elaboration
or explanation. The writer of the *Huth Merlin* went to the trouble of
composing an extended romance about an unlucky knight, Sir Balain,
who brings misfortune to all those he tries to help. His friends and
companions are struck down one after another by an invisible knight,

[52]   Vinaver's edition, III, 1039-98.

whom he finally tracks down and kills, for he is only invisible when
he rides. The knight's brother, however, is King Pellehan, and when
he sees his brother dead, he attacks Balain. Balain's sword breaks in
the middle of the combat and he makes the terrible mistake of rushing
into a nearby room and picking up a sacred sword. He smites King
Pellehan with it, the King falls maimed, and the castle collapses,
crushing most of its inhabitants. When Balain rides out he sees that
the land has been laid waste, and all because of the Dolorous Stroke.
And thus, of course, there had to be a Grail and a Sir Galahad to
restore King and land back to health. Balain goes on from there to his
luckless end: he and his brother, failing to recognize one another, enter
into a combat in which both receive mortal wounds.

The purpose of this story is apparently to set up a sequence of
episodes, all of which by their constant theme of unforeseen misfortune,
will give an appearance of design to the Dolorous Stroke when it
finally occurs. After that, the only problem is to get rid of Balain himself so that other matters may be taken up.

Malory, in handling this same story, shifts the emphasis significantly.
The story of the Dolorous Stroke is more clearly presented. It is given
a beginning and an end.

As for the beginning, the French romance and Malory agree that
early on his way Balain was challenged by an Irish knight, Sir Launceor,
whom he killed. Then the knights beloved appears, sees the dead body
and runs herself through with his sword. Merlin appears and asks who
is responsible for the two deaths. Balain answers, explaining that he
slew the knight, but that he had not time to prevent the lady from
killing herself. At this point there is a serious divergence in detail. In
the French text, Merlin simply says:

Tu ne seras mie si lens, fait Merlins, comme tu fus chi, quant tu ferras le
dolereus cop par coi troi roiame en seront a povreté et en essil vint et deus
ans.[53]

This is a simple prediction. It is not apparently connected with the
incident in question. However, when Malory treats the same material,
he writes:

"Me repentis hit," seyde Merlion, "because of the dethe of that lady thou
shalt stryke a stroke moste dolerous that ever man stroke, excepte the stroke
of oure Lorde Jesu Cryste. For thou shalt hurt the trewyst knyght and the
man of moste worship that now lyvith; and thorow that stroke, three kyng-

---

[53] *Le Roman de Balain*, ed. D. M. Legge, p. 25.

domys shall be brought into grete povrete, miseri and wreccednesse twelve
yerys. And the knyght shall nat be hole of that wounde many yerys." Then
Merlion toke his leve.[54]

Malory has thus picked on this particular incident as a cause for the
Dolorous Stroke. The reason he chose this incident rather than another
is simply that Merlin's prediction of the Dolorous Stroke appears in
the French text at this point. And so by juxtaposition, and a form of
post hoc ergo propter hoc reasoning, Malory assumed or invented this
detail. The Dolorous Stroke now appears as the result of an event within the Balain story itself, having no connection with anything outside
the story. The circle is completed when we come to the episode of the
Stroke itself. Here the French text makes no mention whatever of
Galahad and of the future quest for the Grail. Nor is it by any means
clear why that sacred sword should have caused so much trouble.
Malory, on the other hand, ties all the threads together. We need not
wait until we read the *Quest of the Holy Grail* to understand what all
this preparation is about:

And King Pellam lay so many yerys sore wounded, and and myght never be
hole tylle that Galaad the Hawte Prynce heled hym in the quest of the Sank-
greall. For in that place was parte of the bloode of oure Lorde Jesu Cryste,
which Joseph off Aramathy brought into thys londe. And there hymselff lay
in that ryche bedde. And that was the spere whych Longeus smote oure
Lorde with to the herte. And King Pellam was nyghe of Joseph his kynne,
and that was the most worshipfullest man on lyve in tho dayes, and grete
pite hit was of hys hurte, for thorow that stroke hit turned to grete dole,
tray and tene.[55]

The changes involved in these two cases are simple enough. But
what they indicate about the way Malory's artistic mind worked in
adapting his material is very far-reaching. Malory's intent is clearly to
make the story of Balin a completely self-contained thing, depending on
nothing outside the story itself. He was not writing one long romance
in the style of the French writers, preparing hundreds of pages in
advance for events the writers knew would be there because they had in
fact already read the end and were simply expanding the story backwards by adding explanatory material. On the contrary, Malory was
writing a series of independent stories, whose presentation as one
continuous romance was due entirely to Caxton, who systematically
took out the *explicits* at the ends of the various stories, and left only

[54]   Malory, I, 73.
[55]   *Ibid.*, 85-86.

the last, which is why the compilation appeared with the title *Le Morte Darthur*. The final *explicit*, "Here is the end of the *Deth of Arthur*" originally referred, of course, only to the last of the romances. Caxton's revision, "Here endeth this noble and joyous book entitled *Le Morte Darthur*", was an attempt to make the last *explicit* refer to the whole book.

Vinaver feels that Malory's work thus stands as the starting point in modern fiction. I should move the starting point a bit further back, to Boccaccio's *Filostrato*, for the same process is clearly in evidence there. The whole development, beginning with crude and simply told stories in the early Middle Ages, gradually becoming transformed into longer and more complex structures, both by rhetorical and material amplifications, finally reaches a point of unwieldly complexity in the chivalric romances, and a compensatory movement of analysis begins to operate. By a process of differentiation into coherent units, now long enough to stand alone as pieces of autonomous fiction, the cyclic romances begin to assume the form of the short novel. It is not, however, until Tasso's definitive attack on the medieval form that well-made narrative acquired a theoretical basis which eventually developed into a system of rules.

CONCLUSION

The structural style of medieval narrative may be said to have developed through three major phases. In the first, simple stories – such as we see in the first part of Chrétien's *Erec* and the first part of the *Chanson de Roland* – became compound. The impulse to amplify narrative, to give it fullness and magnitude, appears to have been the most important determining factor in this development. But while the minor writers allowed their stories to become diffuse *romans à tiroirs*, the more gifted ones controlled the process of expansion by their compensatory concern with symmetry and design. The basic structural pattern they chose to confer on their compound stories was bipartite, a tendency we can see as early as *Beowulf* and in the eleventh-century *Vie de Saint Alexis*.

The second phase is a passage from the compound to the complex. Again the impulse to amplify appears to have determined the direction of the development, but in this case the compensatory control is managed in good writers through a systematic use of narrative interlacing. We can see early indications of this technique in the late romances of Chrétien de Troyes, but the movement reaches its fullest development in the thirteenth-century prose *Lancelot*, which, for all its length, is yet an intricately constructed work, one less characterized by disunity than by a controlled multiplicity.

The third and final phase is a movement from complexity back to simplicity. We see it especially in Boccaccio's *Filostrato* and in Malory's Arthurian tales. In both cases, the writers composed according to a principle of analysis, disengaging coherent units of narrative from the complex web in which they had been enmeshed. The structural implications of this final phase ultimately find their theoretical formulation in Tasso's *Discorsi del poema eroico*.

However, as Tasso learned, and as the subsequent history of narrative fiction clearly shows, it is one thing to devise a general theory for the structure of narrative, but quite another to put it satisfactorily into practice. In Tasso's case, it was perhaps fortunate that his genius did not lend itself to the creation of the sort of heroic poem he was able to describe so well. His masterpiece, the *Gerusalemme liberata*, while considerably less diffuse and complex than the *Orlando furioso*, is in fact strikingly similar to it in its structural outline. There are three interwoven actions: first the epic action, the war of the crusaders led by Goffredo against the pagans; second, the love and subsequent hatred of the pagan enchantress Armida for the Christian hero Rinaldo d'Este, in the course of which she transports the spellbound Rinaldo to her bower in the Fortunate Isles, thus putting the victory of the Christians in jeopardy; third, the parallel but unconnected love story of another Christian hero, Tancredo, and the pagan damsel and warrior Clorinda, whom he unwittingly slays in combat.

By Tasso's own standards, this was no 'proper' epic. It was neither very edifying nor of unified construction. He hastily provided the poem with a moral allegory to satisfy the ecclesiastical censors, and he worked from 1587 to 1592 to convert it into a correct classical epic. This revised version, entitled *Gerusalemme conquistata*, the only one which in later years he was to acknowledge, was a stiff and lifeless thing in comparison with the original work, whose existence in print we owe to the Promethean thefts of Malespini and Ingegneri, who printed pirated texts of it in 1580 and 1581.

Some time before 1580, Edmund Spenser in England had begun to work on the *Faerie Queene*. Although Spenser was obviously and admittedly influenced by the Italians, the controversies on the question of narrative structure seem not to have deterred him in the least from organizing his poem in the late medieval manner. According to Spenser's preliminary remarks, the whole poem was to consist of twelve books, each having a separate hero representing one of the twelve Aristotelian virtues. Six books were completed. In these we can see at least two distinct but familiar structural patterns, both of which belong to the Middle Ages.

The first two books, which relate respectively the adventures of the Redcrosse Knight and those of Sir Guyon, are similar in structure: there is a single biographical line, although some interlacing occurs in Book I when Redcrosse is separated from Una and their adventures are recounted separately; there also appear in both books some of the standard features of bipartite romance. In both, for example, the central personage passes with moderate success through a series of adventures; then at the end of the seventh canto he is struck down, Redcrosse by Orgoglio, Guyon in consequence of his ordeal in the cave of Mammon. In both cases Prince Arthur intervenes to rescue the hero, who then undergoes a program of moral rehabilitation, Redcrosse in the House of Holinesse, where he learns repentance, Guyon in the House of Temperance, where he appears to regain his strength by reading a history book, the *Antiquitee of Faery Lond*. Each of them then goes on to complete his quest in the twelfth and final canto: Redcrosse kills the dragon and marries Una; Guyon destroys the Bower of Blisse. The general similarity of these books to Chrétien's *Erec* and *Yvain*, with their overall pattern of success, shame, and rehabilitation, is not likely to be entirely fortuitous.

Spenser manages the transition from Book I to Book II by a form of interlacing. In the first canto of Book II, Redcrosse, having completed his quest, is returning to Gloriana's court. His old enemy Archimago tries in vain to lead him astray. When Archimago happens across the path of Sir Guyon, just starting off on his quest, he invents a long story about the rape of a fair virgin by a knight who bears a red cross on his shield. Guyon is doubtful, but Archimago's accomplice, Duessa, plays so well the part of the ravished virgin that Guyon resolves to attack Redcrosse on sight. But when the time comes, the emblem of Redcrosse's shield stays his hand. The two talk for a while and straighten the matter out. Thereafter Spenser follows Guyon through the rest of the book. Again, at the beginning of the third book, Guyon, after destroying the Bower of Blisse, goes off to "make more triall of his hardiment" (III, i, 2). He then encounters Britomart, the knight of chastity and central character of the third book, who knocks him off his horse. When the second and third books have been threaded together in this way, Spenser turns to the adventures of Britomart.

However, in the third book, Spenser abandons the habit of following one central figure and begins systematically to interlace his story in the manner of Ariosto. He intertwines the affairs of several pairs of lovers – Britomart and Artegall, Marinell and Florimell, Timias and Belphoebe, Amoret and Scudamor – in an extended tapestry that also includes a full length novella, the story of Malbecco (cantos ix-x). He continues in this manner, carrying the same stories forward, all through Book IV, into which are introduced in a merely peripheral way the nominally central figures of Cambel and Triamond, the Knights of Friendship.

In the fifth and sixth books, Spenser returns to the biographic

structural pattern of the first two books, although there is a good deal
of interlacing in the sixth. The concluding section, a pastoral romance
centering upon Calidore and Pastorella shows clearly the influence of
late Greek romance, a thoroughly non-Aristotelian genre.

In undertaking the enormous task of writing the *Faerie Queene*,
Spenser was certainly aware of the tenor of the Italian controversies,
even though Tasso's work had not yet been published. We have as
witness Gabriel Harvey's letter to Spenser, printed in 1580, in which
Harvey loftily declines to accord more than a disdainful glance at
Spenser's major effort, which he finds more homespun than classical:

But I will not stand greatly with you in your own matters. If so be the Faery
Queene be fairer in your eie than the Nine Muses, and Hobgoblin runne
away with the garland of Apollo, marke what I say: and yet I will not say
that I thought, but there an end for this once, and fare you well, till God or
some good angell put you in a better mind.[1]

What is a little more surprising than Spenser's preference for
medieval narrative forms is that fact that even Milton, classicist though
he was, appears to have been in some doubt as to whether his major
work should take the form of a classical epic or an Arthurian romance.
This, at any rate, is usually taken to be the import of the well-known
passage in the preface to the second book of his *Reason of Church
Government Urged against Prelaty* (1642):

Time serves not now, and perhaps I might seem too profuse to give any
certain account of what the mind at home in the spacious circuits of her
musing hath liberty to promise to herself, though of highest hope and hardest
attempting; whether that epic form whereof the two poems of Homer and
those other two of Virgil and Tasso are a diffuse, and the book of Job a
brief, model: or whether the rules of Aristotle herein are strictly to be kept,
or nature to be followed, which in them that know art and use judgment is
no transgression but an enriching of art: and lastly, what king or knight before the conquest might be chosen in whom to lay the pattern of the Christian hero.[2]

Milton's opposition of nature to the rules of Aristotle is not without
its ambiguities, but it would appear that he saw the matter in a
common-sense way. Of all the epics of the sixteenth and seventeenth
centuries, Milton's is the only one that is both a successful poem and
reasonably 'correct' in its structure. Before it, the only successful epics

---

[1] *The Complete Poetical Works of Spenser*, ed. R. E. Neil Dodge (Boston, 1908),
p. 773.
[2] *John Milton: Prose Selections*, ed. Merritt Y. Hughes, 2nd ed. (New York,
1947), p. 105.

had been the 'irregular' works of Ariosto, Tasso, and Spenser. The correct imitative epics had all been failures. Not much later than Milton's tract on church government, in the fifteen years between 1650 and 1665, there were produced in France alone no fewer than ten imitation classical epics, the most noteworthy failures of which were Scudéry's *Alaric*, Lemoyne's *Saint Louis*, and Chapelain's long awaited epic on Joan of Arc, *La Pucelle*, which upon publication was damned by Boileau and consigned to oblivion.[3]

Milton's epic is perhaps not entirely regular. There are examples of interlacing: the scene shifts from Hell to Earth and Heaven and back again; but in general Milton managed with admirable consistency to relate everything to his announced subject, the Fall of Man. The most serious structural flaw in *Paradise Lost* is not so much a question of unity as one of proportion: the last two books present a dense lump of history, the story of mankind from the Fall to the Last Judgment. Here, of course, Milton is imitating Virgil, passing from the relatively brief action that forms the core of his epic to its further consequences in subsequent history. But the matter is disproportionately heavy, and coming at the end, as it does, it has been found distressing by many critics.

Apart from Milton, then, I think we may say that the promulgation and application of Aristotle's principles of narrative structure accomplished little in the way of making possible the production of a great modern epic. The happiest application of the Aristotelian rules of structure was perhaps in the dramatic genre. French literature itself knew its greatest period of dramatic creation at a time when the rules were taken in their most absolute form. With slight modifications now and then, these same rules have persisted down to modern times, and their influence has been generally salubrious.

Although it is not part of my study, it may be of some interest for purposes of continuity to cast a brief glance at the highly complex question of the application of the rules of well-made narrative to the novel, or *roman*, the descendant of medieval romance. During the neo-classical period, the *roman* suffered from its lack of standing as a classical genre. As Giraldi and others had argued, the romance was a genre unknown to Aristotle and therefore not subject to his rules. Giraldi had not meant to imply that it was therefore a less legitimate genre than the epic and the drama, but it seems to have been under-

---

[3] See J. Duchesne, *Histoire des poèmes épiques français du XVIIe siècle* (Paris, 1870).

stood in this way, particularly in France, through most of the seventeenth and eighteenth centuries. The romance fell into disrepute and came to be considered an amusing genre for ladies of leisure, a genre characterized by total lawlessness and extravagant length. Honoré d'Urfé's *L'Astrée* endlessly interlaces the stories of seven pairs of lovers in a make-believe world that derives from Italian pastoral through the *Diana enamorada* of Montemayor. Other interminable pastoral and historical romances – *Clélie, Le Grand Cyrus, Cléopâtre* – in spite of their enormous popularity, never attained genuine literary status.

The passage from frivolous romance to serious and well constructed novel appears to be inextricably tied into the problem of the development of realism in fiction. Von Grimmelhausen's *Simplicissimus* (1669), Lesage's *Gil Blas* (1715), and Fielding's *Tom Jones* (1749) were all under the influence of the Spanish picaresque novel, and structurally speaking, were hardly more than *romans à tiroirs*. These works introduced a strong realistic tone into the writing of fiction, without, however, taking on the rigid narrative structure of epic and drama, and also without becoming particularly serious. It would appear that only after the French Revolution, when it became possible to treat the realistic and the bourgeois with the high seriousness previously accorded only to the idealization of the high nobility, was it possible to bring to the novel some of the structural regularity of epic and drama. Thus it is essentially in Stendhal and Balzac that we begin to find the consistent, though by no means universal, application of the Aristotelian rules to the novel. Up to and even beyond the writing of *Madame Bovary*, the long novel thus took on the form of the well-made story. This tendency was formulated by Poe in his review of Hawthorne's *Twice Told Tales*, an essay in which he repeats what Tasso had already formulated centuries earlier.

Isolated examples of the well-made novel before the Revolution will occur to everyone. *La Princesse de Clèves* (1678), by Madame de Lafayette, is probably the earliest example. Prévost's *Manon Lescaut* (1728), Diderot's *La Religieuse* (1760), and Goethe's *Die Leiden des jungen Werthers* (1774) are all reasonably clear cases. But a consistent habit of logical and unified construction is not at all typical of the 'novels' of the seventeenth and eighteenth centuries.

It is equally possible to cite examples of great and serious narrative after the French Revolution whose construction is anything but Aristotelian. The reasons for this are profound and complex, but hardly inaccessible. To simplify greatly, it would appear that the Naturalists found the habit of writing well-made stories too artificial a procedure adequately to represent reality. It had become impossible to reconcile reality with an overly logical view of structure. The further introduction of the irrational element in human behavior, following upon the work of Freud, made it even more difficult to construct stories on the principle of logical motivation. Thereafter the 'correct' novel seemed to serious writers to be a falsification of reality – rich, complex, often absurd, seldom, if ever, reducible to simple mechanics. And so, with the passage of time, we have returned to a structural disorder that is not without its analogies to the narrative works of the Middle Ages. The wheel has come full circle.

BIBLIOGRAPHY

A. ABBREVIATIONS

ALMA   *Arthurian Literature in the Middle Ages: A Collaborative History,*
          ed. Roger Sherman Loomis. (Oxford, 1959).
AR   *Archivum Romanicum.*
CFMA   *Classiques Français du Moyen Age.*
DV   *Deutsche Vierteljahrsschrift für Literaturwissenschaft und Geistes-*
          geschichte.
GRM   *Germanisch-Romanisch Monatsschrift.*
MLN   *Modern Language Notes.*
MLQ   *Modern Language Quarterly.*
MLR   *Modern Language Review.*
MPh   *Modern Philology.*
PBB   *Beiträge zur Geschichte der deutschen Sprache und Literatur (Paul/*
          Braunes Beiträge).
PMLA   *Publications of the Modern Language Association.*
R   *Romania.*
RF   *Romanische Forschungen.*
RG   *Les Romans du Graal aux XIIe et XIIIe siècles.* Colloques Inter-
          nationaux du Centre National de la Recherche Scientifique, III
          (Paris, 1956).
RPh   *Romance Philology.*
RR   *Romanic Review.*
SATF   *Société des Anciens Textes Français.*
SPh   *Studies in Philology.*
ZdA   *Zeitschrift für deutschen Altertum.*
ZFSL   *Zeitschrift für französische Sprache und Literatur.*
ZRPh   *Zeitschrift für deutsches Altertum.*

B. BIBLIOGRAPHICAL REFERENCES

Baldensperger, F. and W. Friedrich, *Bibliography of Comparative Literature*
    (Chapel Hill, 1950).
Bateson, F. W., *Cambridge Bibliography of English Literature*, Vol. I (New York,
    1941).
Bossuat, R., *Manuel bibliographique de la littérature française du moyen âge*
    (Melun, 1951, supplements, 1955, 1961).

Cabeen, D. C., *A Critical Bibliography of French Literature*, Vol. I, *The Medieval Period*, ed. U. T. Holmes, Jr., 2nd ed. (Syracuse, 1952).
Eppelsheimer, H. W., *Bibliographie des deutschen Literaturwissenschaft* (Frankfurt a/M, 1945-53, 1957-).
Klapp, O., *Bibliographie der französischen Literaturwissenschaft* (Band I: 1956-58; II: 1959-60; III: 1961-62; IV: 1963-64; V: 1965-66; VI: 1967-68; VII: 1969).
Palfrey, T. R., *et al.*, *A Bibliographical Guide to the Romance Languages and Literatures*, 4th ed. (Evanston, 1951).
Bulletin bibliographique de la société internationale arthurienne (published yearly at Paris since 1949).
Jahresbericht über die Erscheinungen auf dem Gebiet der germanischen Philologie (1877-1939; 1954-).
Modern Language Quarterly. Annual Arthurian Bibliography (June issue).
Publications of the Modern Language Association of America. Annual Bibliography; since 1956 has been international in scope.
Zeitschrift für romanische Philologie: Bibliographische Supplementehefte (1875-1964).

C. TEXTS CITED

Aliscans, eds. E. Weinbeck, W. Hartnacke, P. Rasche (Halle, 1903).
Altprovenzalische Chrestomathie, ed. C. Appel, 6th ed. (Leipzig, 1930).
Ariosto, L., *Orlando furioso*, ed. S. Debenedetti (Bari, 1928).
Arts poétiques du XIIe et du XIIIe siècles (Les), ed. E. Faral (Paris, 1923).
Beowulf and the Fight at Finnsburg, ed. Fr. Klaeber, 3rd ed. (Boston, 1950). Ed. E. V. K. Dobbie (New York, 1953). Trans. into modern English by J. R. Clark Hall, Rev. ed. (London, 1950).
Béroul, *Le Roman de Tristan*, ed. E. Muret, 4th ed., rev. by L. M. Defourques (Paris, 1947 [*CFMA*]).
Biographies des troubadours, eds. J. Boutière and A.-H. Schutz (Toulouse, 1950).
Boiardo, M. M., *Orlando innamorato*, ed. A. Zottoli (Milan, 1936).
Chanson de Guillaume (La), ed. D. McMillan, 2 vols. (Paris, 1949-1950 [*SATF*]).
Chanson de Roland (La), ed. J. Bédier, 2 vols., I, Text and Translation (Paris, 1922); Commentary (Paris, 1927). Ed. A. Hilka, *Das altfranzösische Rolandslied*, 3rd ed. (Halle, 1948).
Chevalerie Vivien (La), ed. A. L. Terracher (Paris, 1923).
Chrestomathie de l'ancien français, ed. K. Bartsch, 12th ed. (Leipzig, 1927).
Chrétien de Troyes, *Romans, édités d'après la copie de Guiot (Bibl. nat. fr. 794)*. I: *Erec et Enide*, ed. M. Roques (Paris, 1956). II: *Cligés*, ed. A. Micha (1957). III: *Le Chevalier de la Charrete*, ed. M. Roques (1958). IV: *Le Chevalier au lion*, ed. M. Roques (1960).
——, *Li Contes del Graal*, ed. G. Baist (Freiburg, 1909).
——, *Guillaume d'Angleterre*, ed. M. Wilmotte (Paris, 1927 [*CFMA*]).
——, *Philomena*, ed. C. DeBoer (Paris, 1909).
——, *Le Roman de Perceval*, ed. W. Roach (Geneva, 1956).
[Cicero]. *Ad C. Herennium: De ratione dicendi (Rhetorica ad Herennium)*, Eng. trans. by M. Caplan (Cambridge, Mass., 1954 [Loeb Classical Library]).
Couronnement Louis (Le), ed. E. Langlois, 2nd ed. (Paris, 1925 [*CFMA*]).
Du Bellay, J., *La Deffence et Illustration de la langue françoise*, ed. H. Chamard (Paris, 1904).
Enéas: Roman du XIIe siècle, ed. J.-J. Salverda de Grave, 2 vols. (Paris, 1929 [*CFMA*]).

Giraldi Cintio, G. B. *Scritti estetici: De' romanzi, delle commedie, delle tragedie, ecc.*, 2 vols. (Milan, 1864).
Girard de Vienne, ed. F. Yeandle (New York, 1930).
Jakemon, *Le Roman du Castelain de Couci et la dame de Fayel*, eds. M. Delbouille and J. Matzke (Paris, 1936 [*SATF*]).
Malory, Sir Thomas, *Works*, ed. E. Vinaver, 3 vols. (Oxford, 1947).
Merlin: Roman en prose du XIIIe siècle (Huth), eds. G. Paris and J. Ulrich, 2 vols. (Paris, 1886 [*SATF*]).
Mort le Roi Artu (La): Roman en prose du XIIIe siècle, ed. J. Frappier (Paris, 1936).
Nibelungenlied, ed. K. Bartsch (Leipzig, 1870, 1880).
Peletier du Mans, J., *Art poëtique*, ed. A. Boulanger (Publications de la Faculté des lettres de l'Université de Strasbourg, LIII, 1930).
Queste del Saint Graal (La), ed. A. Pauphilet (Paris, 1923).
Raoul de Cambrai, eds. P. Meyer and A. Longnon (Paris, 1882 [*SATF*]).
Roman de Balain (Le), ed. M. D. Legge, introd. E. Vinaver (Manchester, 1942).
Roman de Renart (Le), ed. E. Martin, 3 vols. (Strasbourg, 1882-87). Ed. M. Roques (Paris, 1948- [*CFMA*]). I: Br. I (1948). II: Br. II-VI (1951). III: Br. VII-X (1955). IV: Br. X-XI (1958). V: Br. XII-XVII (1960).
Roman de vrai amour (Le) and *Le Pleur de saint âme*, ed. A. Bates (Ann Arbor, 1958).
Rudel, J., *Chansons*, ed. A. Jeanroy, 2nd ed. (Paris, 1924 [*CFMA*]).
Tasso, T. *Prose*, ed. E. Mazzali (La letteratura italiana: storia e testi, XXII) (Milan, 1959).
Thomas, *Le Roman de Tristan*, ed. J. Bédier, 2 vols. (Paris, 1902-1905 [*SATF*]).
Vie de Saint Alexis (La), eds. G. Paris and L. Pannier (Paris, 1887); ed. J.-M. Meunier (Paris, 1933).
Vulgate Version of Arthurian Romances, ed. H. Sommer, 8 vols. (Washington, 1908-16).

D. SECONDARY WORKS

Auerbach, E., *Mimesis*, trans. W. Trask (Princeton, 1953). German edition (1946).
——, Review of A. Fierz Monnier, *Initiation und Wandlung*, in *RR*, XLIII (1952), 208-210.
Bédier, J., *Les Légendes épiques: Recherches sur la formation des chansons de geste*, 4 vols. (Paris, 1908-13); 3rd edition (1926-29).
Bentley, R., *The Works of Richard Bentley*, ed. A. Dyce, 3 vols. (London, 1836-38).
Bethurum, D. (ed.), *Critical Approaches to Medieval Literature* (New York, 1960).
Bezzola, R. R., *Le sens de l'aventure et de l'amour: Chrétien de Troyes* (Paris, 1947).
Bloomfield, M., "Symbolism in Medieval Literature", *MPh*, LVI (1958), 73-81.
Bossuat, R., *Le Roman de Renard* (Paris, 1957).
Brodeur, A. G., *The Art of Beowulf* (Berkeley, 1959).
Bowra, C. M., *Heroic Poetry* (London, 1952).
Bruce, J. D., "The Composition of the Old French Prose Lancelot", *RR*, IX (1918), 241-268, 353-395.
Bumke, J., Review of H. Eggers, *Symmetrie und Proportion epischen Erzählens*, in *Euphorion*, LI (1957), 222-227.
Casella, M., *Il Chisciotte*, 2 vols. (Florence, 1938).
Chambers, R. W., *Man's Unconquerable Mind* (London, 1930).
Cottaz, J., *Le Tasse et la conception épique* (Paris, 1942).
Crosby, R., "Oral Delivery in the Middle Ages", *Speculum*, XI (1936), 88-110.

Curtius, E., *European Literature and the Latin Middle Ages* (New York, 1953). German ed. (1948).
——, "Zur Interpretation des Alexiusliedes", *ZRPh*, LVI (1936), 113-137.
De Boor and R. Newald, *Geschichte der deutschen Literatur von den Anfängen bis zur Gegenwart*, Vols. I-II (Munich, 1955).
Delbouille, M., *Sur la genèse de la Chanson de Roland* (Brussels, 1954).
——, "Le Système des Incidences", *Revue Belge de Philologie et d'Histoire*, VI (1927), 617-641.
Delehaye, M., *Les Légendes hagiographiques* (Brussels, 1927).
De Riquer, M., "La composición de 'Li Contes del Graal' y el Guiromelant", *Boletín de la Real Academia de Buenas Letras de Barcelona*, XXVII (1957-58), 279-320.
Duchesne, J., *Histoire des poèmes épiques français au XVIIe siècle* (Paris, 1870).
Dubs, I., *Galeran de Bretagne: Die Krise im französischen höfischen Roman* (Bern, 1951).
Eggers, H., *Symmetrie und Proportion epischen Erzählens* (Klett, 1956).
Emmel, H., *Formprobleme des Artusromans und der Graldichtung* (Bern, 1951).
Faral, E., *La Chanson de Roland: Etude et analyse* (Paris, 1934).
Fierz-Monnier, A., *Initiation und Wandlung* (Bern, 1951).
Fourquet, J., "Littérature courtoise et théologique", *Etudes Germaniques*, XII (1957), 35-39.
——, "La Structure du Parzival", *RG*, 189-213.
Frappier, J., *Les Chansons de geste du cycle de Guillaume d'Orange* (Paris, 1955).
——, *Chrétien de Troyes, l'homme et l'œuvre* (Paris, 1957).
——, "Sur la Composition du *Conte del Graal*", *Moyen Age*, LXIV (1958), 67-102.
——, "The Vulgate Cycle", *ALMA*, 295-318.
Frey, D., *Gotik und Renaissance als Grundlagen der modernen Weltanschauung* (Augsburg, 1929).
Gardner, E., *The Arthurian Legend in Italian Literature* (London, 1930).
Gautier, L., *Les Epopées françaises*, 4 vols., 2nd ed. (Paris, 1878-92).
Gilson, E., "La Mystique de la grâce dans *La Queste del Saint Graal*", *R*, LI (1925), 321-327.
Hart, M. W., "The Narrative Art of the Fabliaux", *Anniversary Papers to George Lyman Kittredge* (Boston, 1913), 209-216.
——, "Narrative Techniques of Fabliau and Prose Tale", *PMLA*, XXIII (1908), 329-374.
Hatcher, A. G., "The Old French Poem Saint Alexis: A Mathematical Demonstration", *Traditio*, VIII (1952), 111-158.
Hatzfeld, H., "Esthetic Criticism Applied to Medieval Literature", *RPh*, I (1947-48), 305-327.
Heusler, A., *Nibelungensaga und Nibelungenlied* (Dortmund, 1922).
Hoepffner, E., "Matière et sens dans le roman d'*Erec et Enide*", *AR*, XVIII (1934), 433-450.
Hofer, S., *Chrétien de Troyes: Leben und Werke des altfranzösischen Epikers* (Graz-Koln, 1954).
——, "La Structure du Conte del Graal examinée à la lumière de l'œuvre de Chrétien de Troyes", *RG*, 15-16.
Huizinga, J., *The Waning of the Middle Ages* (London, 1924).
Hytier, J., "La Méthode de M. Leo Spitzer", *RR*, XLI (1950), 42-59.
Hurd, R., *Letters on Chivalry and Romance*, in *The Works of Richard Hurd* (London, 1811).
Jackson, W. T. H., *The Literature of the Middle Ages* (New York, 1960).
Kellermann, W., *Aufbaustil und Weltbild Chrestiens von Troyes im Percevalroman*

(Beiheft zur *Zeitschrift für romanische Philologie*, LXXXVIII, 1936).

Lachmann, K., *Uber die ursprungliche Gestalt des Gedichtes von der Nibelungen Noth* (Berlin, 1816).

LeGentil, P., *La Chanson de Roland* (Paris, 1955).

Loomis, R. S., *Arthurian Tradition and Chrétien de Troyes* (New York, 1949).

—— (ed.), *Arthurian Literature in the Middle Ages* (Oxford, 1959).

Löseth, E., *Le Roman en prose de Tristan* (Paris, 1891).

Lot, F., *Etude sur le Lancelot en prose* (Paris, 1918).

Malone, K., *The Old English Period*, Vol. I of *A Literary History of England*, gen. ed. A. C. Baugh (New York, 1948).

Maurer, F., Review of B. Mergell, *Tristan und Isolde*, in *Archiv für das Studium der neueren Sprachen*, CLXXXVIII (1951), 131.

Menéndez Pidal, R., *La Chanson de Roland y el neotradicionalismo: Orígenes de la epica románica* (Madrid, 1959).

Mergell, B., *Tristan und Isolde* (Mainz, 1949).

Misrahi, J., Review of R. R. Bezzola, *Le sens de l'aventure*, in *RPh*, IV (1950-51), 348-361.

Müller, G., "Gradualismus", *DV*, II (1924), 681-720.

Novati, F., "Un nuovo e un vecchio frammento del Tristan di Tommasso", *Studi di filologia romanza*, II (1887), 369-514.

Paris, G., *Extraits de la Chanson de Roland* (Paris, 1887).

——, *Histoire poétique de Charlemagne* (Paris, 1865).

——, *Poémes et légendes du Moyen Age* (Paris, 1900).

Pauphilet, *Le Legs du moyen âge* (Melun, 1950).

——, *Etudes sur la Queste del Saint Graal* (Paris, 1921).

——, "Sur la Chanson de Roland", *R*, LIX (1933), 161-198.

Ranke, F., *Tristan und Isold* (Munich, 1925).

Robortelli, F., *In librum Aristotelis de Arte poetica explicationes* (Florentiae, 1548).

Rychner, J., *La Chanson de geste: Essai sur l'art épique des jongleurs* (Geneva, 1955).

Schutz, A.-H., "Were the *vidas* and *razos* recited?", *SPh*, XXIII (1939), 565-570.

Schwietering, J., *Die deutsche Dichtung des Mittelalters* (Potsdam, 1932).

Smalley, B., *The Study of the Bible in the Middle Ages* (Oxford, 1952).

Spingarn, J., *A History of Literary Criticism in the Renaissance*, 2nd ed. (New York, 1908).

Stronski, S., *La Légende amoureuse de Bertrand de Born* (Paris, 1914).

Thorp, M., *The Study of the Nibelungenlied* (Oxford, 1940).

——, "The Unity of the Nibelungenlied", *Journal of English and Germanic Philology*, XXXVI (1937), 475-480.

Titchener, F., "The Romances of Chrétien de Troyes", *RR*, XVI (1925), 165-173.

Tolkien, J. R. R., "Beowulf, the Monsters and the Critics", *Proceedings of the British Academy*, XXII (1936), 245-295.

Vinaver, E., "A la recherche d'une poétique médiévale", *Cahiers de Civilisation Médiévale*, II (1959), 1-16.

——, *Etudes sur le Tristan en Prose* (Paris, 1925).

——, "Sir Thomas Malory", *ALMA*, 541-552.

——, Introd. to *Le Roman de Balain*, ed. D. M. Legge (Manchester, 1942).

——, Introd. to *The Works of Sir Thomas Malory* (Oxford, 1947).

Weinberg, B., *A History of Literary Criticism in the Italian Renaissance* (Chicago, 1961).

Wellek, R. and A. Warren, *Theory of Literature* (New York, 1948).

Witte, A., "Hartmann von Aue und Chrestien von Troyes", *PBB*, LIII (1929), 65-192.

Witte, A., "Der Aufbau der ältesten Tristandichtungen", *ZdA*, LXX (1933), 161-195.

Wolf, F. A., *Prolegomena ad Homerum sive de opera homericorum prisca et genuina forma variisque mutationibus et probabili rationi emendandi* (Halis Saxonum, 1795).

Woods, W. S., "The Plot Structure of Four Romances of Chrétien de Troyes", *SPh*, L (1953), 1-15.

Young, K., *The Origin and Development of the Story of Troilus and Criseyde* (London, 1908).

Zumthor, P., *Histoire littéraire de la France médiévale* (Paris, 1954).

INDEX